Pyramind

TRAINING SERIES

Audio Fundamentals

Alfred Music Publishing Co., Inc.

Los Angeles

Alfred Music Publishing Co., Inc., Los Angeles

Copyright © MMXI by Alfred Music Publishing, Co., Inc.
All Rights Reserved.

ISBN-10: 0-7390-6647-1 Book & DVD
ISBN-13: 978-0-7390-6647-8 Book & DVD

Interior by Stephen Ramirez.

Edited by Sarah Jones and George Petersen.

Cover photograph by Trevor Traynor.

Produced in Association with Lawson Music Media, Inc., Nashville, TN
www.lawsonmusicmedia.com

Contents

Acknowledgements

Everyone at Pyramind knows that we're a part of a larger musical community. As part of that whole, we've learned that no art is created alone. It's the people around us that make the art special. These books are the result of the work of all the good people in the Pyramind community. From the authors, to the graphic designers and audio collectors, to all of the support staff that keeps the place humming day in and day out, these works represent the collected efforts of our entire team.

There are some teammates who deserve special mention for their extra efforts and dedication in providing this high-quality product for you, our special customer! It's been a pleasure to work with all of them at Pyramind and I am extremely proud of every contributor. I've listed them here to give them a written pat on the back and heartfelt thanks for everything they've done—both for this project and for Pyramind every day.

Thank you!

—Matt Donner
mix and mastering engineer, author, teacher, producer,
CAO Pyramind, project manager, guitarist, bassist, pianist

At Pyramind:

Steve Heithecker:	chief engineer, Pro Tools expert, author, art director, teacher, producer, keyboardist
Cliff Truesdell:	media creator, producer, guitarist, teacher
David "DJ" Rankin:	assistant media creator, student producer
Fred Stark:	drummer, rock star
Charles Geogehegan:	photographer, composer, video editor
Bryan Dale:	Pro Tools expert, copy editor, teacher, engineer, guitarist

At Large:

George Petersen:	editor, coach
Mike Lawson:	executive producer
Stephen Ramirez:	art director, book design

Preface

Over my 17-year career, I've witnessed radical changes in many aspects of the sound industry. The artistry has changed, the business has changed, and the technology has certainly changed—the only thing that hasn't changed is sound itself!

These days, technology has never been so powerful and affordable. Newcomers to music and audio production have the lowest cost of entry ever, with more power per dollar coming every year! We're continually bombarded with cool new hardware products that become "must-have" items for studios and producers, and much of that hardware stays valuable for life. In fact, some of the most prized studio microphones and outboard processors are more than 50 years old! On the other hand, manufacturers of digital software tools debut amazing new versions every eight to 12 months, so keeping up is both an exciting and challenging process! While each version may only last 12 months or so, the tools become more powerful and easier to use with each release. Fortunately, many newcomers to audio production are already technically savvy, and can readily understand the software and achieve solid results quickly.

Widespread accessibility of such powerful recording technology makes this an exciting time to become involved in music and audio production, yet there's never been a harder time to get started. The tools are affordable: building a professional music and audio production studio used to cost millions of dollars for the gear alone—never mind the cost of building the space—but these days, a professional rig can be assembled for roughly $25,000, and semi-professional and hobbyist studios (we call them "project" studios) can come together for less than $5,000! But just because you can build it, doesn't mean they will come. You've got the same tools as 25 other producers on your block, but what makes *you* so special? Why should someone pay *you*?

The world of music and audio production is like a diamond— it may be dazzling and brilliant, with dozens of facets to stare at, but it's really only one stone. If you stare at one facet, you'll miss the others. By simply turning the diamond a bit, a whole new set of colors is presented, making it seem like a whole new stone—but it's not. Only when you've examined the whole stone, facet-by-facet, will you truly understand what you're seeing.

Many people in our industry simply stare at one facet, thinking they have the diamond nailed. Most often, it's the technology facet. Users get lost in the features and functions of their gear and forget about the listener. But simply having the tools does not make you successful—you need to understand the whole process behind successful productions before making it a career. In other words, you've got to keep twisting the diamond to see *all* the facets before truly knowing it.

We Made These Books for Producers

To describe the producer's role, one has to describe the production process. It usually starts at the artist with the song. Good producers work the song with the artist to script the flow of the song, the instruments that will play and the performance nuances so a certain sonic goal can be achieved. The producer takes the artist and project from the rehearsal space into the studio to work with an audio engineer. Afterwards, the producer then takes the final product and moves it to the market. This process can happen in conjunction with a label or manager, but isn't always that way. Long and short, the producer's job is to take this song idea, produce a recording, and then market it.

This is *not* what an audio engineer does. Audio engineers have a fairly clear job description: they're responsible for the capture, manipulation, and delivery of audio. That job starts and ends in the studio, while the producer's job started long before the studio and ends long after it. Producers have the widest responsibility set, and they usually take a good portion of the song and production ownership for their efforts and risk. Their role is also the most complex, as it involves aspects of songwriting, engineering, marketing, sales, and a whole lot of personality management—to name a few functions!

We at Pyramind have been doing this a long time, and we've already made the mistakes most producers make as they begin their careers. What makes us unique is that we offer a world-class training program, partnered with the industry's leading manufacturers, and we produce music and audio all day, every day. We practice everything we preach for our clients, because it works. Now, we are presenting our knowledge to you in these books.

Why Create a Book Series?

☞ Getting information is easy, but getting the *right* information is hard. The Internet has no shortage of "how-to" examples. However, for every 20 free videos, you'll be lucky if one will give you a clue about what to do in *your* situation. There's no way to get personalized coaching from videos—especially free ones! That's why we hire coaches and mentors, go to school, etc. Books can be hard to learn from because they "tell you" rather than teach you. Knowing what something is doesn't tell you how to use it—these books give you the tools to use the information. After all, the results are all that matter, so knowing the tech talk is useless until you can actually use it!

☞ We want to be your "on-call" coaches. We've done this long enough to know that there are no right answers for every situation, and the only method that really works for you is yours. We always say there are four ways to do things—the right way, the wrong way, the Pyramind way, and *your* way. Good coaches help you develop your own sense of workflow based on your creativity so that you can make the right call every time. Until the time comes when you're ready to craft your own workflow, you can just use ours to get through—they work every time.

☞ Writing these books helps us give back to our community in ways we weren't lucky enough to have when we were learning this stuff! From our self-earned knowledge, we've become excellent at teaching—a very different skill from simply knowing or even doing. A good teacher creates a framework for you to operate under until you're ready to operate on your own. These books offer just that framework.

☞ Selfishly, we want better producers out there. Music and audio production is a glorious art form and we all deserve great art. We also believe that there's an artist in each of us. Simply stapling loops together doesn't make great art—it makes collage art. We want to hear what *you* think—not what the presets think.

☞ We want to buck the "starving musician" category. We make great music that everyone should enjoy. Music makes our lives richer, and artists should be paid for their works. This is not a podium rant on the state of file sharing; rather it's the overall comment that music is valuable and creating it can be a viable career. In fact, some people become wildly rich in our business! It's not just a pipe dream—there are real opportunities out there if you're willing to bust your hump to get them.

How to Use These Books

This series is comprised of nine books in three levels—beginning, intermediate, and advanced—with books on creative, technical, and business issues in each group. We believe that the blend of all three of these disciplines is the key to success in our industry. Having wild creativity won't move your career forward if you can't execute your ideas. And if you can execute your wild ideas, you won't earn any money if you misunderstand the music-purchasing marketplace. And without money, you can't buy more gear.

You can't separate the creative and technical aspects of a project—these must work together to achieve a goal. You can't separate the creative and business sides, either—making something great and selling it to no one does nothing for your career. Having a great idea for a piece of music and having the market to sell it to won't do you any good if the music doesn't sound good when you release it. We know—we've made all of these mistakes ourselves, and we see others making the same mistakes every day.

Having each of the three disciplines (creativity, technology, and business) in an easy-to-digest form with references to each other is the best way to provide the teaching and coaching we want to give. We love to teach; we're extremely focused on giving real-world, practical, highly effective training to our students, and we wanted to offer the same approach here.

These books are written in plain language—we're not trying to dazzle you with facts, figures, or overly technical information in an effort to show you how smart we are. In fact, how smart *we* are doesn't even matter! The only thing that matters is *your* results—making *you* smarter about how and why you work. The language is used to help you get into the information easily and

---

NOTE

Throughout the book you will see the following icons which refer you to supplemental video or audio material found on the accompanying DVD disc. The disc is in DVD-Video format with embedded audio and can be viewed using any DVD player.

put it to use. Knowing the difference between dB SPL and dBfs is great—as long as it has some application that can make your productions sound better. Otherwise, it's just jargon—words that get tossed around at conferences to make people sound like they know what they're doing.

Keep in mind that some information will be duplicated across these books. This helps reinforce the commonality of the subjects and the information itself.

One of our training techniques is cross-referenced learning, which means that hearing the same thing three times from three teachers in three different classes should tell you that something is true—and it's something you really need to know. By covering the same subject across each of the books, your understanding of the material (the "why") is much greater than if you just read it once.

By that same reasoning, some of the same material is occasionally covered more than once within each title. In this case, you're getting the same information—or something similar—from two or more sources. Each book has several authors covering the subject, each presenting facets of the diamond in their way.

We hope that you enjoy these books, and more importantly that you find them useful. If this first series covers information that you already know, then congratulations—you're ready for the next series! It's likely that even if you already know this information, there are bound to be a few nuggets of wisdom that you didn't have at the start. We always have students who already have a lot of experience, yet we find that their body of homegrown knowledge is made up of little "bubbles" of information with thin connections between them. These books are perfect for these folks to help erase the boundaries of the little bubbles and make one big bubble out of them. So even if you know many of the pieces, these books should help you wrap all of this knowledge up into a single body of knowledge you can use every day.

And we hope that your productions shine as brightly as a diamond!

—*Matt Donner*

mechanical vibrations traveling through an elastic medium, traveling in air at a speed of approximately 1087 ft (331 m) per second at sea level, that can be produced or caused

s o u n d
[s o u n d] – n o u n

1. the sensation produced by stimulation of the organs of hearing by mechanical vibrations transmitted through the air or other medium.

Free Versus Captured Sound

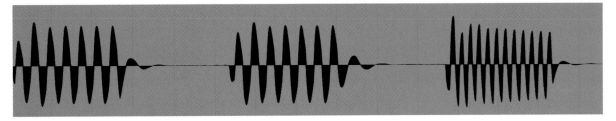

"the sensation produced by stimulation of the organs of hearing by mechanical vibrations transmitted through the air or other medium . . ."

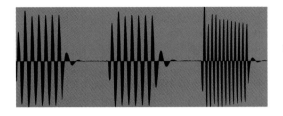

What Is Sound?

Understanding Sound

Everything you hear is sound. Whether you're listening to speech, music or ambience (such as traffic or nature), if you can hear something, then you are perceiving sound. It's important to define sound this way, so we can define all other terms related to it, each having its own set of rules and parameters.

Constantly moving and changing in its environment, sound is a living energy, which contributes to its magical quality that attracts us. Think of sound as existing in two forms: *free* and *captured*. Free sound is what happens "live" in a room as it's being created. Captured sound is sound that we literally capture, as in recordings. The biggest difference between them is the medium in which the sound exists—that is, the environment in which it is created.

For example, the quality of sound generated in a room depends on its interaction within the acoustical environment (the walls, the ceiling, the air, the furniture, people in the room, etc.), while the quality of sound generated from a recording is affected by the recording medium. Different recording media—from cassette tapes (remember those?), to 2-inch multitrack recorders, to digital audio captured into your computer recorder—will all interact with sound differently. Of course, once the captured sound plays back out of the speakers, it then behaves like free sound again as it interacts with the acoustical environment. All of these interactions add up to determine the final quality of the sound that we hear, whether at a club, a recording studio or in our living rooms.

This forms the foundation of understanding sound, and is the basis for every decision we make in the studio, on the stage or in the field. We should begin every project with the realization that we must first understand the nature of free sound, and then make choices about capturing and playing back the captured sounds.

There are exceptions to the rule of course, especially with much of today's dance, hip-hop and electronica music, where the production often starts from previously captured sounds (such as samples or loops) or begins as an electronically generated sound (synthesizers, etc.). Only when such sounds play back through speakers does a free sound-style interaction occur with the environment.

Note that the difference between free and captured sound has nothing to do with the creativity put into the sound. This simply describes the different ways that sound interacts with its medium. That medium could be air, tape or analog-to-digital converters.

COACH'S CORNER

While we can generally accept that the term "sound" is a catchall for everything we hear, free or captured, we don't necessarily all agree on the difference between *sound* and *audio*. At Pyramind, we define the two much in the same terms that we define "sound"—free or captured. "Audio" is captured sound. "Sound" is free (live) sound. In either case, what we hear can be music, or, at least, musical. Some schools of thought define "music" as having a set form or structure, or standardized instrumentation like violins or drums. Other schools of thought think of music as having a clearly defined rhythm or repetition, while audio can be rhythmically void, like wind or streams babbling. For us, the musicality is more of a personal experience—does it envoke an emotional response? Did you feel anything from it? If so, it's music.

Tech-Speak: *Sound*

Sound is a three-dimensional mechanical energy wave where molecular vibrations travel through a medium such as air, water, or walls. Sound is transmitted when molecules of the medium are pushed into each other serially, until the energy dissipates and they return to their normal, unexcited state.

Sound is an energy wave traveling through a medium. Basically, this means that sound is a vibration that requires the medium (air, for example) to vibrate in order to be heard. So, sound only happens when a burst (or wave) of energy is emitted and vibrates the medium surrounding the burst. Water is an efficient sound-conducting medium, which is why you can still hear things underwater. However, in vacuums (like space), no sound can be heard, as there is no material for the sonic vibrations to excite. This takes some of the fun out of watching alien space ships flying by in the movies and wondering why they sound so huge . . .

COACH'S CORNER

Keep in mind that the density of the medium can change the way in which sound works. For example, air is not very dense compared to the ocean, and, as such, sound travels much farther underwater. This is how whales can communicate with each other over a span of miles. In air, sound travels at a speed of about 770 miles per hour (approximately a foot for every millisecond—1/1,000 of a second). Through water, sound travels at about 3,300 mph!

It's very important to understand that sound travels in spherical waves outward from the source. These sound waves are much like ocean waves, which have a ridge and a trough (a high point and a low point). The curve of an ocean wave, as seen in **Figure 1.01**, seems to move horizontally across the ocean until it reaches the shore and starts to tilt forward until the ridge falls over into a crest (and hopefully a tube if you surf!).

Figure. 1.01: View of an ocean wave with ridge and trough detail. Sound waves move in a similar shape but out from a central point rather than in a single direction.

Sound is very much like this ocean wave in that a burst of energy first pushes, then pulls, much like when you drop a pebble into a calm lake and the ripples go up and down. Unlike the water, sound doesn't just move across the surface, it moves outward in a sphere, completely filling the space it's in. If ocean waves are two-dimensional, sound is three-dimensional! Therefore, sound moves in a sphere outward from the source, while ocean waves only travel horizontally across the surface, as seen in **Figure 1.02**.

Figure 1.02: 3D and 2D representations of a sound wave.

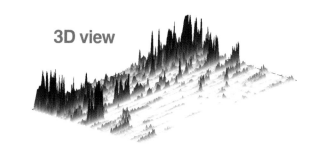

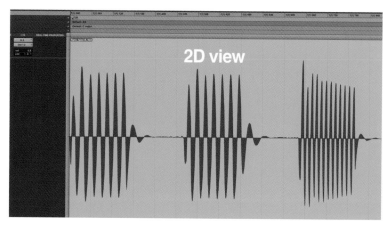

Another key aspect is that sound is a burst of mechanical energy. This means the energy literally moves the medium around it by mechanically transferring energy, particle by particle. Consider the desktop trinket of five silver balls swinging from strings. If you pull one of the balls back and let it go, it strikes the next ball and the energy transfers through the middle balls to the end ball, making it swing outward. Sound works much this way, where the original burst of energy pushes the molecules around it outward (air, in most cases) and those molecules transfer the energy to the molecules around them.

Once the molecules hand off their energy, they pull back to their original position, creating both a pushing energy and a pulling energy at the same time. This is what gives sound waves ridges and troughs (as in the crest and valleys of the ocean wave). If a sound hits a wall, some of its energy will transfer to the wall and some will bounce out the other side (in your angry neighbor's apartment usually!). The remaining energy bounces off the wall and back into the space, like a racquetball. This continues until all of the energy is dissipated, or spent.

Frequency: Timbre

Sound can be quantified by three measures: *amplitude, frequency* and *time*. These are the three components of sound, whether captured or free. Amplitude should be a familiar term (aka volume) as should time, but timbre and frequency might be new terms for some. The frequency of a sound defines its *pitch* (musical note value), while timbre (pronounced "TAM-bur") is the overall tonal quality of a sound that allows the listener to distinguish one instrument or voice from another. Timbre cannot be quantified solely through measures of pitch or amplitude; it is the *quality* of the sound, the timbre, that lets humans differentiate a saxophone from a trumpet, even when both instruments are playing the same pitch at the same loudness.

The most basic form of sound is represented by something called the *sine wave*. Remember that sound is a 360-degree mechanical energy burst through a medium, and as such, its pushing, then pulling, behavior causes peaks and troughs in the energy wave. This is exactly the same as a familiar mathematical function called the sine wave, as seen in **Figure 1.03**. The sine wave is an even energy wave whose ridges and troughs are the same size and shape and do not change over time. Each rotation through the up and down portions of the wave is called a *cycle*. This simple one-cycle sine wave is literally the building block of sound, much like the atom is the building block of matter.

Figure. 1.03: A standard sine wave, measuring 1 Hz, meaning 1 cycle per second (cps). This is called the *wavelength*.

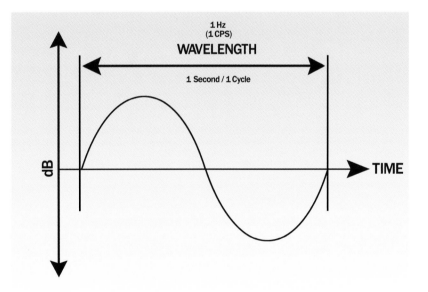

When drawn as a mathematical expression, a sine wave demonstrates this pushing and pulling energy, as seen in **Figure 1.04**. The curve of the wave is perfectly even and the top and bottom of the wave are exactly the same distance away from the zero line. This means that the energy starts at zero (standing still) until the burst is created, at which point the wave pushes outward, called *compression*, and then pulls back, called *rarefaction,* just as hard as it pushed out. In other words, the wave pushes and pulls repeatedly at a fixed rate, measured over the course of a second. Each repetition is called a "cycle." Frequency can thus be defined as the number of times a wave pushes and pulls in one second, which is expressed in, *Hertz* or *cycles per second.*

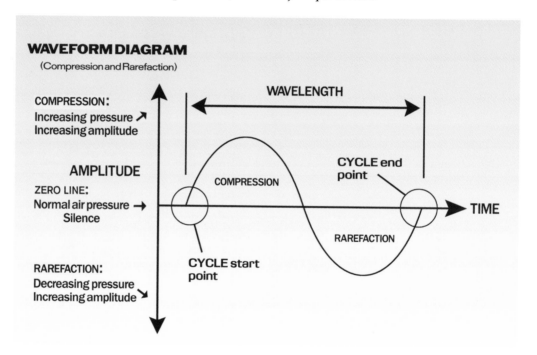

Figure 1.04: A simple sine wave showing the beginning and end of a cycle, as well as compression and rarefaction.

COACH'S CORNER

The sine wave is important to us for many reasons, but is most important mathematically because it represents a circular motion over time. Envision a world map where the world is laid out horizontally with funny curves as it tries to take the circular globe and represent it on a flat page. The math behind sound waves is called trigonometry. Trigonometry defines several functions, including cosines and tangents, but for audio purposes, we will concentrate on the sine wave.

- -

The common term used to define the speed of a sine wave or sound wave is Hertz—*sometimes called* cps *or cycles per second. One Hertz (Hz) represents one cycle of a sine wave. A frequency of 440 Hz repeats its cycle of compression and rarefaction 440 times per second.*

The sine wave is the simplest form of sound measurement. It would be amazingly useful if all of the sounds we heard were as simple as singular sine waves that came one after the other. Unfortunately, this is not the case. Sound is extremely complex and just about every sound you've ever heard is made up of dozens or more of these simple, individual waves. The combination of simple sine waves defines the *timbre* of a sound.

Tech-Speak: *Timbre*

- -

Most sound is comprised of a combination of individual sine waves. The unique defining quality of the combined sound is called its timbre.

Amplitude: Loudness and Volume

Okay, we now understand that sine waves push and pull in even amounts at different speeds (frequencies) until they run out of energy. The next question to ask is, "by how much?" The *amplitude*, or volume, of the sound is determined by how high and low the wave ridges and troughs rise or fall from the zero line. Back to the ocean analogy, a two-foot wave is playful and fun for some, but small and weak for others. Conversely, a 20-foot monster is playful for some and deadly for others. The amplitude of a sound is similar—it can be too loud for some (you're too old!) or not loud enough for others (get your hearing checked!).

The measurement of the amplitude of a sound over time is called *dynamic range*—the difference between the loudest point and the softest point in the lifecycle of the wave. There are several measurements of amplitude, but we generally use something called the *decibel* (dB) to measure volume. A decibel is a deci-Bel—that is to say, $^1/_{10}$ of a relative unit of measure called the "Bel."

COACH'S CORNER

Originally used as a measurement of signal level in telephone cables, the Bel was defined by Bell Labs during the early days of the phone. The "Bel" became shorthand for the level related to the Miles of Standard Cable. The Bel became a difficult number to use as the ranges of values became too large for telephone development, so its range was shrunk, via a mathematical formula called the logarithm, into the *decibel*.

Remember that sound is a three-dimensional mechanical energy wave moving through a medium. The level of the movement of this wave is its pressure; that is, the pressure of the moving molecules of the medium is what helps move the wave along. The dB SPL (sound pressure level) measurement defines the level of sound in the listening environment at any given time. **Figure 1.05** compares SPL ratings of common sounds.

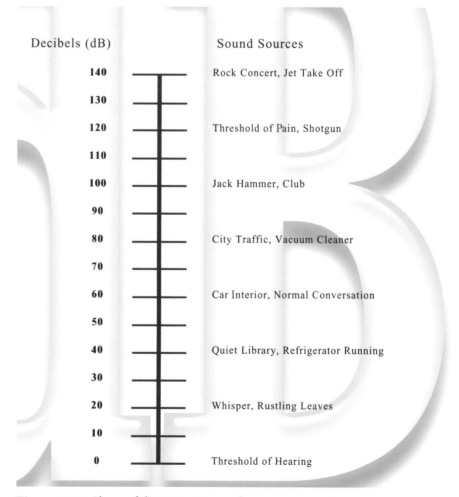

Figure 1.05: Chart of dB SPL ratings of common sounds.

The unit of decibel usually has no meaning on its own. It's actually a ratio—the relationship between two numbers. A decibel measures the difference between the input and output of a component (such as a microphone preamplifier or equalizer)—if the dB value is positive, the signal got louder, and if the dB value is negative, the signal got quieter. Another thing to note about the decibel is that it is measured in many different ways, all of which relate to each other. There will be much discussion on this later but for now, let's focus in on one type of dB—amplitude in the listening environment. This is known as dB SPL.

COACH'S CORNER

You might have noticed that audio equipment uses many different types of measurements to determine its quality, known as *specs* or *specifications*. These specs, when referred to in dB, often have strange monikers that refer to different types of measurements we will discuss later. Here are some common examples:

S/N: 108 dBu

THD: ±0.0003% (@ 1kHz, +4 dBu)

-10 dBm

@ 77 dB SPL

For now, don't worry about whether or not this makes sense—it may not right now, but it will later. Suffice to say, the dB is relative. Its real meaning is determined by the way you compare it to some reference standard, measured in distance from a standard set value—either higher (+), lower (-), or above *and* below (±).

Time: Morphology and Rhythm

When we've discussed frequencies, dB SPL measurements have been assumed to be a constant level, meaning that they stay at the same energy level. Most sounds don't generally stay the same, though, and how they change over time is one of the key components of understanding sound and amplitude. This is called *morphology*—the study of change over time.

When the change becomes symmetrical, or repetitive, it's generally thought of as *rhythm*. All sounds conform to some kind of time pattern in the sense that they have a beginning and an end, but many sounds don't repeat a pattern. They burst their energy once and follow their time pattern but never repeat, thus avoiding rhythm. Whether or not a sound is rhythmic, all sounds live and die over time. The evolution of sound's time/life cycle is called its envelope.

Tech-Speak: *Envelope*

The dissipation of a sound's energy burst follows a pattern called its envelope. *The envelope is a sound's life-cycle, where there is a beginning, a shrinking, a leveling off, and an end.*

The amplitude (SPL) of a sound isn't the only thing that changes over time; so too does the frequency of the sound. As if it weren't enough to try to keep up with the volume changes, keeping up with the frequency changes makes the study of sound quite complex. Thankfully, we are all equipped with amazing tools called ears! These amazing little things do a great job of following all of the nuances of sound and all of the changes over time.

COACH'S CORNER

We hear a tremendous amount of information; from frequency and its changes, to amplitude and its changes, and time and those changes. There's a huge amount of information within every sound. Even though we might oversimplify what we hear because it's so ordinary to us—a car horn, a drum, a person's voice—by definition, these are all very complex sounds, yet we can instantly recognize them as the commonplace sounds we hear. Ask yourself how long it takes you to recognize who's on the phone when you get a call (caller ID aside, wiseguy). A second? Two? Less? Our ears and brain have the ability to almost instantly recognize familiar sounds. This brings up one question: What is it about the sounds that we hear that makes them so familiar?

The sonic possibilities created through combinations of frequency, volume, and time are infinite. The ear and brain's ability to recognize a sound so quickly is due to the fact that every sound has a unique combination of these three components. The combination of the three make up a sonic imprint and our brain stores a huge repertoire of these sound "maps" (and has since birth), which allow us to instantly recognize who or what is being heard.

COACH'S CORNER

It is generally accepted that the human ear can accurately capture sound from 20 Hz to 20,000 Hz (20 kHz). It is also generally accepted that humans can comfortably hear sounds as quiet as 12 dB SPL through 115 dB SPL. However, it's also generally accepted that:

1. All people DO NOT hear these tones and volumes equally

   —and—

2. All people DO NOT hear tones equally at all sound pressure levels/SPLs (More on this later—read on at Fletcher-Munson!)

The only given is to say that no two people hear things the same way. This is one reason why some people are born with perfect pitch (the ability to recognize a given pitch without a reference) and others have to study and train their ears to hear with perfect pitch.

> ### RECAP
>
> Sound is a 360-degree mechanical energy wave that vibrates the medium through which it travels. All sound is composed of an elemental unit—the sine (sinusoidal) wave. Sine waves have even peaks and valleys, which represent the pushing and pulling energy of the wave. Each repetition of a sine wave is called a cycle and is defined in Hertz (Hz) or cycles per second (aka frequency). Humans generally hear sine waves between 20 Hz and 20,000 Hz. The volume of sound is measured by the decibel, a logarithmic scale, and the evolution of sound over time conforms to a pattern called its envelope.

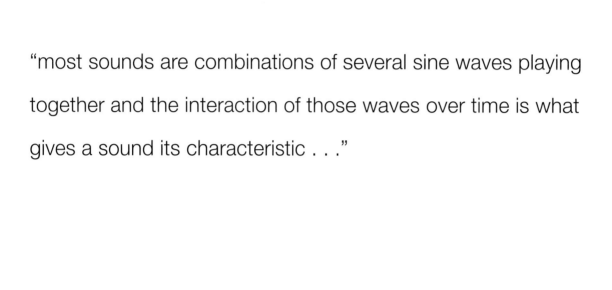

"most sounds are combinations of several sine waves playing together and the interaction of those waves over time is what gives a sound its characteristic . . ."

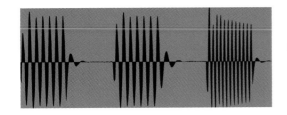

Timbre–Sound Waves

The Single Sine Wave, in Detail

Let's get properly acquainted with the sine wave in the way that really matters—by listening.

The following section refers to the accompanying DVD, which has recordings of several sine waves at fixed volumes and fixed lengths of time so we can focus on the sound of the frequency. The first few frequencies are presented in three groups of tones, also known as *bands*. These bands are likely to be already familiar to you—*bass, midrange* and *treble*. Each track has three frequencies within the band so you can hear the low, mid, and high ranges of these bands. While there are no rules defining which frequencies belong in each band, there will likely be some debate as to what constitutes the difference between bass and midrange, as well as midrange and treble. For now, we will use the (somewhat) arbitrary figure of 220 Hz to separate bass from the mids, and 2,200 Hz to separate the mids from the treble. There are good reasons for choosing these tones, but for now, let's just accept these boundaries as true.

COACH'S CORNER

Imagine a basketball bouncing up and down on the floor. The energy of the ball striking the floor translates into an upward motion, and the ball falls again until it hits the floor again, repeating until the energy runs out. Remember that we generally hear from 20 Hz to 20,000 Hz, so in the case of the bouncing basketball, imagine that it bounces between 20 times per second and 20,000 times per second—that would be considered the frequency of the bouncing basketball! With complex sounds, imagine sine waves as thousands of basketballs bouncing at different speeds all at once. The combination of all of those speeds and bounces makes up the timbre of the sound—its complex collection of frequencies.

DVD Track 1: The Bass Tones. The first three tones are all bass tones and are good reference tones to see how low your monitors, speakers, or headphones can play back audio. These tones may not sound great, as everyone's monitors are different and some simply can't reproduce low frequencies. This track will play 55 Hz, 110 Hz, and 220 Hz, which represent the low, mid, and upper portions of the bass band.

 DVD Track 2: The Midrange Tones. Midrange is very important for clarity of a variety of instruments, including the voice. Knowing that your monitors and listening environment can accurately and pleasingly reproduce these tones is a key ingredient to verifying that your productions will sound great, in your studio and elsewhere. This track will play 440 Hz, 880 Hz and 1,760 Hz. These represent the low, mid, and upper portions of the mid-band.

 **DVD Track 3:** The Treble Tones. Often referred to as the "highs," these tones can be the difference between clean and shiny productions and harsh and painful productions. People who consistently listen to music too loud—or have been exposed to high volumes of sound over long periods of time—are likely to lose their treble hearing first. You'd be surprised at how much treble might be missing from your hearing, so it's a good idea to have your hearing checked often. This track will play 3,520 Hz, 7,040 Hz, and 14,080 Hz. Can you hear the last part at 14,080 Hz?

COACH'S CORNER

You may have noticed that all the tones in tracks 1–3 are multiples of 55 Hz, the first frequency. Did you notice that they all sound the same as the original, just at different "levels"? These are known as *octaves*, meaning the same pitch at higher frequencies. This demonstration shows you that, as you move up the frequency range, the same pitches keep coming around over and over again. What this means is that there are only so many frequencies within a band, and that as you move up the frequencies, you eventually hear the same groups of tones in the same order, over and over.

The octave phenomenon is often called the "miracle of music"—it's that important. However, not all frequencies line up in perfect octaves. In fact, there is a very set relationship between frequencies that are multiples of each other. This is known as the *harmonic series* or the *overtone series*.

Tech-Speak: *Harmonic Series*

The harmonic series is the musical and mathematical relationship between frequencies that are multiples. It is comprised of a fundamental tone (the lowest in the series) and frequencies at multiple values (2×, 3×, 4×, etc.) of that fundamental.

Tech-Speak: *Octave*

An octave (8va) is a pitch at double or half the frequency of another frequency. In musical terms, it's the same note at a higher or lower level, as in from C to the next C, etc. Mathematically, it refers to a frequency that is double (or half) the original frequency as you go up (or down) in Hz.

The harmonic series is another of those "miracles" of music, in that this collection of tones provides the foundation of certain disciplines in music, instrument design, equipment manufacturing, acoustics, and synthesis. This concept is very important to understand and become familiar with, so let's refer back to the CDs, to listen to various harmonics and hear what they are.

Let's start with a simple sine wave vibrating at 110 Hz. The wave of energy is pushing (via compression) and pulling (via rarefaction) 110 times per second. Listen to the accompanying **DVD Track 4** to hear about 20 seconds of 110 Hz.

DVD Track 4: A 110 Hz sine wave being played for about 20 seconds. Can you find the note on the piano?

In this case, the fundamental is the 110 Hz tone. Multiplying 110 by 2 gives us 220 Hz—known as the first overtone or the *second harmonic* (the first fundamental is the harmonic). Now listen to it next to its fundamental and see what it sounds like.

DVD Track 5: Two sine waves played one into the other—110 Hz, then 220 Hz. Can you find the note matching 220 Hz on the piano?

Surprisingly, it's actually the same note, played an octave higher. But what happens if you do the math again, one step higher? Now, let's listen to the fundamental, 110 Hz, ×3—which is the second overtone, 330 Hz.

DVD Track 6: Three sine waves played back to back—110 Hz, 220 Hz, and then 330 Hz. Can you find all three on the piano?

Now, we have three notes, all built from the same fundamental, but not all at the same pitch. You can imagine that this can go on for a little while. So let's shortcut the process and go up to the eighth harmonic.

DVD Track 7: Eight sine waves played back to back—110 Hz, 220 Hz, 330 Hz, through 880 Hz. Can you find them all on the piano?

COACH'S CORNER

You might notice that these pitches all fall perfectly onto various keys of the piano. You might have heard this sequence of sounds before—or at least some of them—if you've ever heard Richard Strauss' *Also Sprach Zarathustra*. Some people know it better as the theme music from Stanley Kubrick's film *2001: A Space Odyssey*. (If you don't know this movie, you should. It was released in 1968, one year before the first moon landing. Mindblowing . . .)

The Harmonic Series

Tone	Frequency	Pitch	Interval
Fundamental	110 Hz	A	
First Overtone	220 Hz	A1	8va
Second Overtone	330 Hz	E1	perfect 5th
Third Overtone	440 Hz	A2	8va
Fourth Overtone	550 Hz	C#2	major 3rd
Fifth Overtone	660 Hz	E2	perfect 5th
Sixth Overtone	770 Hz	G2	flatted 7th
Seventh Overtone	880 Hz	A3	8va

COACH'S CORNER

This harmonic sequence rule applies to oscillating sound generators. This includes guitars, pianos, pipes, flutes, and a whole assortment of other instruments. Many instruments and sound-producing devices (such as drums) don't conform exactly to this math, but it holds true for a lot of instruments and certainly holds true for the basic waveforms of common synthesizers.

Figure 1.06: Diagram of a fundamental sine wave and its first 7 overtones.

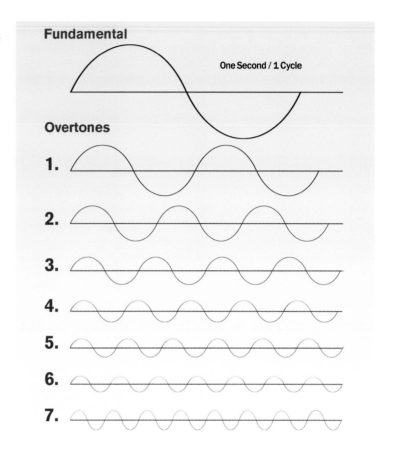

Two Sine Waves

Earlier, we mentioned that most free sounds are extremely complex—they almost never play as pure sine waves. Most sounds are combinations of several sine waves, and the interaction of those waves over time is what gives a sound its defining characteristic. Before we get ahead of ourselves, let's understand what happens when two sine waves interact. Two waves playing together generally combine to make the resulting complex wave. However, two waves playing together don't necessarily add together well. Even two waves of the same frequency won't add together perfectly every time!

Figure 1.07 shows two simple sine waves in perfect sync— that is to say, they are the same frequency and their peaks and valleys line up perfectly. This is known as being *in phase*. When these two waves play together, they add up perfectly and the result is the same wave frequency, just twice as loud. This is called *summing*. This means that their energies add to each other as they play together, creating a larger energy wave as a result.

Figure 1.07: Two simple sine waves (red and yellow) playing together in phase. The resulting wave (green) is the same frequency but twice as high in amplitude (twice as loud).

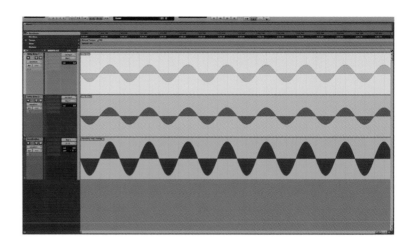

Tech-Speak: *In Phase*

Two waves are said to be in phase *when their peaks and valleys start and finish at the same points in time. Their phase refers to their starting position in time.*

Tech-Speak: *Summing*

When two waves play together and the resulting sound gets louder, the two waves are said to be summing.

DVD Track 8: This track contains 10 seconds of a single 110 Hz signal, then 10 seconds of two 110 Hz signals, played in phase. You'll hear when it happens because the result is an increase in the loudness of the sound. The resulting sound is nothing more than simply turning on the second wave and not the result of simply turning up the volume of one sound.

Not all waves will play together in phase, nor will the resulting energy wave always sum together positively. Another possible result of two waves interacting is a phenomenon known as *phasing*. When two waves play together but their cycles are offset,the resulting energy is smaller than the original two. This is a result of the two waves beginning at different phases in time—their peaks and valleys don't line up perfectly like they do in summing.

Tech-Speak: *Phase Cancellation*

When two waves play together and interact negatively, they are said to be phasing—*or* phasing out. *Since the phase, or timing, of the two waves don't line up, the peak of one wave might correspond to a valley of the other, thus cancelling each other out—appropriately called* phase cancellation. *This occurs when the two waves are out of phase by 180 degrees. Waves can be phasing without cancelling out if their phase is offset by less than 180 degrees.*

In **Figure 1.08** you can see two waves phasing against each other where the peaks and valleys line up exactly opposite to each other. The resulting wave is a flat line, indicating that the energy of the one wave exactly counteracts the energy of the other. The result is no wave at all! This is called phasing out or phase cancellation.

Figure 1.08: Two waves exactly out of phase (red and yellow) and the resulting wave (green), which contains no energy at all due to phase cancellation.

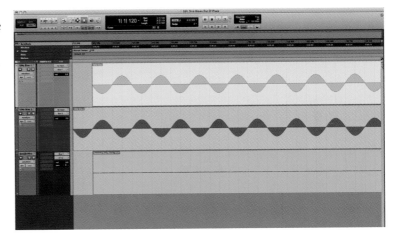

COACH'S CORNER

The level at which two waves line up is known as their *phase degree*. Two waves that sum perfectly are said to be at 0 degrees of phase to each other. Conversely, two waves that cancel each other out perfectly are said to be at 180 degrees to each other.

Figure 1.09: Two waves (yellow and red) that are 90 degrees out of phase and the resulting, complex wave (green).

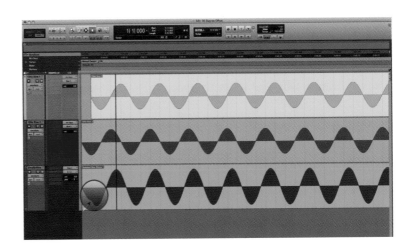

Usually, two waves don't line up perfectly to each other where the peaks and valleys interact cleanly. Most waves line up somewhere in between, resulting in waves that are more complex than simply larger versions or flat lines. **Figure 1.09** shows the result of two waves that are out of phase by 90 degrees, that is, one wave cycle starts at the point where the other is already at its peak.

The previous examples have pitted two waves against each other, but each wave is at the same frequency. In most cases of real-world sounds, any two waves that play against each other are not at the same frequency. In this case, the two waves wouldn't sum or phase against each other in the same way as two waves of the same frequency. Cases like this result in a phenomenon known as *beating*.

Tech-Speak: *Beating*

When two waves of different frequencies play together, their resulting energy wave fluctuates at the rate of the inverse of their difference. For example, if 110 Hz and 112 Hz play against each other, the resulting wave is said to beat *at a rate of once every ¹/₂ second. The resulting sound is often referred to as* vibrato, *or vibration of frequency.*

DVD Track 9: On this track, the first frequency of 110 Hz plays for 10 seconds, then 111 Hz plays for another 10 seconds. At the end of the second frequency, the two play together for 15 seconds and the beating between them is apparent. The difference between them is 1 Hz, so they beat once every second.

DVD Track 10: Here, the first frequency of 110 Hz plays for 10 seconds, then 112 Hz plays for another 10 seconds. At the end of the second frequency, the two play together for 15 seconds and the beating is apparent. As the difference between them is 2 Hz, they beat once every ¹/₂ second.

DVD Track 11: On this track, the first frequency of 110 Hz plays for 10 seconds, then 114 Hz plays for another 10 seconds. At the end of the second frequency, the two play together for 15 seconds and the beating is apparent. Since the difference between them is 4 Hz, they beat every ¹/₄ second.

DVD Track 12: This track demonstrates the first frequency of 110 Hz playing against a sweep of frequencies from 110 Hz through 220 Hz. In this case, the beating frequency increases until a tone is heard, which is the beating frequency.

In real-world situations, there are usually dozens of waves playing against each other at any one time. Consider a simple phenomenon like phasing or summing with two waves. If this concept is extended to 12 or 24 waves at once, the process becomes very complicated. The mathematical formula used to analyze the relationship between multiple waves in a complex wave is known as the *Fourier transform*—also known as the *fast Fourier transform*, or *FFT*.

Tech-Speak: *Fourier Transforms*

Named after French mathematician Joseph Fourier, the Fourier transform *is a mathematical process by which complex waves are broken down into their component sine waves. A fast Fourier transform is just that—a faster version of the original formula, which is more efficient for audio purposes.*

In **Figure 1.10,** check out the FFT analysis of a single kick drum recording. As you can see, there are many frequencies in this sound. While the graph shows a concentration of energy in the low end, there is also energy in the mid band as well as some in the treble band. This should give you a sense of the complexity of every sound we hear in the world! Every sound is comprised of dozens of individual sine waves that play together—some phase and others sum, but all combine to make unique and rich sounds that, in turn, become the building blocks of the music we create!

Figure 1.10: An FFT of a kick drum sample. The FFT in this case is derived using RND Digital's Uniquelizer plug-in.

<u>**DVD Track 13:**</u> A recording of a single kick drum, played several times. This is the kick drum recording that was used to create the FFT chart in **Figure 1.10**.

FFTs are very handy in the studio, offering the ability to analyze any captured sound and give a sense of where that sound's energy is concentrated. They also help new producers learn where certain frequencies reside by literally showing listeners what they hear. However, FFTs are *not* very handy for measuring the frequencies of a free sound in a space; that is, they don't help you understand what's happening in your control room, rehearsal room or live room. This information is useful for determining what your recordings and productions will sound like when performed in other spaces.

COACH'S CORNER

An FFT can come in handy for compositional purposes as well as mixing, as it can tell you if there's too much (or not enough) energy in a particular frequency range within the sound, which might necessitate changing the chosen sound. For example, if a kick drum is too strong in the 220 Hz range, you might find it fighting the bass for "space" in a song where the bass also plays strongly at 220 Hz. In this case, you might choose a different kick that has stronger energy at 110 Hz, so the two can happily coexist!

While FFTs are great for analyzing captured sound, we use another tool for analyzing free sound—the *real time analyzer*, or *RTA*. A microphone is connected to an RTA that effectively performs an FFT-like analysis on the sound. All incoming sounds are measured at varying resolution, and the result is a chart of frequencies that looks a lot like an FFT. Very accurate RTAs will show as many as 24 frequencies per octave band while others may only show six or less. This means that, for every doubling of frequency, the RTA may show 24 lines or six lines between the two points.

RTAs are used in control rooms to listen to pre-configured sounds as a method of determining the acoustic behavior of the room. If, for example, an RTA reading says that your control room has a tendency to sum frequencies at around 220 Hz, it means that you are hearing more sound at 220 Hz in your room than actually lives in your production. This can cause you to undershoot the level of 220 Hz in your production and your music will sound lighter at 220 Hz than it should!

One of the most interesting parts of observing RTAs or running FFTs is noting the dense harmonic content of everyday sounds. For example, **Figure 1.11** shows the FFT of a recording

COACH'S CORNER

RTAs usually come bundled with a calibrated test microphone and a display system. The display is hardware-based with some systems and software-based in others. The key is to use a test microphone and not an over-the-counter music microphone. Since most microphones have a certain sonic "coloration," they will not respond with the accuracy needed for RTA work. Several manufacturers make measurement-grade RTA microphones, which range in price from $99 to $2,000. How to calibrate your control room is an advanced subject of a later book. There are several free resources available that can help you build a basic understanding of control rooms and acoustic design and they are a great place to start. There are also manufacturers offering all-in-one analysis/correction tools that require little expertise to run but, overall, are fairly simple to use.

of a piano playing a simple 440 Hz note (concert pitch A). Note that the FFT display shows a lot more than just the 440 Hz tone! Strings (like piano strings) behave like oscillators; their vibrations create overtones in multiples of the fundamental. So if the fundamental is 440 Hz, there are overtones at 880 Hz, 1,760 Hz, and so on, up the line. These overtones play at different volumes and sum in different ways depending on the construction of the piano, the type of wood, age, the tuning, and a host of other factors. However, the collection of overtones is what makes one piano sound different from another—and that's what we look for!

Figure 1.11: An FFT of a recorded A-440 Hz tone played on a piano.

DVD Track 14: A repeated playback of a single piano note playing A-440. This is the piano sound that was used to create the FFT seen in **Figure 1.11**. Try using your favorite FFT (or download a free one/trial version) and compare notes. Does your FFT look like ours?

As you can see in **Figure 1.11**, the single note and its collection of overtones is very harmonically rich. In fact, the single note could be seen as a chord unto itself. In this case, you'll see a strength of energy at several points in the FFT, many of which comprise notes that are not A. It could be said that for every note played on the piano (and lots of other instruments, for that matter), a miniature chord is created!

COACH'S CORNER

As you continue to train your ear to correlate frequencies to musical notes, there are several websites that can help this process. Some are more colorful than others, but a generic web search for something like "Pitch to Music" or "Frequency to Music Converters" will display several of them We recommended two sites:

   The first, at http://www.independentrecording.net/irn/resources/freqchart/main_display.htm, correlates frequency ranges of instruments to pitch es. As you move your mouse over the different areas, the frequency ranges and loudness responses are given too, making this a very interactive and informative site. The second useful resource is http://peabody.sapp.org/class/st2/lab/notehz/. This site is very direct, listing only frequencies and notes side by side in octave ranges. This one is great for fast information about this relationship.

RECAP

There are myriad different interactions between sine waves, depending on whether or not you are inspecting one, two, or more waves. Sometimes, waves add nicely together, called *summing*. Other times, they combine together poorly, resulting in *phasing*. When two waves of differing frequency add together, they often achieve a *beating* where the difference between the two frequencies is audible in a rhythmic pattern. When multiple waves combine, a variety of all three interactions often occur in unique ways, making a very complex, characteristic sound, referred to as the sound source's timbre.

Combining Sine Waves to Create Noise

When trying to determine the nature of sound in a room or in a particular piece of equipment, acousticians and manufacturers use a variety of sounds to test the space or gear. These collections of sounds range in types and purposes, but often, they use specific collections of frequencies known as noise.

   One very common type of noise is *white noise*, which is represented by a collection of all frequencies (often limited to 20 Hz to 20,000 Hz) playing at the same level. This noise is often used in manufacturing, where a piece of equipment's spec is measured electrically. In this testing, white noise is fed into the device and then measured on its output. As white noise is very specific in its frequency content, it can be easy to measure any affect the device has on the sound.

Tech-Speak: *White Noise*

White noise is a sound in which every audible frequency is represented at even amplitude. It is often used by manufacturers for to test equipment.

If the output of the device is significantly different from the pure white noise input, the manufacturer may choose to re-design and re-build the device to try and get the output to match the input more closely or they can choose to keep the design as-is, if testers think that the subjective audio quality is pleasing. Overall, the change of the sound by the device is known as its total harmonic distortion or THD. It is measured in percentages of change from the original input of white noise to the resulting noise output.

COACH'S CORNER

Many engineers refer to a change of sound as a device's "color," defining the resulting frequency shape as the colorization of the sound. This is entirely subjective and the subject of much debate around the studio, but suffice to say that a sound-coloring device is loved, hated or simply ignored over time. The un-colored ones tend to be used for a long time in studio productions as most people agree that they are high-quality products, but the colored devices also last the longest in studios when they have the most fans. Ask fans of Neumann microphones or Neve equalizers why they prefer the "sound" of this gear and they'll often talk on and on, delivering a very personal—and almost religious—dissertation of their experience. Ask the same folks about their least favorite products, and you'll find a list of gear that often finds its way to the discount bin at your local retailer!

While white noise is very useful for testing equipment electrically, it is not much good for measuring acoustics, or things that we "hear" (the quotes emphasize the differences when sound is manipulated by its medium). In the case of equipment testing, the medium is electrical—be it tubes, transistors, or both, the process is all voltage, so white noise is the appropriate testing agent. For human ears, however, white noise isn't an accurate measure of equal sound. For these circumstances, we use *pink noise*.

Pink noise is similar to white noise, but there has been an accommodation for the logarithmic (exponential) nature of frequencies. Frequencies, like the decibel, are measured logarithmically since the range of frequencies is too large to measure linearly. This means that as you move up the frequency range, there are more and more collections of tones that fall within a band or even within an octave.

As such, you'll find that there are more tones between 220 Hz and 440 Hz than there are there are between 110 Hz and 220 Hz, etc. Pink noise accommodates for this logarithm by adding more weight (or volume) to some of the lower frequencies so they are not "drowned out" by the upper frequencies. **Figure 1.12 and Figure 1.13** show FFT comparisons of white noise and pink noise.

Figure 1.12: FFT chart of white noise showing every frequency at equal amplitude.

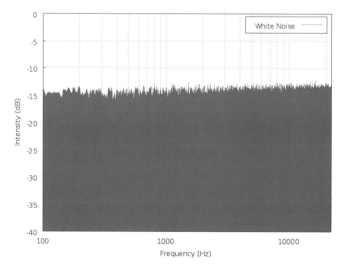

Figure 1.13: FFT chart of pink noise showing the amplitude across the frequency spectrum.

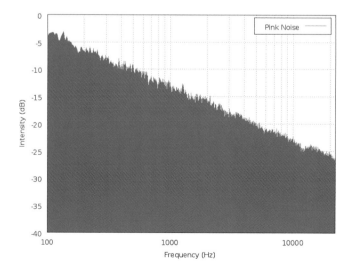

DVD Track 15: This track has 10 seconds of white noise, then pink noise after a short gap. Notice the difference between their sounds and the balance of the high frequencies in each.

Tech-Speak: *Pink Noise*

. . . .

Pink noise is the complete collection of sine waves from 20 Hz to 20,000 Hz, where the loudness of each higher octave of frequencies is diminished relative to the lower octaves.

Because the logarithmic nature of frequencies is not accommodated for in white noise, you'll find that it is very strong in the midrange and treble frequencies compared to pink noise. Thus, when we test any device that captures or reproduces free sound, we tend to use pink noise as it is more related to the "real world" of the frequency response.

COACH'S CORNER

Noise is a helpful tool for ear training and sound design. Often, a certain amount of noise is added to a sound to represent a collection of frequencies that occur in nature. Many modern and classic synthesizers have an oscillator channel that is dedicated to noise generation for just this purpose. For fun, note what happens as we take white or pink noise and play only selected bands of frequencies. Imagine what uses you have for these sounds!

DVD Track 16: White noise played through three bands only—20 Hz to 220 Hz, 220 Hz to 2,200 Hz, and 2,200 Hz to 20,000 Hz.

DVD Track 17: Pink noise played through three bands only—20 Hz to 220 Hz, 220 Hz to 2,200 Hz, and 2,200 Hz to 20,000 Hz.

RECAP

Noise is a collection of all frequencies playing at the same time. The two most common forms of noise are *white noise* and *pink noise*. White noise is the collection of all frequencies playing at the same volume and pink noise is the collection of all frequencies, but with diminished volume as the frequencies get higher. Pink noise compensates for the logarithmic nature of human hearing, and the fact that higher octave bands contain more frequencies than lower octaves.

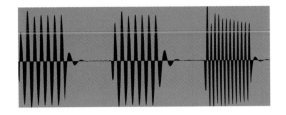

Dynamics: The Decibel

Defining the dB

With the exception of dB SPL, which has a very real meaning to your ears, the dB is a relative measurement of change between the input and output of a box, device, or process. There are two important things to consider about the decibel:

☞ The decibel is measured in several ways.

☞ The decibel is a ratio—it generally has no meaning on its own without being referenced to some other value.

Understanding the decibel as a relative term is difficult at first, because all the equipment we're used to using is well-marked with decibel numbers that have no relation to anything else. For example, if you look at common pieces of gear like microphone preamplifiers or mixers, there is always a set of marked numbers denoting the decibel value. It is easy to assume that these numbers mean just what they say—some fixed dB amount—but that's not exactly the case.

You'll notice that on most standard mixers, for example, each fader has a series of numbers along it, denoting the decibel level. **Figure 1.14** shows a common mixer fader with decibel markings. Notice how the numbers get bigger as the fader moves lower, toward the bottom. This seems counterintuitive—shouldn't the numbers get lower as the faders move lower, as the sound gets lower?

Figure 1.14: A fader on a common mixer showing a range of decibel numbers along the side.

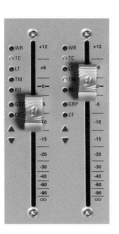

What's really going on here is that the decibel numbers along the side are actually negative numbers, meaning that the decibels denote signals less than zero. This too is counterintuitive. How can sound be less than zero? Isn't that silence? What's quieter than silence?

The mystery is fairly simple. What's really happening is that the negative decibel figures denote that the signal is simply getting smaller. The decibel is a relative figure, so the negative figures mean that the signal going into the fader has been lowered by the decibel amount. The ratio in this case is the difference between the input to the fader and the output from the fader. In the example where the fader is lowered by 3 dB ("-3 dB"), the result is that the output signal is 3 dB quieter than the input. Along these lines, every dB figure can be thought of as either an increase or decrease in volume. Every time the dB level is changed, we call it a gain change. Don't confuse gain change with a strictly positive number—a gain change can be a negative, too, like -3 dB. Remember that 0 dB is nothing more than 0 gain change.

Tech-Speak: *Gain*

Gain *is the change of voltage in a signal whether positive or negative. Gain changes are denoted with "-" or "+" to indicate a negative or positive gain change, respectively. Many positive gain changes are simply noted as "x dB" and do not bother using the "+" sign.*

Remember that the decibel is logarithmic. Meaning it does not increase or decrease, evenly or in a linear manner. In the studio, small adjustments in volume can translate to potentially large volume differences. Conversely, large adjustments in decibel can translate to small differences in volume. **Figure 1.15** shows a logarithmic curve that represents the decibel.

Figure 1.15: The logarithmic representation of the decibel.

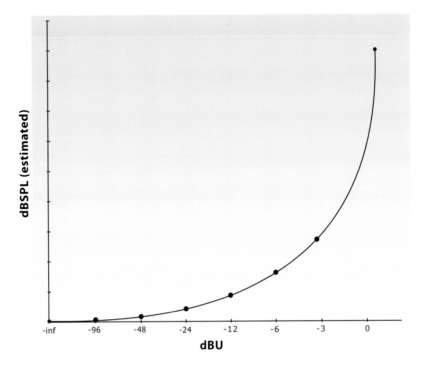

Let's review the mixer example. Whether hardware or software, every fader represents this logarithmic range of volume linearly—that is, along a straight line. The faders don't twist or turn—they move up and down in straight lines. However, the straight line is not a linear layout of decibel figures—the fader moves straight but the differences in dB do not.

COACH'S CORNER

Generally, with hardware, faders come in two sizes: 60mm and "long-throw" 100mm lengths. The main difference is that the 100mm fader throw gives the user an extra 40mm to play with, allowing a bit more room to make volume adjustments. Think of the long-throw version as a luxury-sedan fader, while the 60mm one is a compact! Software tools don't often hold the same standards, and what might look like a tiny movement in the software fader might actually be a huge change in dB! Practice adjusting the fader of your favorite DAW (digital audio workstation), and get comfy with the range of volume changes available with small (or large) fader moves.

Fletcher-Munson Curves

The two most common forms of the dB are dB SPL and dBu. One is how we measure volume by ear (dB SPL), and the other is how we measure volume changes in volts (dBu). We've also looked at frequencies as a function of the pulsating nature of sound energy. We have yet to correlate the two in any way other than to say that they relate . . . until now.

Earlier, I stated that people don't hear the same way and that a person doesn't hear frequencies the same way at different volumes. This important correlation between amplitude and tone (decibels and frequencies) is found in the *Fletcher-Munson curves*. First studied by Harvey Fletcher and W. A. Munson, these curves show the results of tests run on people in an attempt to uncover how people hear tones differently. Different tones were played at different volumes and the participants were asked to raise their hands when the new tone played matched the volume of the previous tone. The results were unexpected

Figure 1.16: Fletcher-Munson curves.

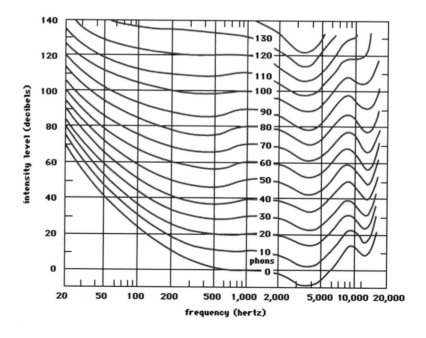

and consistent—on the whole, people do *not* hear tones evenly across all volumes. Take a look at **Figure 1.16** to see the resulting curves.

Notice that, at first inspection, the lower tones (to the left) seem to be louder, because they are drawn higher than others. Along the same lines, the midrange tones appear softer because they are lower, and the high tones are louder once again as they too are higher. This is, in fact, the exact *opposite* of what the curves actually say! The real meaning of the Fletcher-Munson curves is that our ears are most sensitive in the midrange; similarly, the bass tones require greater dB SPL energy to sound as loud as the midtones. Sadly, the ear is simply *not* a very accurate machine in which all tones are as audible as others at the same dB SPL levels.

COACH'S CORNER

While the Fletcher-Munson curves tell us where we are more sensitive to frequencies and where we are less sensitive to frequencies, it should be noted that the curves are the results of testing hundreds of people. Your own hearing might not actually follow along these lines, but all humans follow them closely enough that the curves can be called accurate. These curves are the foundation of many home theater stereo systems, which generally reproduce the bass tones and high tones more aggressively than the mid tones in an effort to compensate for the ear's response. In most production studios, we call that equalization response the "home theater smile," as the EQ curve looks like a smile, with boosts in the lows and highs!

COACH'S CORNER

The ear varies in sensitivity more out of design than out of aesthetics. The tones found in the mid band, where our ears are most sensitive, directly correlate to the bands where the frequencies of the human voice live. In fact, we are most sensitive to the frequency range where most baby cries are heard. It's been argued this is a genetic defense mechanism developed so that prehistoric humans could hear baby cries across greater distances, allowing them to respond immediately to a baby's needs. I'm sure any distraught and sleepless new parent would second this theory—I know I did for each of my children!

Another key ingredient to understanding the Fletcher-Munson curves is that, as the loudness increases, the "flatness" (linear response) of our ears improves. Have you ever noticed that music sounds better when turned up loud? This is partly because it's cool to rock out loud, but also because our ears hear the full range of frequencies more accurately at louder volumes.

This phenomenon is a potential hazard if you think that you should mix everything while listening at a high volume since your ears "work better." The fact is that exposure to loud, consistent sounds over time not only fatigues the eardrums, but can also cause long-term hearing damage and permanent loss! When setting up your studio, setting an appropriate listening volume is a key ingredient. Choosing the dB SPL level that is the "standard" for each room is a bit arbitrary but it should generally be set at a point where the volume is full enough to hear the subtleties of music without making you deaf while soft enough so you don't have to scream to be heard. Common values here range from 75 dB SPL to 87 dB SPL.

COACH'S CORNER

There are many debates about proper music listening levels in the studio. Film mixers often use the standard of 85 dB SPL as a reference for dialog; i.e., when they mix movies, they aim to have the dialog play consistently at or around 85 dB SPL. Music studios, however, have no such standard and as you go from facility to facility, the loudness of the music mixing varies. Part of this variance is due to room size and some is due to personal taste. At what level are you comfortable mixing?

The Different Types of dB

Other than dB SPL, the dB generally refers to a relative number—the gain addition or subtraction as the sound flows through something (EQ, compressor, plug-in, etc.). This is nice, but means nothing without knowing what standard to compare it to. Consider the dollar as an example. The dollar is only worth what you can buy with it (less and less these days, sadly!) and without referencing the bricks of gold in Fort Knox, the dollar's meaning would be even more arbitrary! Luckily, our "Fort Knox" is easy to get into! For us, the magic number is 0.775 volts. This may not be the Holy Grail you were expecting, but there it is. (Insert choir sound here . . .)

Heads up, music types—we're about to start doing some math and using a lot of terms, so put on your science geek hat and hold your breath. I promise it won't hurt that much and it'll all be over soon.

Remembering the relative nature of the dB and the fact that it's measured in many ways, the 0.775-volt reference is mostly useful in measuring—you guessed it—the dB in volts. What this means is that the 0 dBv—also known as dBu (don't ask right now, I'll explain later) is the result when a signal (0.775 volts in this case) is circled through a resistor of 600 ohms, resulting is a heat loss of 1 milliwatt. More on this later, but for now, what's important is to take away that the standard of volts measured in dB is 0.775 dB.

COACH'S CORNER

Note that 0.775 volts is just about ¾ of a volt. The power coming out of a wall outlet is roughly 110 volts, so you can see immediately that the 0 dBu standard of 0.775 volts is tiny in comparison. The whole world of audio in recording and producing is a world of these tiny voltages, which should show you even further that small adjustments in dB (or volt fractions) will yield large results in gain to our ears.

The concept of 0 dB is something like Valhalla—all sounds want to go there gloriously. It was mentioned earlier, when discussing white noise, that audio manufacturers like to build boxes that exhibit no additional color or noise to the frequency spectrum. In similar fashion in the volume world, manufacturers like to build boxes that don't change the volume—unless they're designed to. When they say that the knobs are at 0, they mean it—there should be no change to the levels going through the circuit.

Studios are wired so that all the signals flowing through them are at similar levels, so there should be a 0 dB standard there too. It would be weird if some devices in the studio worked at higher levels and others worked at lower levels. There could be a huge difference as sound moves between them and the result could be noise in the signals, or worse. This is a key component in understanding how to properly connect your devices within the studio to achieve the best results from each device. This is covered in detail later in this book in the "Electronics Basics" section.

Figure 1.17 is a chart of a variety of dB measurements and what they mean—both in terms of electricity and relative to each other. It's important to understand that all of these dB measurements relate to each other in some way. In fact, this relationship is the foundation for calibrating a studio's operating levels and improving the *translatability* of your productions—that is, making sure that what you hear in your room is what others will hear in theirs.

Take a look at the "dBfs" (dB Full Scale) row in **Figure 1.17**— this is the one that you are probably most familiar with, without even knowing it! Anyone who's been using a DAW in the past 20 years (yes, it's been that long since DAWs were first brought into the studio) has been looking at meters measuring dBfs. If you've ever seen a set of analog VU (volume units) meters, you know that the numbers are black until the needle hits 0, then they get red and they only read up to about 3 dB. All of these numbers are relative to the 0 dBu figure, which relates to 0.775 volts. **Figure 1.18** shows a typical VU meter, with the top measurement being +3 dBu.

Figure 1.17: A comparison of dB levels and measurement types.

dBV represents the level compared to 1 volt RMS. 0dBV = 1V. There is no reference to impedance.

dBu represents the level compared to 0.775 Volts RMS with an unloaded, open circuit source (u = unloaded).

dBm represents the power level compared to 1 mWatt. This is a level compared to 0.775 volts RMS across a 600 ohm load impedance. Note that this is a measurement of *power*, **not** a measurement of *voltage*.

dBfs relative to digital Full Scale (digital)

dB SPL a measure of sound pressure level. Example, a jet taking off registers around 120 -130 dB SPL

Figure 1.18: A typical VU meter showing the 0 and +3 dB markings.

Tech-Speak: *dBfs*

dBfs is a relative term for the dB measured in the Full Scale. Digital audio is, by its nature, as much as 20 dB hotter than classic analog audio gear. As a result, dBfs is a scale of dB measurements that is as much as 20 dB larger than scales that top out at 0 dBu.

Since the 0 VU measurement correlates to 0.775 volts, it should stand to reason that the 0 measurement in your DAW is the same 0 dB, right? Well as you might have guessed, it isn't.

Digital audio has the capacity to handle much larger dB levels than analog 0 (at least today's digital audio can!) and as such, the 0 dB in your DAW is not even close to the 0 VU on the analog meters. Without getting too deep into the math, suffice to say that 0 dBfs is roughly +20 dBu—literally 20 dB hotter! Since hotter means louder and louder is better, digital audio must be better than analog audio! Right?

COACH'S CORNER

Debating the "hotter is better" discussion with any old-school engineer can be a lot of fun. Watch them shake their heads and start speaking more loudly as they pontificate about the ignorance of today's youth. They have a completely valid point—while analog audio is quieter than digital audio, it can sound just as good as digital audio—if not better. The real point is to compare the two at the same listening volume and then decide which sounds better! For the record, this is a common comparison technique used by mastering engineers today.

Note that 0 dB measured in one way—like dBfs—has a relative measurement in some other form, like dBu. Relating the two is important as you connect the analog world to the digital world, so you understand how the two work together. So far, we've explored 0 dBu as a relative term to dBfs, which is roughly 20 dB away from the other. With this in mind, it is safe to say that in general, 0 dBu = -20 dBfs. That means an analog device plugged into your DAW's inputs will potentially be giving 20 dB less signal than your DAW can handle. This can lead to the potential of 20 dB of noise in your signal—certainly an unwanted piece of sound in your music!

RECAP

We hear frequencies differently at different loudness levels and should be aware of how loud to set our studios prior to making critical listening decisions. The dB is measured in many ways and all of they relate to each other in some way. 0 dB in volts is related to 0.775 volts for analog equipment and is related to 0 dBfs (digital) by -20, in that 0 dBu = -20 dBfs.

Operating Levels

It was mentioned earlier that different pieces of gear operate at different levels and knowing the level at which any piece of gear works is key to understanding how to connect them together. Getting this wrong can lead to noise (the input signal is too quiet, requiring a lot of amplification to boost levels) or heavy distortion (the input signal is too loud, thus overloading the next stage) from such mismatches. **Figure 1.19** shows a comparison chart of different types of gear and a generalization of their operating levels. There are, of course, huge variances within each category, and you should compare the specs of your gear before jumping to any conclusions.

Figure 1.19: A chart of gear types and their generalized operating levels.

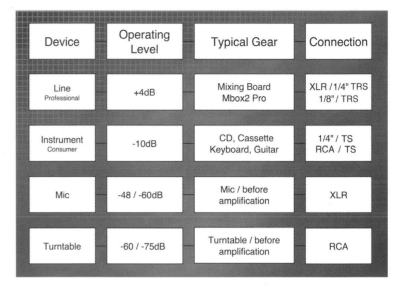

Device	Operating Level	Typical Gear	Connection
Line Professional	+4dB	Mixing Board Mbox2 Pro	XLR / 1/4" TRS 1/8" / TRS
Instrument Consumer	-10dB	CD, Cassette Keyboard, Guitar	1/4" / TS RCA / TS
Mic	-48 / -60dB	Mic / before amplification	XLR
Turntable	-60 / -75dB	Turntable / before amplification	RCA

The level issue is less of a problem these days, as many pieces of gear are designed better than their historical counterparts, but the mismatching of gear and operating levels has historically been a huge issue in studio design. And with the resurgence in the use of turntables in DJ performances, the turntable has been brought back into the studio. This is one of the biggest offenders in the operating level wars, as a phonograph output is so much lower than current professional operating level standards.

COACH'S CORNER

Turntables were among the original recording playback media and as such, set the standard in audio for 50 years. The technology has stayed the same since the beginning, with the one exception being the advent of stereo in the '50s. During the turntable's heyday, electricity brought to your home was a different standard than it is today, and back then there was no use of the ground wire. Today, turntables require a dedicated ground wire be connected to some metallic contact to ensure its safe (and low-noise) operation.

In the case of a turntable, a dedicated preamp is generally required and most certainly suggested if not required. As we saw in **Figure 1.19**, the turntable output is generally 45 dB (or more) quieter than the expected line level of other playback devices and as such, requires a pre-amp to boost the signal to line level. Most DJ mixer manufacturers understand that today's DJ is likely to mix and match CDs, vinyl and laptops all in one session and modern DJ mixers are designed to accommodate several types of inputs at once. They are usually well marked and are generally labeled things like "tape," "line," and "phono" for clarity. **Figure 1.20** shows the back of a common DJ mixer and the types and labels of the connections.

Figure 1.20: The back row of connectors on a typical DJ mixer.

It is generally accepted that the two standards in use within professional and project studios today are -10 dBm (some professional, but mostly *pro-sumer* gear) and +4 dBu (professional). Remember that the goal is still 0 dB—the perfect operating level where there is no change between the input and output. Also remember that even though 0 dBu is the original analog professional audio standard, that standard has since been upgraded, as gear has gotten hotter and hotter. Today's standard is +4 dBu.

COACH'S CORNER

Since +4 dBu is hotter than 0 dBu by 4 dB (hence the "+" symbol), it must be better as the studio standard, right? If your entire gear list operates at -10 dBm (dB measured in milliwatts) except the monitors, logic should tell you that the decision to operate at +4 is probably a mistake. The odds are, however, that this is a rare situation, and if you've done any shopping for gear made in the past 10 years, it won't apply in your case!

RECAP

Audio is measured in several forms of the dB, which all relate to each other in some way. The voltage standard is 0.775 volts, which translates to 0 dBu (analog), which is roughly the same as -20 dBfs (digital). Most studios operate at a level of +4 dBu, making them "hotter" than consumer/project studios, which sometimes operate at -10 dBm. Knowing the operating level of your gear matters when you connect things together so you can avoid noise and/or distortion.

Power Rules

Not to be confused with the golden rule ("He who has the gold makes the rules" or "Do unto others as you'd have them do unto you"—which is *your* golden rule?), power rules are simply standards in measuring the dB and how much power each dB measurement offers. There are a few power rules to know and they have very real implications on our mix decisions. These rules will explain some production phenomena that you might have experienced already, and others that—if you re-create the experiment—you will experience now.

Doubling

We've already seen that studios operate at different levels, and that each piece of gear within the studio operates at a different level within the overall studio level. This can add confusion and potentially unwanted signal artifacts, such as noise or distortion. Assuming that you've gotten all the connections and operating levels worked out, you should know what happens when you connect everything together. For example, if you need to connect a preamp from a DJ rig to a DAW, how much gain would you need to add? If you need to lower the gain to connect from a DAW back to the DJ rig, how much gain are you losing?

The amount of gain that always seems to resonate best with people is the ever-popular *doubling*—at what point are we twice as loud or twice as soft? As you might have guessed, the answer here is . . ."It depends!" Yes, depending on which type of dB you are measuring, the answer varies. For example, in amplifier design, the rule is that to increase the dB output by 3 dB, you'll need to double the power within the amp to get it. By this standard, a doubling of power is 3 dB.

However, a doubling of voltage within a circuit is actually 6 dB. For our studio purposes, this is more likely what you'll experience. In other words, turning the fader up by 6 dB represents a doubling of the voltages that are passing the signal from one device to another. Only when that signal hits an amplifier and plays to speakers does the 3 dB power rule apply. Note that neither of these actually means louder to your ears! For a doubling of acoustic power, the answer is 10 dB SPL!

So what does this mean to us in the studio? Generally, it means that 6 dB of fader increase on any track will double the voltage going to the outputs. In order for a sound to really be twice as loud to your ears, the fader needs to be pushed up 10 dB. Neither answer really matters, as the concept of doubling is somewhat arbitrary—in general, you simply turn up the signal until it's loud enough, relative to everything else in your session. You might not think that 6 dB is very loud (it's not double to your ears, after all!) but it might be too much for the session or even the mixer (digital or analog), and the result might be distortion. Keep these figures in mind as benchmarks to be used when choosing how much gain to add or subtract from any sound.

COACH'S CORNER

In many cases, sounds will be recorded too quietly when compared to the other sounds in a session. For example, consider the case where a vocal was recorded in one session and a section was overdubbed at a later time. It's likely that the energy level of the first session was much higher than the energy level of the second session. As a result, the overdubbed file may be quieter than the others. In this case, you may need to increase the gain on the file, as opposed to automating the volume curve, and you should start in increments of 3 dB—a 50% increase in voltage power. If this isn't enough, increase by 3 more dB, making a total increase of 6 dB—a double of the voltage power.

The Haas Effect (aka Precedence Effect)

Understanding the doubling of power rules is an important foundation when approaching the next power rule—the *Haas Effect*. Named after Helmut Haas, the Haas Effect says a few things at one time, but the most notable point is that a sound coming from one speaker is noted to be -3 dB (3 dB quieter) than if the same sound played equally out of both speakers. This means that in a stereo field, a sound panned to the left or right will play -3 dB versus playing in mono out of both speakers.

The original tests run by Mr. Haas measured the results when a signal was presented to a listener from within a pseudo 180-degree space. The Haas effect is the cornerstone of panning perception and spatial imaging when listening to stereo material. Stereo was not commercially available at the time (mid-1940s) and Haas' tests were pioneering research in the field. Even though stereo was not yet commercially available, some home stereos did employ two speakers—one for each ear (although the sources were usually mono). Haas set out to find the results of the signal played through the two speakers at different levels and at different times.

His results were as follows:

☞ Sounds that play from one speaker reach the closest ear first and the farther ear second.

☞ When the same sound is played out of two speakers and one arrives to the ear sooner than the other by a few dozen milliseconds (ms) or more, the ear perceives the sound to come from the closest source only, effectively ignoring the farther source.

☞ If the delayed sound is offset by roughly 25 ms or less, the ear cannot distinguish the second sound from the first. Events more than 25 ms apart are perceived as two distinct events.

Tech-Speak: *The Haas Effect*

The Haas Effect states that people perceive the localization of a sound by precedence—closest sound is perceived first. When a sound is played out of two sources (each equidistant from each ear) and one is delayed by less than 30 ms, the listener will perceive only one sound source, the first to reach the ear.

COACH'S CORNER

There is no rule stating that 25 ms is the defining time period at which people hear events as separated. For some, this figure is closer to 20 ms and for others, it may be closer to 30 ms.

DVD Track 18: plays a speaking voice for 10 seconds in dual mono. The same signal is played equally in volume and time from both speakers. Where do you perceive the tone to be coming from?

DVD Track 19: plays a speaking voice for 10 seconds in mono—first panned left, then middle, then right. Did you perceive any volume difference? Were you able to track the vocal as it moved? Are your speakers wired backwards (left is right, right is left)?

DVD Track 20: plays a speaking voice for 10 seconds where the signal is played 10 ms earlier on the right than on the left. Both tones are at the same dB level. Where do you perceive the tone to be coming from?

DVD Track 21: plays a speaking voice for 10 seconds where the signal is played 50 ms earlier on the right than on the left. Do you hear the two voices separately? Where are they coming from?

RECAP

The dB is measured in different ways and, as such, each dB measurement has its own meaning and scale. We hear frequencies differently at different volumes, with a higher sensitivity in the upper midrange. A doubling of a sound's power means different things, depending on whether you're measuring amps, volts or SPL. We have the ability to localize sounds—to audibly discern where they're coming from.

When two sounds are played within 25 ms of each other, the ear prioritizes the one that hits first or is closer in precedent. We hear sounds as being 3 dB SPL louder when played evenly out of two speakers, as opposed to played from only a single speaker. Headroom is the amount of dB "space" between the loudest delivered signal and the maximum capacity of the medium.

Understanding Audio Headroom

Fletcher-Munson curves could be argued to predict that "louder is better." After all, our ears perform better when sound is played louder—isn't that enough? While the answer on the surface might look like "yes," the answer is, "it depends." Louder is better when comparing the flatness of our ears' responsiveness to different frequencies, but over time, your ears will fatigue (the eardrum literally gets tired and becomes sore, like muscles). Over very long periods of time and really high SPL levels, our ears lose their performance—permanently.

COACH'S CORNER

Loudness being "better" is a historical phenomenon that is not rooted in technology as much as it is rooted in finances. Remember that one goal of making records was (and still is) to sell lots of them. The way you found listeners back in the day was two-fold: you played live shows (which performers still do), and you got heard on the radio (not so much these days). Radio was the big equalizer—if you could get your record heard in Boise, you could sell records there and develop a fan base. You could then support a tour, which would earn more money and sell more records. Sound familiar? Some things haven't really changed that much over time.

Getting on the radio was—and still is—a daunting task, and being heard is no guarantee of record sales. The DJ and/or program director had to like a tune enough to play it again and the audience had to like it, too. But was that it? When AM radio gave way to FM radio, three things happened—songs were playable in stereo, stations could extend their reach to new audiences, and songs got louder. FM is simply better than AM at reproducing a wider frequency response and

COACH'S CORNER continued:

larger dB amounts, and, as such, songs played louder. Louder songs caught more people's ears and, in turn, sold more records. On and on this went, and it still applies. Hence, the notion that louder is better is because you'll sell more records!

COACH'S CORNER

Along the way to today's loudness wars, engineers like Bruce Swedien (Michael Jackson's *Off the Wall*) were praised and lambasted for making more dynamic records. Rumor has it that Bruce, at one point, was the target of a lawsuit by club owners who kept blowing speakers because his records were too loud!

What does this mean in terms of today's records? Can't you just turn down the volume on the speakers and listen more quietly? Or turn them up? Of course, yes you can. What "louder" really means is "louder than the other guy's record, when played at the same volume." Simply play your record next to someone else's but don't touch the volume knob. Which one is louder? Which one is better? That's an example of comparative volume, or the A/B test. Switch between songs "A" and "B" and see which is better.

Remember when I told you that telling some "old-school" engineers that louder is better would make them get grumpy? Well, do the A/B test again, but this time, turn up the volume on the quieter song to match the louder one and then judge. Is the same song still a hands-down winner? Harder to tell? This should give you a clue: Listening decisions are best made when the A/B comparison is performed at the same listening volume (dB SPL). What this really means is find an SPL level that works for you (75, 77, 85, etc . . .) and make that the standard by which everything gets listened. By comparing things at the same volume, you'll have a better sense of how your record will stack up against others.

Along these same lines, we should take a look at the DAW. The maximum level achievable in digital audio is 0 dBfs, which is as much as 20 dB hotter than analog 0 (0 dBu). Should every sound be recorded or processed to the point of hitting (and staying at) 0 dBfs? Isn't that loudest? Isn't that best? Some would argue—yes.

While it is true that 0 dBfs is as loud as it gets in digital audio, it is arguable that it is not best. As you'll see later in this book (in the section—Digital Audio Primer"), you simply cannot record over 0 dBfs with good results. At best, you'll only distort your sound a little bit; at worst, you'll destroy your recording. If you could somehow predict how loudly your talent will perform, then you'd know whether the talent will exceed 0 dBfs during their recording. Sometimes you can, but more often than not, the talent changes their mind (how dare they!) and they perform louder than the time before (or even the note before). In this case, your recording will go over 0 dBfs and will likely distort. You may have ruined the best take your talent has in them.

What most engineers do in cases like this is build in what we call *headroom*. Headroom is literally the difference ("room") between the loudest sound the talent will deliver and 0 dBfs. The metaphor comes from the small space where your head is close to the ceiling—how high can you jump until you run out of headroom, bonking your head on the ceiling in the process? In the recording case, the metaphor is, how loud can your talent's volume jump until it hits the ceiling (0 dBfs) and "bonks" the signal into distortion?

Tech-Speak: *Headroom*

Headroom *is the amount of dB "space" between the loudest signal and the maximum capacity of the recorded medium.*

For more on the specifics of digital audio, skip forward to the section under "Captured Sound—Digital Audio Primer." Many people have different views on headroom, but the general consensus is to leave yourself as little as 3 dB of headroom (-3 dBfs) or as much as 12 dB of headroom (-12 dBfs) when recording into your DAW. Much of this is dependent on how you calibrate your DAW's input/output sections—if you even can.

"sound evolves over time in a very specific pattern,

referred to as its "envelope" . . ."

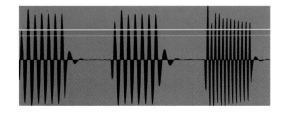

Morphology and Time

Sound Over Time: The Envelope

Sound evolves over time in a very specific pattern, referred to as its *envelope*. The envelope is made up of four main parts, and all sounds follow these four parts: the *attack*, the *decay*, the *sustain* and the *release*—known as the ADSR.

Tech-Speak: *The ADSR Envelope*

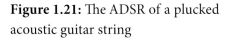

The way in which a sound evolves over time—its envelope—can be broken down into four phases that occur in this order: the attack, the decay, the sustain, and the release—aka the ADSR.

The *attack* is the length of time it takes for a sound to increase its pressure from zero to its loudest point, while the *decay* is the time it takes to attenuate from the highest point to its average point. The *sustain* is the average level maintained from the decay to the beginning of the *release*, which is the ending of the sound. **Figure 1.21** shows a typical ADSR of a plucked acoustic guitar string.

Figure 1.21: The ADSR of a plucked acoustic guitar string

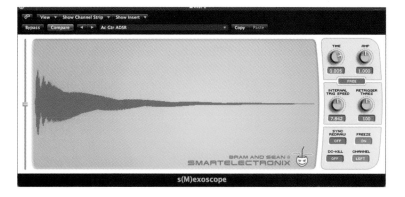

DVD Track 22: A plucked acoustic guitar string, matching the envelope shown in **Figure 1.21.**

Keep in mind that the ADSR is the time involved in a single sound impulse and that every sound conforms to some kind of ADSR. Not every sound has a clearly defined envelope—some have practically no attack or decay, and others have a really long release, to the point where the sustain and release are almost the same. Other ADSR examples are shown in **Figure 1.22**.

Figure 1.22: Varying ADSRs with shortened and elongated sections.

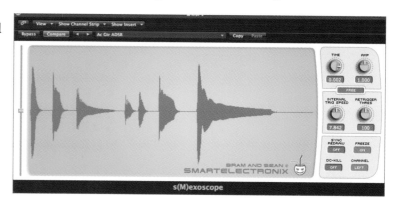

When sounds are repetitious, their envelopes get strung together and sometimes the release of one sound never really occurs because it is overlapped by the attack of the sound after it. **Figure 1.23** shows overlapping envelopes, both as simple ADSR and as standard waveforms.

Figure 1.23: Overlapping ADSRs on a waveform.

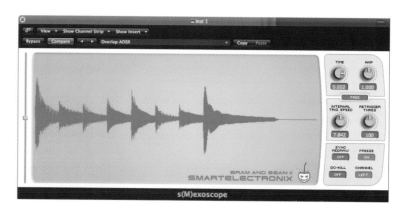

DVD Track 23: An acoustic guitar part, demonstrating overlapping ADSRs, as shown in **Figure 1.23.**

Looking at the waveforms of the various ADSRs of sounds demonstrates one of the key links between frequency and time—the cyclical nature of the sine wave. Going back to

Figure 1.21, notice that the waveform goes above and below a central *zero-crossing line* (ZCL) and is similar to the line delineating the positive and negative portions of a wave. In other words, like a simple sine wave, complex waves have positive and negative energy where the positive energy "pushes" and the negative energy "pulls" the sound.

Tech-Speak: *The Zero-Crossing Line (ZCL)*

The zero-crossing line *is the horizontal line in a DAW indicating where a recording's energy is neither positive nor negative.*

COACH'S CORNER

If you could listen to just the sound that exists at the zero-crossing line, you'd actually hear nothing—there is no energy there! Try highlighting a small piece of a sound where the highlighted section is only at the zero-crossing line. Play it and see if you can hear anything!

At the zero-crossing line, the energy of the wave has "stalled" and actually produces no sound. Sound is a mechanical energy wave where the molecules of the medium literally bounce into each other and pass the energy onward. Remember the bouncing basketball? As the basketball reaches its apex, it neither falls nor rises—it simply hangs in the air, floating for the briefest of moments. This is the equivalent of the ZCL—the point at which the sound has no energy (or more specifically, it is in between pushing and pulling the molecules of the medium it is in).

COACH'S CORNER

While it is almost always advisable to perform edits at the ZCL, there are occasions when it is desirable to cut your audio in the middle of the wave. The results are a very audible clicking sound, known as the *Fourier click*. In some electronic music productions, where multiple edits are made in a short period of time, hearing the click is a desired effect.

The Basics of Time Shift

Remember the Haas effect? Briefly stated, Haas tells us that our ears prioritize sounds coming to the closest ear first and effectively ignore information entering the ear that's farther from the sound source. What's implied here is that the ear further from the source receives information a tiny bit late compared to the closer ear. Now, the question at hand is: At what point do we perceive the sound going into the far ear? Are we always deaf to sounds arriving at the farther ear?

The answer lies in understanding time and its relationship to Haas. In normal cases, like in the studies of Haas, a sound source is moved across a pair of speakers and the listener tries to pinpoint the location of the sound within the pair. Usually, the speakers are fairly close to the listener (average distance of 6 to 8 feet), which puts the sound in both ears only milliseconds (or less) apart from each other. Remember that sound travels approximately one foot per millisecond. Our ears are good, but we can't hear sounds that close together in time as separate sounds, which is another reason why Haas works.

The general rule of thumb is that when two sounds arrive at our ears 25 to 35 milliseconds apart, we don't hear them as separate events. We might experience the combined sounds in different ways like phasing or flanging (defined below). For many, the experience is something of a "smearing" of the sound—the individual "punch" or impact of the sound is diminished as if the attack was smeared.

Tech-Speak: *Phasing*

Phasing *is the result of two similar sounds that play together at slightly different times (usually less than 25 to 35 ms apart). The two sounds sum acoustically (their point of phase within the sine wave), yet many of their component frequencies cancel each other out acoustically. The phasing changes over time as the waves are shifted slowly back and forth, changing the frequency at which the phasing occurs. The rate of the shift is what gives phasing its cyclical sound.*

Tech-Speak: *Flanging*

Flanging *is similar to phasing—it's the result of hearing two like sounds playing together but at slightly different times. The term comes from the manipulation of tape machines, where someone would lightly touch the flange of the tape reel, (the metal circular plate that holds the tape) and change the speed of the playback. When one flange was slowed and the other was not, the result was a shifting in time between the two. Flanges could be sped up and slowed down repeatedly for a shifting "flanging" sound.*

DVD Track 24: A guitar part, first played clean, then with a phasing sound, then a flanging sound. Note how the phasing smears the attack of the guitar and the flanging smears the attack even more.

In the '70s, many vocalists sought this smeared sound on their productions. The smearing of the attack created a softness in their vocals that often fit the soft and mellow tone of the music they were creating. The easiest way to achieve this effect was to sing the part at least twice and play the two tracks together. This is called *doubling*, for obvious reasons. It is safe to say that only the best singers can repeat a performance perfectly (or pretty close), and most singers—even good ones—would always vary slightly. Either the timing would be off a bit or the pitch (or both) and the results were tiny variations of the two performances that changed unpredictably over the course of the song. Since the waves of the two performances rarely lined up perfectly, they cancelled each other differently from moment to moment, creating a randomized phase-shifted sound.

This technique is still used often today, sometimes to extremes. Many producers have their singer sing the part three, four or even eight times to blend them together for a thick and rich sound. Clearly, the parts need to be very close to each other to be perceived as a single voice, and this process can take time.

DVD Track 25: A short vocal stanza performed first as a single, then as a doubled, tripled, and then quadrupled voice. Notice how at first the part gets a slight smear to the attack and then a thickness appears.

RECAP

The evolution of a sound over time is measured by its *envelope*. Every sound has an envelope, although every sound's envelope is unique. The envelope consists of attack, decay, sustain, and release values that make up the overall time image of the sound. The envelope is only one part of the "time" portion of sound,—and the way sounds play against each other in time affects the impact of the sound. Shifts in the time of a sound that's played twice can either be a *phasing*, *flanging*, or *doubling* sound.

pro•duc•tion

[pruh–duhk–shuh] – noun

1. the organization and presentation of dramatic entertainment.
2. the act of producing; creation of a work of art

Captured Sound

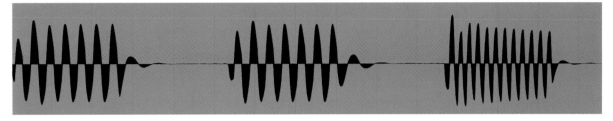

"the act of producing: creation of a work of art . . ."

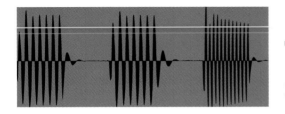

The Life Cycle of Sound in the Studio

Basic Electronics

In the studio, two key concepts to be aware of are *voltage* and *resistance*. The voltage part is fairly common—we've already discussed the relationship between voltage and the dB—but resistance is new for us. Resistance describes the electrical "friction" that tries to stop the flow of electricity.

Tech-Speak: *Voltage, Amperage, and Resistance*

In terms of physics (in this case, electricity), activity is measured in a few ways: the potential for the flow of energy, the resistance or friction against that energy, and the actual flow of energy. Electrically, the potential flow of energy (electrons) is voltage, *the force against that flow is the* resistance, *and the actual flow is* amperage.

COACH'S CORNER

Have you ever noticed that cable manufacturers try to sell expensive cables that are either plated in gold or wired with gold? The reason is that gold is an excellent conductor of electricity, which implies that it has less resistance against electrical flow. Additionally, gold is a fairly inert metallic element that does not readily corrode, as do copper and silver conductors. But all cables and connectors (including gold) have some measure of resistance, and lowering this figure is key to keeping high-quality audio passing through your wires. Knowing the resistance of the cables is important because connecting pieces of equipment incorrectly can seriously impact the quality of your sound.

Keep in mind that there is a difference between the wires that connect pieces of gear and the operating level of the gear itself. Many people confuse the connector on the end of the wire with the type of equipment you can use it with. For example, the XLR connector is often assumed to be exclusively for microphones—so much so that wires with XLR connectors on both ends are casually referred to as "mic" cables. This is a misnomer—the connector is in no way indicative of a single usage.

The connector is, however, a good indication of the type of wire between the connectors and that gives us a clue as to what type of gear it might be connected to and how. It's not a rule, mind you—just an educated guess. **Table 1** shows a list of cables and connectors and their general uses. One key ingredient in cables is their resistance, which is a measurement of how hard the electrical signal must work to travel the length of the cable without changing its power or losing quality.

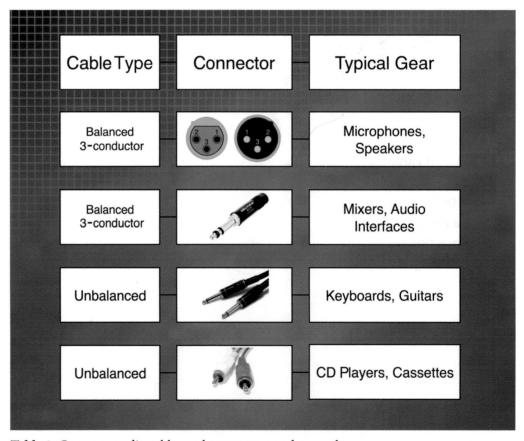

Cable Type	Connector	Typical Gear
Balanced 3-conductor		Microphones, Speakers
Balanced 3-conductor		Mixers, Audio Interfaces
Unbalanced		Keyboards, Guitars
Unbalanced		CD Players, Cassettes

Table 1: Common audio cables and connectors and general uses.

Audio cables generally come in three types: *balanced, unbalanced,* and *speaker.* Let's use the term "cable" in reference to the finished product and the term "conductor" to mean each of the individual wires within the cable. Speaker cable has two conductors separated by some sort of insulation, usually plastic or rubber,—that is non-conductive and somewhat heat resistant. The two conductors are exactly the same and work very well for audio monitors or sound reinforcement/musical instrument speakers, where each conductor should represent even signals—one to push the speaker out (compression wave) and one to pull the speaker back (rarefaction wave).

In the case of cables connecting different pieces of gear to each other, speaker wire rarely works—at least not very well. A dedicated ground wire is needed to flow the noise contained on ground wires to the earth and drain it out of the system. (Don't worry if this doesn't make sense—just go with it for a minute.) Other conductors in the cable carry the actual signal and are protected with a plastic coating—the ground wire is not. Many cables carry only two conductors—one for the ground and one for the actual audio signal. These cables are called *unbalanced*, or *single-conductor*, and are often used in short-run applications such as electric guitar cables or between components in home hi-fi systems.

COACH'S CORNER

Unbalanced cables tend to have very high resistance levels and are not good for uses beyond 15 feet. They will work, but as the length increases, the high frequency response diminishes significantly. In cases where an unbalanced cable needs to bring the signal further than 15 feet, a device called a *direct box* (aka *DI*, or *direct input box*) is often used. The DI converts the signal from a high-resistance signal to a low-resistance signal, allowing it to run for literally miles. The DI is also known as a *balancing kit*, or *balancer*.

The term *balanced* refers to the fact that there is one conductor carrying the signal (called the *lead wire*) and a matching conductor carrying the returning signal (called the *neutral*). In the case of balanced wires, having three conductors within the cable presents advantages and disadvantages. One of the advantages is that having the neutral connected drops the resistance on the cable from 10,000 ohms to roughly 600 ohms and, as such, allows the signal to run much longer distances without signal degradation—hundreds of feet for low-level microphone signals, and up to a mile or more for line-level signals.

Tech-Speak: *Balanced Line*

A balanced line *is an audio line consisting of three conductors: two signal wires and a ground (shield) wire, where one of the signal wires carries the sound signal and the other carries a copy that is 180 degrees out of phase. When the signal reaches the destination, the inverted copy is "flipped" (via a balancing circuit or transformer) and brought back into phase with the other. Any noise (such as electrical hum or buzz) that is picked up by the cable along the way is also inverted with the signal on one leg of the cable, resulting in phase cancellation of the noise with a subsequent summation of the original signal.*

COACH'S CORNER

Consider today's digital and wireless signals. More than ever, radio, Bluetooth, cellular, and general wireless signals float throughout the air, infiltrating everything. This type of noise and interference is indiscriminate and will certainly find its way into your wires at some point. Remember that, if wireless signals can pass through the walls of your home, they can most certainly pass through the protective coating around the cable.

One of the disadvantages of the balanced line is that there are three conductors in the cable, which presents three opportunities for unwanted noise to find its way into the signal. This being the case, three-conductor balanced wires like this need some form of noise-rejecting power in order to be useful. In our case, the solution is called a *twisted pair*—simply twisting the lead and neutral within the cable in a braided fashion.

Tech-Speak: *Twisted-Pair Cable*

Twisted-pair *cable consists of three conductors within the wire: one for the "hot," one for the "cold" (neutral), and one for the ground, where the hot and cold are twisted around each other.*

Twisting of the wires has the effect of alternating a magnetic field around the wire at every twist. This flipping of the magnetic field causes a pushing of unwanted signals within a wire to the outer edges, where the ground lives. So, unwanted noise like cell phone transmissions or radio frequencies that enter the cable are magnetically rejected and pushed onto the unshielded ground conductor. The ground carries the noise to the earth and away from the rest of the studio. As a result, balanced twisted-pair wire has the best results in audio performance—low impedance for long travel runs and noise rejection to keep the signal clean over those long runs!

One of the most common mistakes in understanding audio cables lies in the difference between stereo and mono cables. Let's take a moment to first understand the differences between stereo and mono so we can understand how to identify the cable, connector, and uses among them.

Mono is defined as a single sound source. When thought of electrically, it's a single cable, carrying a single sound, that is eventually interpreted as a single sound. Even at this point, however, mono can be confusing. For example, if a sound plays out of the left of two speakers, is it mono or stereo? Since the sound is coming from somewhere other than the center, isn't it creating a stereo image?

By simply panning a sound to one side or the other, the source does not change, although the listener would be able to identify the sound in a unique location within a stereo field. In this view, a mono source playing out of one speaker more than another is not enough to define the sound as stereo. For example, if the same mono source sound played out of one of five speakers in a surround sound setup, would the sound be considered surround? The answer here is still no. The source is still mono.

Tech-Speak: *Mono Sound*

Mono refers to a single sound or single channel. When the sound is played evenly out of two speakers, the listener perceives a single source—they hear it in mono, which is known as monaural sound.

Tech-Speak: *Stereo Sound*

Stereo refers to two sounds or channels. In situations where there are two speakers, the sound plays uniquely from each speaker.

The key ingredient in identifying a sound source as stereo is the number "2". What this means is that a sound would have to be captured using, at minimum, two microphones, recording information to two channels, to be played out of two speakers. However, this definition alone is not enough to define stereo.

Traditionally, stereo imaging is recognized when experiencing a sound source that is wide—wider than the width of your ears, to be more specific—and plays back uniquely across the two speakers. In the case of a drum set or a piano, the sound source extends beyond the width of your head. When the instrument is played, you can hear the sound "move" across the landscape in front of you as the player moves. On a piano, the low notes would be on the left (from the player's position) and the high notes would be on the right (also from the player's perspective). **Figure 1.24** shows the inside of a piano.

Figure 1.24: A piano shown from the player's perspective, where the low and high notes are heard on the left and right, respectively.

In the case of the piano, the concept of stereo is very direct—when you play back the recording, you should hear the sound move just as you do at the piano itself. The same would apply for drums—as the drummer plays the kit, moving from one drum to the next, the sound source moves along with the performance. This would be reproduced in the recording—translating the stereo image of the drums to the same stereo image of the recording.

Not all stereo works this way. What has been described is a true stereo image, where the stereo source is reproduced faithfully in the recording. Taking a look at a vocal scenario, where two mics are used to record a single vocalist, we don't have the luxury of the simple definition—the sound source is not wider than our ears. However, you might find that moving one mic slightly closer to the vocalist than the other and panning them differently causes a stereo effect. While the perception of the panned vocal recording is stereo (unique sounds in each speaker), the result is indeed an effect and not a reproduction of a stereo instrument. In this case, the best term is *dual panned mono.* The result may be stereophonic, but the source is still mono. The singer still has only one mouth, after all. Many recordings like this are indeed dual mono and not true stereo.

It's important to understand the concepts of mono and stereo when dealing with both your DAW and your studio in general. The definition of stereo and mono can help us understand certain cables better and avoid confusion when trying to connect equipment. For example, let's look at a "stereo" cable. I use quotes here because the cable itself is not stereo—it is meant to carry a stereo signal. **Figure 1.25** shows a stereo cable where one end has separate left and right RCA connectors and the other end has a "mini" 1/8-inch connector. This cable is actually two cables in one, carrying both the left and right sides of a stereo sound at once.

Figure 1.25: Mini 1/8-inch to dual RCA cable.

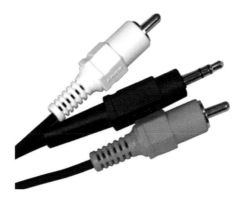

Whereas XLR cables have three conductors and are balanced carrying one mono signal, other three-conductor cables are used to carry stereo signals. The cable above is one, where one end has two unique two-conductor connectors and the other end is a single 1/8-inch connector housing all three conductors. When this connector is 1/4-inch, it is known as a TRS connector—tip/ring/sleeve. TRS connectors are just like XLRs—they house connections to each of the three conductors in a balanced cable. The connector has two black stripes, or insulators, to separate the three conductors, and each conductor is connected either to the tip, the ring (the metal piece in between the two stripes), or the sleeve.

In the $\frac{1}{8}$-inch stereo cable, the three conductors are joined at the $\frac{1}{8}$-inch end but separated along the cable—the tip and ground are sent to the left connector, while the ring and ground is sent to the right (the ground conductor gets split in two, so it's shared by both the left and right connectors). Cables with TRS connectors on each end are NOT stereo as each end has only one connector. The $\frac{1}{8}$-inch TRS connector in stereo cables is more a function of space than anything else—trying to add two RCA connector ports on a device as small as something like an iPod would ruin the portability of the device.

So far, we've only referred to three-conductor XLR cables used for analog mic and line connections. Three-pin XLRs are also utilized for connecting a serial stereo datastream in the AES/EBU digital audio protocol and look like analog mic cables, but require specialized 110-ohm cabling. And other, less-common forms of connectors using the XLR housing exist, such as five-pin XLRs used for the output of professional stereo microphones. (These typically connect to specialized "Y" cables that break the connection out to separate standard three-pin, 2 XLRs for the left and right signals.) Four-pin XLRs are often used for connecting stage intercom systems, and are standard for power plugs supplying 12-volt DC voltage to pro film and video cameras. Multi-pin XLRs are also typically the choice for connecting tube microphones, to carry both power and the mic's output signal. However, aside from these and a few other custom, non-audio applications the term "XLR cable" almost universally refers to a three-pin cable used for balanced mic and/or line connections.

TRS cables are balanced, mono cables, as are XLR cables. Essentially, they are the same cable with different connectors on the ends. Again, the connectors are more for convenience than anything else. These cables can be used interchangeably in the studio in many circumstances. At line level (0 dB), either the XLR or TRS connector can be used—some equipment manufacturers need to save space on the back panel and choose to use TRS jacks (female connectors) as they take up less space. Others use XLR connectors for their line-level inputs, if there's adequate space on the unit to support the larger connector type. The XLR connector is superior to the TRS in that the connector is locked into place when attached. This prevents slippage and accidental disconnection.

While TRS cables are often confused for stereo cables, XLR cables are often mistakenly referred to as mic cables. Yes, XLR cables are used to connect microphones to preamps, but they are really just balanced cables. They are perfectly happy connecting line-level equipment, too! **Figure 1.26** shows the back of a professional mic preamp that also has an EQ and compression function.

Figure 1.26: Back view of an Avalon VT 737 preamplifier, showing XLR mic and line inputs. Notice how the back inputs are all XLR, but only one is for the microphone? Even the output is XLR—dedicated to a line level (not mic level) output!

The chart of cables and connectors on page 58 is very handy for understanding the connections between pieces of gear, the operating level of those connections, and the resulting sound quality. Getting this right the first time is a big time saver in the studio—especially if something goes wrong.

RECAP

Balanced cables use three conductors within the cable to carry a single sound from the source to the destination. Two of the conductors are twisted, creating a reversing magnetic field, which helps reduce the resistance of the cable to 600 ohms (down from 10,000 in unbalanced cables) and rejects noise that finds its way onto the cable. Balanced cables are mono, which can be confusing when looking at TRS balanced cables since the TRS connection is the same on one side of a stereo cable.

"a microphone is the first (and arguably the most important) transducer in the studio as it is closest to the free sound being emitted from the source . . ."

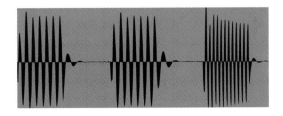

Microphones

Introduction to Microphones
Chapter 2:
Types of Microphones

Microphone Basics

Anyone in the production business, at some point, makes recordings, and at the head of every recording is the microphone. This is the single most important element of any signal chain that records audio—whether it's a recording studio, production studio, or voice-over studio. The microphone is likened to a camera lens—change lenses and you can change the quality or perspective of the picture. In this way, microphones are the "eyes" of the studio. How you hear your recording is a direct result of how the microphone hears the performance. This single point of transition from free sound to captured sound is the essence of recording.

Tech-Speak: *Transducer*

A transducer *is a device that converts one form of energy to another.*

A microphone is the first (and arguably the most important) transducer in the studio as it is closest to the free sound being emitted from the source. A *transducer* coverts energy from a source to a destination. In this case, the microphone is a transducer that converts free sound (mechanical energy) to electricity. At the other end of the studio is the other important transducer—the speakers, often referred to as audio monitors. At this end, the conversion is from electricity back to acoustical energy—essentially returning to its free sound form.

Microphones tend to be delicate instruments. Again, many people liken them to cameras or at least camera lenses, as they are the eyes of the studio. Lenses easily scratch and break and once they sustain damage, they no longer provide the high-quality picture you seek—and paid for! Great care should be taken with using microphones—before, during, and after the recording session.

One extremely common source of mic damage has nothing to do with the actual usage of mics—it's the time when you put the mic on the stand! This is the time when the mic is most exposed to damage, as it is neither safe in its box, resting on a flat surface, nor secured to the stand. Many first-timers (and studio interns, sadly) make the mistake of putting the mic under their arm or in one hand insecurely while they struggle to get the mic clip onto the stand. This process usually takes two hands, so you can guess that holding the mic secure during this struggle starts to take lower priority. Eventually, one of three outcomes occurs: the clip gets on the stand just fine and the mic soon after (whew!); the clip falls and the mic almost falls—caught just in the nick of time (WHEW!); or boom, it falls to the ground (DOH!). It happens every day, all over the world.

Showing a lack of respect and consideration for a mic is a sure sign of a studio newbie—mistakes like that will get you fired, and fast. The best rule of thumb is this: don't even take the mic out of the box until the clip is secured on the stand. That makes sure that both hands are on the mic at all times. Following this, make sure the mic is secured to the clip very well before letting it go. All too often, the mic gets most of the way onto the clip (but just barely), only to slowly slip over time. Again, it's more common than you think to put the mic on the clip, walk away, then come back to find that it's lying on the floor (hopefully, not in pieces!).

Lastly, make sure the stand itself is secure before walking away. Many mic stands have a few different points of adjustment where you can extend the arms so the mic gets into the right position—these are often called telescoping arm stands. The cheap ones are light—usually some form of painted/anodized aluminum or graphite. While they are strong stands in that they won't bend, they are often lighter than the mic that's connected to them! If the arm gets over-extended, the mic stand itself can tip over, bringing down the mic with the stand on top! Again, it's all too common, as are the words that follow: "you're fired—and you owe me $2,500 (or more)."

Assuming you followed the rules and secured the clip to the stand, then the mic to the clip, and then you verified that everything is stable and secure, you're only halfway to mic safety at this point. You will still need to position the mic and the stand where they need to go—*vis-à-vis* the instrument being recorded—and connect the XLR cable. This is where the telescoping arm and the weight of the mic and stand can still potentially damage the mic by falling. Many studios have sand bags available to put at the base of the stand to keep it from falling over, and it's a good idea to have some—they're cheap insurance!

Okay, so now let's assume that everything is in place and safe. You still need to run the XLR cable from the mic to the preamp, mixer, or wall plate (which will connect to the preamp in the control room). In haste, many interns and newbies just throw the cable anywhere, trying to simply make the connection. This is another "broken microphone" trap. Anyone who's spent a good amount of time with musicians knows that they don't always pay the most attention to their studio surroundings. Concentrating on the music and their performance tends to make them not notice the cables strewn about the studio. (It's also not their job—so don't expect them to care or notice!)

Being messy with cables in the studio leaves the very high possibility for someone to trip, slip, or catch a cable in their shoe and pull the mic stand down with force. *Always* wrap the extra cable on the floor in a place that's out of major traffic areas. Bunching them up next to the drum throne where the drummer will be going in and out of behind the drum set is a bad idea. Also, for those musicians who do notice their studio environment, seeing the care you take in laying out the cables this way shows them that you take the process seriously and that you're a professional. Most musicians will see that (at least subconsciously) and tend to bring that level of care to their playing. If you're focusing on details, so should they. It's better for everyone—not just the mics!

When connecting the mic cable to the mics, try running the cable along the shaft of the stand, wrapping it once or twice around on the way up. Then, do the same along the arm of the stand, leaving just enough slack at the mic to avoid bending the cable. This helps the wire stay close to the stand, again lowering the risk of someone (or something, like a drum stick) getting caught in a loop of wire. It also looks cool! The important thing here is to avoid crimping, bending, or stressing the cable too much. Cables do break—usually at the point where they've been bent repeatedly, like where the cable is attached to the connector. Good cables have stiffeners inside the wrapping to keep you from doing too much bending and help keep the cable working well over a long time, but damage is always possible when cables are handled without care. Nothing is more frustrating than trying to figure out why the sound keeps going in and out with the mic that was working fine yesterday.

COACH'S CORNER

All studio vets love to tell stories of their favorite session screw-ups. It usually involves an intern underneath them or a story of when they were first starting out—the foibles of their early years. You could guess that someone somewhere tried the Roger Daltry technique of connecting a very expensive mic to a cable and swinging it around his head like a rock star—and it ended very badly. There's the classics of the intern who kept fumbling with the mic clip and the mic, dropping the mic repeatedly, sneaking looks around the studio to make sure that no one saw him. Of course, everyone saw him, and when they fired up the mic and it didn't work, he claimed "no mea culpa" (not my fault) right in front of the witnesses. Oh, by the way, he doesn't work there anymore.

A recent example concerns one of my students who shall remain nameless (you know who you are!). An extremely talented producer who had just bought a very expensive mic mistakenly loaned it to a roommate (NEVER do that!) who, of course, dropped it. The capsule separated from the body but the wires were intact. Seeking to avoid the embarrassment of the repair shop and the ire of the mic owner, the roommate simply glued the capsule back onto the chassis hoping to press onward with his work. The owner couldn't get the right sound anymore and struggled for weeks with it. One inspection at Pyramind revealed that the roommate had glued the capsule on backward and he was singing into the back of the mic the whole time! I'm guessing they don't live together anymore . . .

Microphone Types

In today's audio world, there are four main types of microphones, three of which are used in studios every day.

☞ Dynamic

☞ Condenser (aka Capacitor)

☞ Ribbon

☞ PZM

Each of these mics works differently, and as a result, yield a different sound. Each has a purpose and a situation when it gives great results, and very rarely is there one type of mic (or one mic of any type) that's perfect for every situation. Often, it's the old favorites that we go to every day that get the most use for the common situations. But what do you grab when the common situation become an uncommon one? Let's explore the types of mics, how they work, and what we think we can expect from them.

Dynamic Microphones

The *dynamic* mic is one of the most common types of microphones and is very versatile. Most clubs and live sound venues have a solid collection of them and for a good reason—dynamic mics can take a beating. The basic principle of the dynamic mic is an electrical principle called *inductance*. It's the same principle that electrical generators use in river dams and turbines, which is that when a powerful magnet is wrapped in wire, an electrical current is created or *induced* as the magnetic field around it moves. In turbines, the change is created by its spin.

Tech-Speak: *Inductance*

Inductance *is the difference (potential for energy, or voltage) between the power of a magnetic field and the current through an electrical circuit.*

Inductance has been applied to dynamic microphones as well. Within the capsule, a set of wires are wrapped and suspended in a magnetic field, called the *voice coil*, as shown in **Figure 1.27**. Attached to the top of the wires is a thin piece of material (often Mylar plastic) called the *diaphragm*.

As sound enters the capsule, it hits against the diaphragm and moves the voice coil in and out of the magnetic field, creating an electrical current by inductance. The more the sound waves move the diaphragm, the more the voice coil moves, and the greater the current created. This alternating current is akin to an electrical version of a sine wave—a direct correlation from the sine waves of the acoustical energy, now transformed into electrical energy!

Introduction to Microphones
Chapter 3:
Dynamic Microphones

Figure 1.27: The inside of a dynamic mic capsule and the diaphragm's relationship to the voice coil.

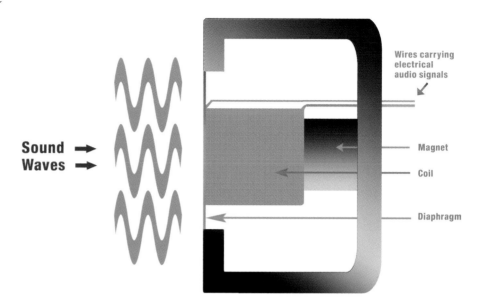

Cross Section of Dynamic Microphone

Wires carrying electrical audio signals

Sound Waves

Magnet

Coil

Diaphragm

The inductance that creates the voltage in dynamic mics is a result of moving the diaphragm and the attached voice coil, and as such requires a bit more energy to make the movement than in other mics. Additionally, the diaphragm itself is usually thicker than in other mics, as it needs to be strong enough to handle the sound coming into it and strong enough to stay attached to (and move) the voice coil. These two technical issues conspire against the quality of the sound reproduced in two ways: dynamics and frequency.

The thickness of the diaphragm tends to make it move somewhat slowly. Quiet sounds coming into the mic (lower SPL levels) have a harder time moving the diaphragm. This tends to make dynamic mics less, well, *dynamic*—although they do a better job of reproducing loud sounds than quiet sounds. Additionally, loud high-frequency sounds have a tough time moving the diaphragm (higher frequencies translate to smaller wavelengths), since the diaphragms are often thicker. As a result, the dynamic mic is not overly sensitive to high frequencies. **Figure 1.28** shows the frequency response of a typical dynamic microphone, demonstrating diminished high-frequency response.

Dynamic mics are very good in situations where a lot of SPL is expected. They perform best when pushed hard by loud signals.

You'll see lots of dynamic mics used in front of loud drums, heavy guitars, and other high-SPL instruments in the studio. On stage, you'll see lots of dynamics as they are also very rugged mics. They can take the rigors of the stage much better than some of their more sensitive cousins such as ribbon and condenser mics.

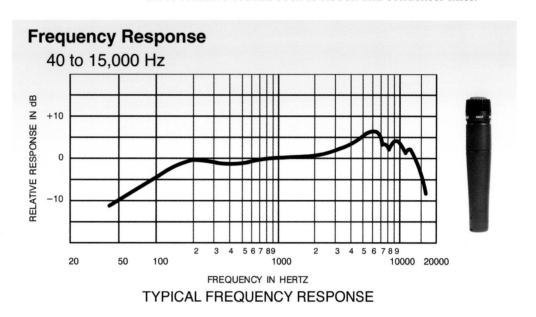

Figure 1.28: A Shure SM57 dynamic mic and its frequency response plot—note the diminished high-frequency response.

DVD Track 26: Acoustic guitar recorded using a dynamic microphone.

DVD Track 27: Acoustic guitar recorded using a condenser microphone.

COACH'S CORNER

One of the most popular mics in the world is the Shure SM57 model. It was designed by the Chicago-based company in 1964 as an answer to a contract request by the U.S. military—one of many that Shure has won. Rumor has it that the 57 won the bid from the military because it was the only contestant to function after a 30-foot drop! The SM57 has been the official microphone of every president of the U.S. since Lyndon Johnson and remains the official mic today.

Introduction to Microphones
Chapter 4:
Condenser Microphones

Condenser Microphones

It is ironic that the dynamic mic is actually not as dynamic as its condenser mic counterpart. The reason for this difference is due to the technology that drives the functionality of the mics. In condenser mics, the electrical principle being utilized is called *capacitance*. Capacitance works differently than inductance, although both rely on voltage being created by a moving diaphragm. In dynamic mics, the diaphragm moves the voice coil through a magnetic field, creating a voltage out of the electro-magnetic field already there. In condenser mics, a voltage already exists within the capsule and the diaphragm movement causes another voltage to be created.

Tech-Speak: *Capacitance*

Capacitance *is the measure of a device's ability to store electrical charge, or the measure of an electrical charge that is already stored in a device. A battery, for example, is a capacitor, and a 9V battery's capacitance is 9 volts.*

The secret of the condenser mic? Its diaphragm is placed in front of a metal "backplate," which holds a charge, as shown in **Figure 1.29**. The diaphragm is coated with a conductive material (often gold dust), and the center of the diaphragm has a wire that's connected to the output of the microphone. The gold dust is sputtered (evenly sprayed) onto the diaphragm, so it evenly coats the surface. As the gold-sputtered diaphragm moves closer and further from the charged backplate, a voltage is created. As there's a charge held at the backplate, the capacitance is the difference between the diaphragm's regular position and the fluctuating distance to/from the backplate. As the diaphragm gets closer, a positive voltage is created, and as it gets further away, a negative voltage is created.

If it moves very close, a higher voltage is created, corresponding to the energy used to move it. Therefore louder sounds move the diaphragm more, which puts it closer to the backplate, creating a higher voltage. Similarly, a quieter sound will also move the diaphragm, but not as much (and therefore not as close to the backplate), creating a smaller voltage. In this way, the movement of the diaphragm corresponds to the volume (SPL) of the incoming signal, much like the dynamic mics.

Figure 1.29: The insides of a condenser mic. Note the gold-sputtered diaphragm.

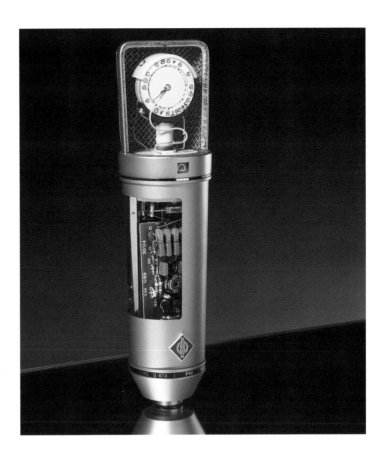

Unlike dynamic mics, the diaphragm in condenser models is usually thin, and a thinner diaphragm moves more sensitively to higher frequencies and to quieter sounds. Therefore, condenser mics are much more sensitive to both high frequencies and quieter sounds than dynamics. For this reason, condensers are used more liberally in the studio for delicate instruments, performances, and instruments with wider dynamics and more high frequncies (or; high-frequency nuances). Acoustic guitars, pianos, strings, chimes, cymbals, and voices are among the common instruments miked with condenser mics.

The charge on the backplate in condenser mics varies mic-to-mic, but is usually set at +48V. I use the "+" here to indicate that the voltage to the backplate is not like audio voltage—it's DC (direct current). When we talked earlier about electrical signals correlating to audio signals because the voltage has a push and pull, like audio waves, we were talking about (AC) alternating current, which alternates between a positive and negative cycle; much like audio. Direct current is a single, all-positive (or negative) charge that has no push or pull—it's just on.

With +48V, the cycle is always on—there's no alternating. Once activated, a solid and continuous 48 volts is always flowing to the mic's backplate. Coined by Neumann, the inventor of this voltage/backplate technology, the +48V charge is known as *phantom power*, because it travels over the same mic cable conductors that carry the audio, there is no separate power cord and the voltage does not interfere with the audio signal. If this voltage ever did find its way to the audio signal, it could yield several results, from destroying the mic, the preamp and your speakers to destroying your hearing and the comfort (and trust) of the client sitting next to you!

COACH'S CORNER

Prior to phantom power, condenser mics had separate power conductors to bring power to the backplate. As such, mics didn't connect to standard 3-pin XLR cables—a proprietary cable was needed to connect power to the mic and to bring the signal down from the mic back to the supply box. The supply box then sent the final audio signal off to the preamp via standard XLR cables. Phantom power has the distinct advantage of traveling along the XLR cable directly to the mic as well as the ability to bring the audio down from the mic. This makes studio operations much easier, as now, there is a method of standardizing the cables between dynamic mics and most condenser mics. However, most condenser microphones using vacuum tube electronics require a separate power supply and proprietary, non-standard mic cables due to the high voltages (often in the 300-volt range) required by the vacuum tubes themselves.

Here are some rules involving the handling of condenser mics and phantom power:

☞ Always handle condenser mics with extra care. These have more internal electronics within the mic body than dynamic mics and are extremely fragile. Also, the diaphragms are thinner and susceptible to damage from being hit, dropped, or blown-in with very high SPL sounds. Some condenser mics are made with built-in windscreens to protect against this; others simply have a metal grille around them to protect against puncture only.

☞ Always connect the mic to the XLR cable and the preamp before activating phantom power. If not, the sudden charge of +48V to the backplate can cause damage to the mic and preamp if the power is on and the cable is then connected. The same applies to the power-down sequence. Monitors should be turned off or muted before disconnecting or turning off any phantom-powered gear.

☞ Always have the channel (or speakers) muted when activating +48V. A loose wire, bad connection, or accidentally unplugged mic can send +48V to your monitors, causing either damage or a VERY loud boom. If this happens while the speakers are on and turned up, you can damage the monitors or your hearing. If the client is next to you and you hurt their ears, not only can they sue you (rare), but they will certainly lose faith in you and your skills. Often, this means they might not come back and you're out some much needed $$$ in terms of repairs and future income!

☞ Very important: Re-read the three items above and then read them again.

☞ Extremely important: Re-read once more, just to be sure. Okay, thanks. (This is also known as the "lather-rinse-repeat" clause.)

Power is required for condenser mics, whether from an external supply in a tube mic, phantom powering on most pro condensers, or an internal battery in some models. The mic simply won't work without the charge to the backplate that creates the capacitance needed. It is worth mentioning that some mic manufacturers have chosen a lower voltage to power their mics (9 volts is common, a battery can be used to charge the backplate in such cases), while a few others have chosen a higher voltage. Know the specs before plugging in your mic and turning on phantom power, just to be sure. You should also be aware that some direct boxes—aka DI/direct input boxes—that contain *active* electronic balancing circuitry (as opposed to transformer-based passive units) can operate using standard +48V phantom power in lieu of internal 9V DC batteries.

A modern variation on the phantom-style powering concept comes in the form of USB mics, which typically include a condenser capsule with onboard preamplification and analog-to-digital converters—all run by 100mA of +5V DC power supplied over the USB bus. Such mics are often convenient for capturing podcast-style desktop narration, "sketchpad" recording of musical ideas, or as field recording mics, but are rarely used for high-end studio work.

COACH'S CORNER

When recording grand piano one day, my client came in with a set of high-quality mics that he had just purchased and wanted to try out. I used my $3,500 mic preamp to power them but was aghast when we got no signal from the connection. After several minutes of troubleshooting, we chose to use the $800 preamps, just to see if there was something wrong with the expensive one. The signal came through fine. I checked different mics with the expensive one and they also worked fine. Now I was confused. Turns out that the expensive preamp put out just a bit less than +48V and the cheap one put out just a bit more than +48V, which was just enough to power the backplate and make the mics work.

Introduction to Microphones
Chapter 5:
Ribbon Mics

You should be concerned with +48V power all of the time—not just when working with condenser mics. Dynamic mics are unaffected by the voltage as it literally has nowhere to go in the mic and effectively disappears in the circuit (yet another reason why it's called "phantom"). However, there is another type of mic that is highly sensitive to phantom power—the ribbon mic.

Ribbon Microphones

Ribbon mics are a type of dynamic microphone in that they consist of an extremely thin (and quite fragile) aluminum or other metal strip suspended between two poles of a strong magnetic field, as shown in **Figure 1.30**. The suspended ribbon reacts to the *velocity* of air particles rather than to the *pressure*, as in the case of dynamic mics. This motion within the magnetic flux field generates a small AC voltage proportional to this velocity. This slight movement creates a fairly small electrical signal (even smaller than that of dynamic mics), so the ribbon mics tend to have a very low output compared to condenser and dynamic mics. With this in mind, ribbon mics typically require a preamp with a substantial amount of gain.

Many ribbon mics are fragile, like condensers, and are easily damaged by bumps, drops, bangs, and even extreme wind or breath blasts. And placing a ribbon mic in a high air velocity location—such as inside a kick drum—can permanently distort or deform the ribbon element. Additionally, many will be damaged or destroyed by the activation of +48V, unlike their cousin the dynamic mic! Some ribbon manufacturers are now making ribbons that are +48V safe, but their older counterparts are not so lucky. Always refer to the manual of the ribbon mic manufacturer (or the Internet) before plugging in the mic, and always refer to the previous list of safety tips before activating +48V.

Figure 1.30: Operation of a typical ribbon mic and the bidirectional field created by the ribbon element.

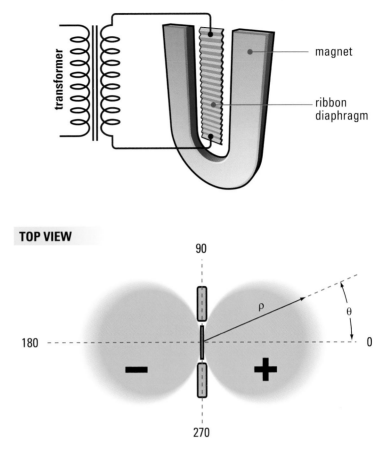

(Graphic courtesy Mix magazine; used by permission.)

COACH'S CORNER

Ribbons have become en vogue recently, as they tend to have a warmer and darker sound than other mics. Ribbon mics lend warmth to the source, which can help smooth out some of the harsh and edgy quality of digital audio. While today's digital signals are much smoother than some of the early CD quality recordings, some people still claim that digital imparts a "coldness" to the audio quality.

Keeping with our "there seems to be an exception for everything" theme, I should mention a new breed of ribbon microphones with on-board preamplification circuits that boosts a ribbon mic element's normally low output to a level comparable to that of condenser or dynamic mics. Such "active" electronic designs—available from manufacturers such as Royer (who also offer standard, *non*-active ribbon mics without onboard electronics) may even *require* phantom power to operate! These active ribbon models are less commonly encountered than passive ribbon mics, however. Here's another case for reading manuals before using unfamiliar products.

One Mic Techniques—
Acoustic Guitar:
Chapters 7–11

Pressure Zone Microphones

The "oddball" of the microphone bunch is likely to be the *PZM®*, or *pressure zone microphone*. Originally mass-marketed (and trademarked) by Crown International, the PZM is effectively a boundary mic with a diaphragm that is not only parallel to an attached wall or floor surface, but also super close to that surface. The PZM typically lies on the floor or on the wall and captures sound that bounces off of the floor or wall. It is very useful in situations where a visible microphone would be a problem, such as a lectern, pulpit, or theater stage. The audience does not desire to see the mic—only the person requiring amplification.

In the case of a lectern or pulpit, the PZM is simply laid on top, with its discreet low profile making it virtually invisible to the audience. As the speaker approaches the pulpit, the speaking voice naturally projects downwards onto the surface of the pulpit and right into the diaphragm of the mic. In the case of the Broadway show, the front of the stage might be lined with PZMs and stage lights; The audience can't see the mics as they are hidden behind the lights. As the actors move across the stage, each mic picks up their voices and alleviates the talent from having to wear a lavalier (clip-on) or headset mic. This works especially well in tap dance performances as the PZM picks up the tapping on the stage directly—no matter where the dancer is!

Polar Patterns

When selecting a microphone for your recording, knowing which type to choose for your application is a big decision. If the situation calls for a high-SPL mic to be put in front of a raging guitar amp, a dynamic might be the best call. However, many condensers can also handle high-SPL sounds—the amplitude of a signal does not necessarily require a dynamic mic in all situations.

Choosing the type of microphone is not your only decision, though. For example, not all dynamic mics are equal, nor do they perform the same way all the time. There is another consideration that needs to be weighed before truly arriving at the right decision—where should I put the mic? Mic placement is a huge undertaking—not because it's difficult, but because there are so many choices.

Consider an acoustic guitar. At first inspection, there might be only one ideal place to put a mic—in front of the sound hole, as shown in **Figure 1.31**. In practice, this is not the optimal spot for mics—the sound is usually boomy and unflattering. A slight adjustment of the mic closer to the neck or further from the neck can result in radical changes to the tonal quality of the recording.

COACH'S CORNER

When working with microphones, there are few rules—experimentation is highly valued. A good rule of thumb, however, is to employ this three-staged process: experiment, observe, and adjust. Try a new mic in a weird place because you read about it in a magazine. Use three mics at once, even though the "book" tells you not to. Observe the results: Does it sound good? Why? If not, adjust by choosing a different mic or putting it in a different place. In the end, the sound you get when the mic is employed is the ultimate decider. If a mic sounds good in front of the instrument, that's all that really matters. If a dynamic works well on the delicate instrument for your needs, that's great—even though conventional wisdom might not predict that result.

Figure 1.31: A small-diaphragm condenser mic pointed directly into the soundhole of an acoustic guitar—an obvious, but not-recommended, placement.

Remember that sound travels in 360 degrees, and in front of the sound hole, the amount of sound pouring out is huge and all frequencies are there, fighting for space. By moving the mic slightly to the side, some frequencies are not as strong as others, and the mic will pick up different ratios of sine waves. Changing the mic angle sometimes improves the sound quality and sometimes makes the sound worse. There are rules here, too—follow the mic's *polar pattern*, also known as the *pickup pattern*.

The polar pattern of a microphone is a diagram that indicates the frequency response of the microphone when sound approaches the diaphragm from different angles. Usually drawn in circles, the polar pattern tracks the different levels of sensitivity of the mic at different frequencies.

The polar pattern is a graph representing how a mic will behave at different frequencies. It's not so much a graph that says, "this mic captures high frequencies well," or "this one is great for mid-range tones," but, rather, a graph that says, "this one picks up high frequencies well from the front, but not from the sides or back." In other words, this graph tells the story of a mic's directionality.

Microphones come in a few different flavors when it comes to polar pattern and some allow you to adjust the polar pattern at the mic. The four main patterns are shown in **Figures 1.32–1.35**: *cardioid, omni, figure-8,* and *supercardioid.*

Figure 1.32: Cardioid (unidirectional) pattern. Named after its similarity to a heart shape, the cardioid pattern basically describes that a microphone performs best when sound approaches it from the front and performs worst when sound enters from the rear. In the preceding guitar-miking example, where an adjustment to the angle of the mic changes the sound, a cardioid mic would certainly change sound quality when angled.

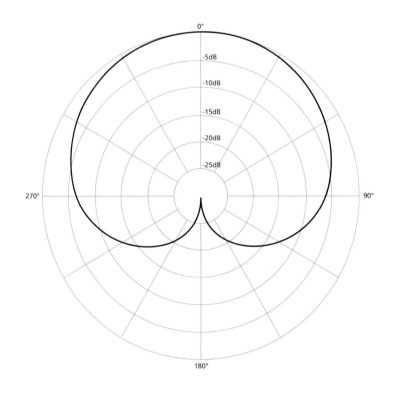

Figure 1.33: Omni (omnidirectional) pattern. A mic that exhibits an omni pattern performs equally well no matter where the sound comes from. Whether sound enters from the front, rear, or from the sides, the omni exhibits the same sound response. In the previous guitar-miking example, where adjusting the angle of the mic changes the sound, an omnidirectional mic would not change its sound if the mic is angled.

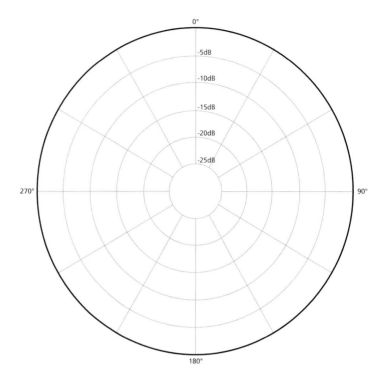

Figure 1.34: Figure-8 (bidirectional) pattern. A mic that exhibits a figure-8 pattern performs best when sound enters from either the front or the rear and performs the worst when sound enters from the sides. If this mic is angled to the source, the sound quality will worsen as the front of the mic is moved away, but as the rear of the mic begins to approach the source, the sound quality begins to improve again.

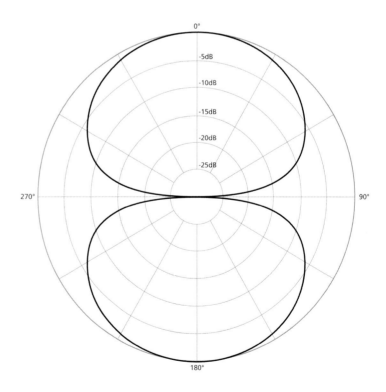

Figure 1.35: Supercardioid (bidirectional) pattern. A supercardioid mic is somewhere between the cardioid and the figure-8 in that the mic performs well from the front but also performs well from the rear. However, in this case, the rear performance is not nearly as good as the figure-8. There is some increase in sensitivity from sound that approaches from the rear over the cardioid pattern, but not as good as the figure-8. The supercardioid has a cousin called the *hypercardioid*, which has better rear performance than the supercardioid but still less than the figure-8.

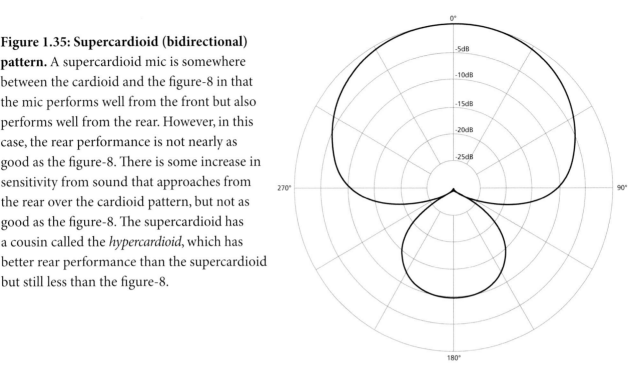

Keep in mind that these patterns are general in use. For most mics, the behavioral pattern changes with frequency. For example, most cardioid mics exhibit omni-like behavior in the low-frequency range. Bass has a tendency to enter the mic from all angles and gets much the same response due to the size of the wave. Mid- and high-frequency sound waves are much smaller and more prone to rejection at certain directions. As a result, mics perform differently at different frequencies.

COACH'S CORNER

One of the benchmarks of a good mic can be found before ever plugging it in and listening—it's in the specifications. Good mics are tested heavily to ensure high standards of quality. While the specs you see on a website may be helpful at first look, a more detailed inspection can show you whether the pattern being claimed is consistent at all frequencies. A good sign would be if either separate patterns are shown per frequency tested, or a single composite pattern graph is shown with different traces for different frequencies, just as you see in **Figure 1.36**.

Polar patterns are created in a few ways but generally relate to two functions: the number of (and interactions of) diaphragms within a mic and the amount of air venting along the mic chassis. Some *shotgun microphones* (supercardioid mics with extremely narrow polar patterns) tend to be very long in the chassis with lots of venting along the side, as seen in **Figure 1.37**. The idea is that sound entering the mic from the side cancels the sound coming from the other side, creating extra phase cancellation at the sides. The result is a narrowing of the cardioid pattern from the front, along with an elongation of the response from the rear. It responds very well to sounds directly in front of it but does not respond very well to sounds even slightly outside the direct angle of the diaphragm.

Figure 1.36: A single plot showing a mic's polar response at different frequencies.

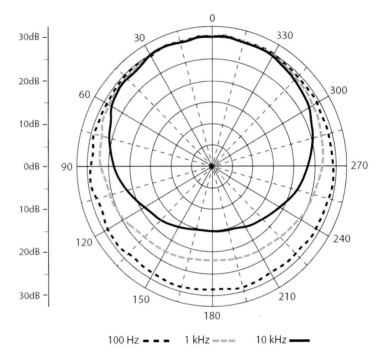

Figure 1.37: A shotgun microphone, showing the long interference tube with vent slots where sounds from the side enter the mic and are effectively cancelled out, while sounds to the front are relatively unaffected.

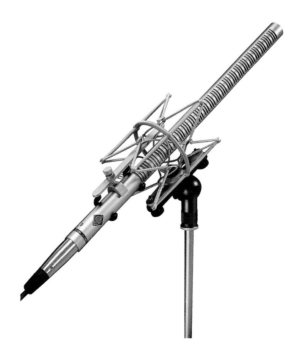

When the air vents are insufficient or the sound at the front of the mic builds up very quickly, the sound cannot escape the diaphragm effectively, creating a build-up of pressure in the diaphragm. This increase of pressure is perceived by the mic to be a build-up of low-frequency information, thus exaggerating the bass response significantly. The result is known as the *proximity effect.*

Tech-Speak: *Proximity Effect*

The proximity effect describes an unnatural build-up of low-frequency energy in a microphone as it gets closer and closer to a sound source. Cardioids are particularly subject to the proximity effect, while omni mics do not exhibit the proximity effect at all.

COACH'S CORNER

The proximity effect is one of the most common sounds made when a handheld mic is used by an inexperienced singer, a would-be impromptu comedian, and wedding singers across the world. It usually involves some one starting with "testing 1, 2 . . . " and by the time "3" rolls around, they've practically shoved the mic into their mouth just to pretend they have a voice as low as Barry White.

While the proximity effect is something to be careful of, it can easily be manipulated in mics with more than one diaphragm. In these mics, the user can often switch between polar patterns by adjusting the way the diaphragms interact. For example, simply adding the cardioid pattern of the front diaphragm to the rear creates an omni pattern response, as demonstrated in **Figure 1.38**.

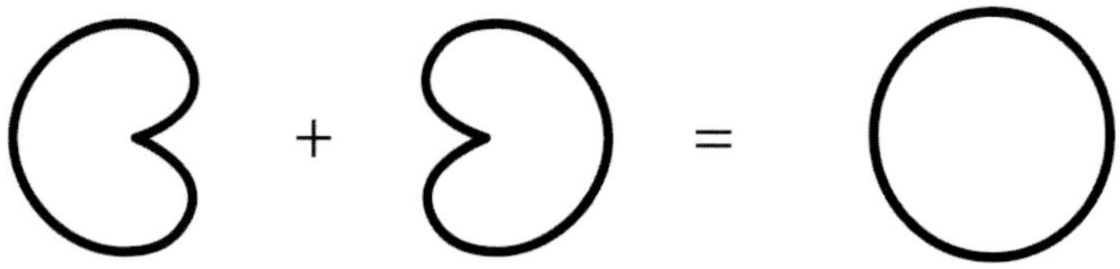

Figure 1.38: The addition (summation) of two cardioid capsules results in an omnidirectional pattern.

In the case where one cardioid is subtracted from the other, the result is a figure-8 pattern, shown in **Figure 1.39**. If the front cardioid is significantly louder than the rear one and they are added together, the result is a supercardioid. Mics with switchable patterns have the circuitry built into them to do this math for you. All you need to do is determine which pattern will work best for you in any situation.

Figure 1.39: A figure-8 pattern can be formed by the subtraction of one cardioid pattern from another.

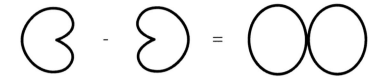

DVD Track 28: A voice recorded in a room at three inches using several mic pickup patterns: cardioid first, then figure-8, then omni. Notice the difference in the balance between the dry vocal and the sound of the room (the room ambience).

RECAP

Mics are thought of in fours—four types and four basic patterns. The four types of mics are *dynamic*, *condenser*, *ribbon*, and *PZM*. The four basic patterns are *cardioid*, *figure-8*, *omnidirectional* and *supercardioid*. All mics exhibit different polar pattern responses at different frequencies, but most behave like omnis for low-frequency sounds.

Introduction to Microphones
Chapter 6:
Types of Microphones
and Their Sounds

Working with Microphones

Choosing the right mic for the right circumstance is something of an art form that's developed through a combination of experience, trial and error, and journeyman apprenticing. It has long been a tradition for senior engineers to impart their favorite techniques upon their interns and assistants—both as a means of training their staff and ensuring that high-quality recordings are made even when the senior engineer is not around. This helps establish a trust among clients and studios, and is a great way to keep quality up and business repeating.

There is one rule above all others in microphone usage and technique: In the end, it just has to sound good. This is, of course, a completely subjective experience—what sounds good to one person doesn't sound good to another. People hear things differently and as a result, it's a good idea to work with people that hear music the way you do. This goes for your audience, as well—if they expect a certain sound from your music (or music in your genre), then don't give them something different if you don't want to risk losing them as your audience.

Finding what sounds good, however, is another art form. Again, you may have been shown a certain technique with a certain mic that works great in that certain situation, but situations don't always repeat themselves, challenging you to come up with a new technique for that new situation. In the end, there's a three-step rule that works well when learning about microphone placement—experiment, observe and adjust.

This rule is based on the assumption that you can identify and understand the function of the sounds you hear. In other words, taking a mic you don't know and putting it in a place you've never tried before will yield a certain set of results. Those results might be good or bad to your tastes. If it sounds good, then why does it sound good? Does it emphasize frequencies that you like? Does it help that sound sit better in the mix? Does it tone down unwanted sounds? Is the audio more dynamic than you expected? Less? Which is better and why? These sorts of questions are going be asked of the recording the second the sound comes through the speakers, and they will need answering. Otherwise, you can just take any old mic, put it anywhere, and say, "That's great—we got sound, so let's roll . . ." without actually determining whether you got the right sound.

This ear training takes a long time to develop. Being able to identify what you hear is a tremendous help for understanding why you like or don't like the sound of that mic in that place. Do you hear phasing? Too much boom? Is the instrument out of tune? Is the performance off? Is the signal too loud? Too soft? The ability to identify the sound leads directly to the ability to fix the sound—not all sounds are bad as a result of the microphone! Again, experiment, observe, and adjust.

Experiment 1: Close Miking

One of the first and most common guidelines is to mic the sound with one mic, up close. No matter the source, using only one mic reduces many of the factors that can negatively impact your sound. For example, with only one mic, you reduce the amount of phase-shifting (phasing) that can happen with two or more mics. In this guideline, the old "KISS" motto holds true: Keep It Simple, Silly.

Before choosing which mic to use for this first step, consider the sound source. Is the sound loud or soft? Is the sound bright or dull? Detailed or full? Is the instrument highly dynamic or consistent in volume? The answers will lead you to good possible first choices. For example, if the sound is loud, dark, and consistent in dynamics, a dynamic mic might be a good choice. These handle high-SPL sounds well, yet don't offer the best high-frequency response, but that's not an issue with this source. If the sound is soft, bright, and highly dynamic, a condenser mic might be a good choice. These handle dynamic range much better than dynamic mics (ironic, I know), capture high-frequency information very well, and will likely capture all of the details in the performance.

Once you've chosen the type of mic, you'll need to consider the pattern. The polar pattern has a direct impact on the frequency response of the mic and its position to the source. If a mic is cardioid, then it should be facing the sound source as a starting place. You can angle the mic from there to change the tone to your liking, as changing the angle changes the frequency response of the mic—depending on the frequency in question. If you need to put the mic in a place where a competing sound will also be playing, say, from the rear of the mic position, then consider that, as well. Do you want to capture other sounds coming from the rear? If so, choose a figure-8 pattern or omni pattern. Keep in mind that the pattern you want may not be available on the type of mic you choose. It's a detailed combination of types and patterns and locations that makes for the overall quality of your recording.

When experimenting to determine the first mic in the first placement, you'll likely need to get very close to the sound source with your mic. Keep in mind that the choice of mic position *should not* interfere with the performer's ability to emote effectively. If your mic is in a great spot for sound capture—say, right above the bridge of a stand-up bass—but the artist can't play around it, that placement is no good. You need to find a spot that's out of their way, yet still provides a result where you like the sound of the instrument. This usually involves moving your head around the instrument while it's playing to hear the sound emanating from it. Does it sound best standing right over it? In front of it? A few inches to the left? Find the sweet spot with your ears and try sticking a mic right there. **Figure 1.40a** shows a Shure SM57 mic positioned in the way of a drummer's performing path. **Figure 140b,** on page 90, shows a Shure SM57 placed out of the way of a drummer's performance.

Figure 1.40a: Shure SM57 dynamic cardioid mic, shown in the way of the drummer's performance.

Figure 1.40b: Shure SM57, placed out of the way of the drummer's performance.

One of the advantages of close miking is that this technique typically results in a high SPL entering the mic. Even if the source is not that loud, being close to the source ensures that any sound coming off the instrument is at a high SPL. This is usually good for the recording in two ways: one is that you're guaranteed to capture most (if not all) of the tones available in the sound. This can be useful later if you choose to accentuate or diminish some of the frequencies—there's bound to be a lot of sound in the sound!

Another advantage of close miking is that high-SPL sound sources need far less gain to get the signal to line level. Remember, mics have a fairly low-level output and need to be amplified to line level before getting recorded in the DAW. With more SPL in the mic before the preamplification stage, the noise in the recording is bound to be lower than if the source was quiet and you had to substantially increase the gain. In fact, sometimes the source is too loud and can overload the microphone itself!

When the SPL level going into the mic is too high, you have three options:

☞ Move the mic away from the source a little bit. At close ranges, a small movement away from the source can have a big impact on the SPL going into the mic. **Figure 1.41** shows mics in two positions at varying distances from the source.

Figure 1.41: Mics in two positions at varying distances from the source.

DVD Track 29: A recording of an electric guitar where the close mic is too loud and distorts the signal. The second half of the track is the same recording with the mic placed a few inches farther away from the source.

☞ Activate the pad switch on the mic. Many mics have a pad, as seen in **Figure 1.42**, where a simple switch reduces the gain at the microphone. This can be the difference between a distorted signal and a clean one.

Figure 1.42: A pad switch on a mic offers flexibility in high-SPL situations.

☞   Ask the player to "turn it down." This almost never works, so try this it as a last resort. Remember, players are the highest priority, and if they don't perform at their best, the overall recording will suffer, no matter which mics you're using.

COACH'S CORNER

As you double the distance from a source, the SPL drops exponentially. So, if you start 1 foot from a source and move the mic to 2 feet, the SPL drops to ¼ of its original level. And moving it 4 feet away drops the level to $1/16$ of that. Moving the mic back a few inches can have a dramatic effect on the sound level going into it and can keep overload distortion out of the recording. Remember that the dB is a logarithmic number, so $1/16$ the sound is not nearly as big a jump as you might think at the loud side of the scale.

COACH'S CORNER

A close microphone to a source is bound to capture a lot of sound—even if the source isn't very loud. Consider a baseball being hit by a bat: even if it's a bunt, if you're only 3 inches away from the bat, the ball will hurt if it hits you!

Experiment 2: The Mid- and Far-Field Mics: A Modest, Then Significant, Distance

Close miking is great, and in many situations, results in a good sound. You can move the mic a small amount left/right, up/down, as well as in/out and experience large sonic differences. However, the quality of that sound is often described as "dead" or "dry." The reason behind this? The mic is engulfed in sound from the source itself, leaving little space for the sound of the room the source is playing in. This is especially true with cardioid mics facing the source—only a tiny bit of other sounds enter the mic, so the sound is almost completely comprised of the direct source. In the case of a figure-8 or an omni mic used up close, the captured sound is less dry, as the sound of the room can—and does—enter the mic from the rear and/or sides. With a supercardioid, a bit of room sound enters from the rear of the mic, but in far smaller amounts than the figure-8 and omni. Therefore a supercardioid pattern might be a good choice if you want an unequal balance of room sound to direct sound, with more direct than room.

When a close mic sounds overly dead or dry, and using a figure-8 or omni mic doesn't help, try setting the mic at a modest distance—also known as a *mid-field* position—from the

COACH'S CORNER

Instruments almost always sound best in a room environment. The instrument acoustically interacts with the room, and this blend comes back to the player instantly. The interaction between the player, the sound and the room combine to make the overall tone that many engineers try to capture. The best studios in the world are the best for the same reason that certain stages are the best in the world—the rooms and acoustics just plain sound great. To this end, dry, close miking doesn't always capture the same sound that the artist hears, and you shouldn't be surprised if they leave the live room, enter the control room and frown—the sound at the close mic isn't as room-heavy as the sound they heard when playing, and getting them used to the dry sound might take some doing. Set their expectations ahead of time by explaining why you chose to close-mic the performance and how it will help the production. This might make them more at ease with the process.

source (start a few feet away and adjust from there). Assuming that the room sounds good and the instrument sounds good in the room, a mic placed at a modest distance will capture both the direct sound and the room sound.

With distance miking, the choice of mic, polar pattern, and position are just as important as they are in close miking situations, but small movements in position don't have as dramatic an effect on the sound. In this case, you'll need to move the mic many feet to make a big difference. To blend the direct sound to the room sound, you'll likely need to change patterns and experiment moving the mic both nearer and farther from the source.

One of the downsides to mid-field miking is that the SPL levels are not as high as when you mic up close. You'll need a bit more gain to bring the signal up to line level, but usually not so much that you'll be introducing noise to the signal. Another difference is that the sound's dynamic range is smaller at a distance than up close. This is a good thing if you have trouble controlling the dynamics up close—a smaller dynamic range is much easier to control.

COACH'S CORNER

In rock and roll, few sounds have reigned as much as the John Bonham drum sound from Led Zeppelin. While John was clearly an amazing player with tremendous power, the bulk of his sound is the room. While that sound has been chased after for years, with varying degrees of success, it's difficult to exactly re-create, due to the locations used in the original records. From Welsh castles to now-defunct auditoriums, the room itself was as much an instrument in the recording as John himself.

Depending on the size of the room you're recording in, you might have several options when it comes to distance miking, including *far-field* miking. As close miking captures mostly direct sound, and mid-field miking tends to blend the room and the direct sound more, far-field miking captures mostly room sound with very little direct sound. The difference between mid- and far-field is completely subjective—how far is far, after all? There are no rules in terms of feet or percentage of distance to the source—the only real determinant is the sound. Remember, the objective is to add *some* of the room sound to the recording to provide a sense of space and to capture the sound of the source interacting with the acoustical environment.

DVD Track 30: Drums in the room. Using only one condenser cardioid mic, a drum set is recorded with the mic right over the set (close mic), then moved back about 5 feet (mid-field), and then at 20 feet (far-field). Listen to the contrast of direct drums, drums and room, and room-only.

Figure 1.43: A drum set with a single overhead mid-field mic focused on the snare drum.

Figure 1.44: The audio file of each drum set recording in DVD Track 30, with the preamp level unchanged between them.

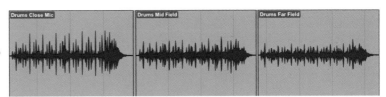

COACH'S CORNER

Whether placing a mic close, mid-field or far-field, it's a good idea to listen to the sound at each position both in the room and through monitors before settling on the position. Many engineers configure mics while listening though headphones in the performance room so they can listen to the microphone sound "live" through the mic while actually being in the room with the player. If you can set this up, you have the advantage of moving the mic while hearing the changes in the sound, thus ensuring that the final position of the mic provides the sound and room-to-direct blend that you're looking for.

Experiment 3: Trying More than One Mic at Once . . .

Most people expect that the secret to high-quality recordings comes from using one mic, in only one place. Sometimes, this is actually true, but in many cases, the sound you might be looking for will come from using more than one mic at a time. Each mic brings with it a tonal characteristic—some are bright, while others are midrange-heavy, and others may have a very flat response, meaning they add no color at all and simply reproduce the sound of the source faithfully. If the tone at the source is exactly what you want, then the job is simple—take the flattest mic you have and put it in the right spot. The job is done!

Ease of workflow is not the only advantage here—using one microphone means that there is no likelihood of negative phase interaction with any other mic. The results are clean and will play well anywhere—even if there's only one speaker! In the scenario of using one frequency-flat mic, the only color that is captured is the color of the source. However, this may not be enough color for your tastes. If a flat mic that provides an accurate representation of the sound source is not colorful enough, you might need to either change mics, or use a second mic to add color and blend with the flat mic.

COACH'S CORNER

The term "color" is used when referring to frequencies. Sound is related to color in that both forms of energy are measured in frequency. To this end, when the frequencies of a sound are completely flat (meaning that no tone or collection of tones is stronger than any other), the sound is referred to as "colorless." When some tones outweigh others, the sound is said to be "colored." Darker tones are heavier bass tones, and brighter tones are higher frequencies.

COACH'S CORNER

Many people have been diagnosed with a medical condition called synesthesia, in which one sense triggers another. A common manifestation of this condition is the process of hearing sound and having that sound "show" you colors. People with synesthesia don't always agree on what color a sound is and those without can hear the same sound and describe it in two (or more) ways. When discussing sound try to use adjectives that are as descriptive as possible—whether it be color or emotion.

Using two (or more) mics to create a rich tone can be both a highly rewarding process and a frustrating process for the same reason—finding the right blend of mics, patterns and positions is tough enough with one microphone, much less two. Consider any two mics with different colorations. Should you blend a darker tone with a brighter tone and hope that they even out? How about two different bright mics? Two dark ones? What about one up close and one far away? One on each side? Just where do I put these mics? Luckily, there are some guidelines here to help narrow the choices down to a few mics.

The Color Blend Rule: Red and Yellow Make Orange!

One of the unspoken concepts when using two mics is that you actually have two mics to choose from! When producers start out, they usually take the "one-mic-to-rule-them-all" approach. After using the mic for a while, they learn its sound but may conclude that the one sound it can capture isn't enough. So they go shopping for another mic. This leads to one of two decisions—get a different mic with a different tonal characteristic, or buy an identical model for stereo recording. (More on this later.)

Assuming that the second mic is different than the first one, you can guess that blending the two mics at once will yield a richer tone, as each one brings a different sound to the blend. Let's assume that mic 1 has a "yellow" tone and mic 2 has a "red" tone. (These arbitrary colors represent that they simply have different tonal characteristics.) When you mix them together, the result is orange. Use more red and the tone is darker, like sunset. Use more yellow and the tone is lighter, like traffic cones. The point is that some colors can only be created by blending other colors together.

When blending two mics to make a complex color, don't think of them as left and right—they're not meant to work that way. Think of them as Layer 1 and 2 in mono. The new color can be determined by adjusting the blend of mic 1 and mic 2—use more of the darker mic for an overall darker sound, and so on.

One way to ensure a clean blend of the two signals is to place them as close to each other as possible, at exactly the same distance from the source. **Figure 1.45** shows two different mics in close position on a guitar amp, with their diaphragms the same distance from the source. Known as *coincident miking*, this technique ensures that each mic is capturing almost the same phase-coherent sound, as they're in the same place and the sound from the source will arrive at both mic capsules almost simultaneously.

Figure 1.45: Coincident miking using two mics on a guitar amp, with their capsules the same distance from the source to ensure the signals are captured in phase.

DVD Track 31: An electric guitar captured with two mics. The first version is mic 1 only, the second is mic 2 only, the third is an even blend of the two mics, the fourth is a 2:1 ratio of mic 1 to mic 2, and the fifth version is a 2:1 ratio of mic 2 to mic 1.

Set Your Phasers to Stun
(A Little Phase Never Hurt Anyone)

In some cases, mis-using mics can yield wildly cool results. Many great techniques have come from happy accidents where someone made a "mistake" in mic position but the results were just too cool to ignore. One of these involves putting the two mics somewhat close to each other but at different distances from the source. By varying the mic distances, you will create a *phase shift*, which can make the sound hollow. You can control how much phase shift you want by raising or lowering the volume of the second mic relative to the first one.

If one mic is moved slightly closer (or farther) from the source while the other stays in position, then the mics are capturing the sound at two different arrival times, even though the time shift may be small. As we read earlier, capturing the sound at two different positions in an energy wave will result in the waves phasing to some degree, which may produce a displeasing sound. However this can be used to your advantage by blending the mics in a way where the phasing is controlled, thus only using as much of the phased sound as you desire.

Figure 1.46: Two close mics at different distances from the source, introducing some phase shift into the recording.

DVD Track 32: The same electric guitar recorded in Track 31, with the same two mics, one back about two inches. Same five mic mixes as Track 31.

Another variation of this method is to point one mic away from the source, while one points directly at it. This is a popular technique used to record electric guitars. The same principle applies—by raising or lowering the amount of the "away" mic, you control how much phase shift is applied to the blended signal. You can also control how far away the second mic is pointed. Shallower angles to the source have less phase shift and larger angles—up to 180 degrees—have a much more dramatic effect.

Figure 1.47: A two-mic technique where the second mic is angled at 90 degrees to the source for intentional use of phase shift.

DVD Track 33: The same electric guitar recorded in Track 31 with the same two mics, one at 90 degrees. Same five mic mixes as Track 31.

The Dual-Mono Rule: Two Mics Don't Make It Stereo!

Remember how we defined stereo earlier? Two unique sounds coming from two microphones capturing a source that's wider than the width of your head and playing back uniquely in each speaker. There are *lots* of stereo techniques designed to give you an accurate stereo response of the source, and nearly all of them require two identical mics. But just because you have two mics, two speakers, and two ears, doesn't mean that using two mics provides a proper stereo image.

COACH'S CORNER

Remember the first 3-D glasses—the ones with the red and blue lenses? These provide a 3-D image, but also give you a headache. They work by emulating a sense of depth in the brain by filtering a different color at each eye. The brain makes up the difference by removing the colors from the final image and compensating by adding a depth of field. So the different colors trick the brain into thinking that each eye is seeing the image from slightly different distances—essentially color filtering the real distance. Using two mics as a means of creating stereo is much the same thing—headache included.

Another manifestation of the mono rule is when two mics capture the sound from two completely different positions to "see" the instrument from two perspectives. This is something like a Picasso painting where you attempt to "paint" two different views of the subject at the same time. Clearly, a person can't be on two sides of an instrument at once, so the idea that two mics in different places can replicate the listener's experience is just not the point.

Consider a drum set. With two mics, you can get a surprisingly good sound even though the set itself can have five or more components! Try placing one mic at the kick drum and the other right over the drummer's head which is commonly known as the overhead technique. (Creative, I know . . .) This technique, shown in **Figure 1.48,** will capture a big kick drum sound with a large amount of low frequencies, as well as the snare drum (and the rest of the kit) as the drummer hears it. It also adds a bit of room sound, as the overhead can be considered mid-field, which adds some space—and often some life—to the recording.

Figure 1.48: A two-mic technique, with one on the kick (close) and the other over the drummer's head (overhead, mid-field).

One of the tricks here is to keep the two tracks panned to the center during playback. Remember, this is NOT a stereo technique, it's a mono technique. Another trick is to minimize phase shift. Each mic unavoidably picks up sounds that are also in the other mic, which will ultimately lead to some phase shift. For example, the kick mic will capture a certain amount of snare, and the overhead mic will hear a bunch of kick drum. However, you can remove some of the snare sound in the kick mic by keeping the mic close (and cardioid, so it only captures the kick) or covering it in a sound blanket. This will minimize the phase shift of the drums, since the one mic is so heavily focused on the direct kick sound that there is simply not a lot of the rest of the kit in the mic signal to phase against!

DVD Track 34: A recording of a drum set—first, the kick mic only, followed by the snare overhead mic, and then, the two together in mono at roughly even volumes.

Let's reconsider the producer who decides to use two mics, of the same mic model. This makes sense for producers who record a lot of stereo instruments, or, at least, instruments that can be recorded in stereo. Remember that stereo is a function of a wide sound source captured at one time, creating unique sounds in each speaker and thus, recreating the width of the source. Using two different mics at the same time and panning them left and right can create a stereo image—it does put unique sounds in the left and right—but is an odd way of working. It's like the red and blue glasses, where the headache comes back.

Consider our ears for a moment. Our ears are designed to operate as a pair, and each ear performs as well as the other (assuming there's no damage to either ear or your hearing as a whole). Neither ear colors the sound compared to the other—any color difference is strictly a result of the sound source and/or its interaction with the room it is in. In this fashion, a true stereo recording is one that seeks to reproduce what the ears would hear in the room at that position. This is simply impossible with two different mics—they just can't reproduce what two of the same ears can do! To this end, capturing stereo sound must be a function of using two of the same microphone.

COACH'S CORNER

In a perfect world, capturing a perfect stereo image requires two identical mics—not simply two of the same mic model, but two mics that are identical in every way, including test results. Many manufacturers produce assembly line mics, where each mic goes through a repeated production process, but tiny variations in this assembly process can yield two slightly different sets of test results from two mics picked off the line. To make true stereo microphone pairs, mics are tested and paired up when their test results are identical. Known as matched pairs, these are usually sold in one box at a higher price than just two off the line. This is a manufacturer's guarantee that the two mics perform exactly the same, removing the possibility of color shift between them.

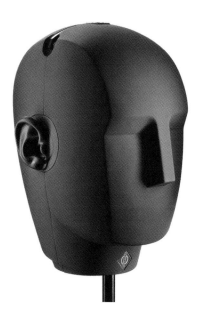

Figure 1.49: The Neumann KU 100 stereo mic—sometimes affectionally known as Fritz—is a dummy head, or *binaural microphone*, that simulates the way a human perceives sound.

Stereo Microphone Techniques

There are several tried-and-true phase-accurate stereo mic techniques, each of which produces a different sound. Here are a few to start with.

X-Y Technique

The X-Y miking technique involves two cardioid mics pointing in different directions by approximately 90 degrees, as shown in **Figure 1.50**. The two mics are placed in a coincident pair so they are extremely phase-accurate. Each mic is pointed to the outer edge of the sound source, so the bulk of the sound falls directly below the pair and the entirety of the sound is likely to be captured by one or both mics.

Figure 1.50: The X-Y mic technique.

DVD Track 35: A stereo drum set recording using a single pair of condenser cardioid mics in X-Y position directly over the snare drum.

Tech-Speak: *Coincident Mic Pairs*

In a coincident pair configuration, the two capsules are as close as they can get to each other without touching, which ensures that the two mics reduce the potential of phase shift to an absolute minimum. For all intents and purposes, they occupy the same space at the same time . . . almost.

The A-B, or Spaced-Pair Technique

Similar to X-Y, this technique uses two mics, either omnidirectional or cardioid, each pointing to the outer edges of the sound. However, unlike X-Y, the A-B pairings are not coincident pairs—they are spaced apart. To effectively employ the A-B technique, it is recommended that you place the two mics at the same distance from the source to minimize potential phase shift. This technique is prone to problems as you not only need to keep the distance the same from the source, but also to ensure that they point in the same direction (usually straight down). Alterations in the *azimuth* (vertical alignment) can also result in phase shift (much less so with omnis, which is why they are often used in this technique). The spaced-pair technique yields a wider stereo image than the X-Y approach. **Figure 1.51** shows an example of a pair of overhead mics on drums, in A-B spaced-pair configuration.

Figure 1.51: The A-B (spaced-pair) mic technique.

DVD Track 36: Stereo drum overhead recording using a single pair of condenser cardioid mics in A-B position at the outer edges of the drums.

The Blumlein Technique

The *Blumlein technique*, named after British engineer Alan Blumlein, is similar to X-Y miking in that two mics are configured as a coincident pair. However, with this technique, the pattern of the mics used is exclusively figure-8. As with any figure-8 pattern, you'll need to blend the room sound to the direct sound by moving the mics closer to or further from the source. And like the X-Y pattern, the Blumlein technique keeps phase shift to a minimum by using a coincident pair. **Figure 1.52** shows a pair of figure-8 ribbon mics in front of a drum set, in Blumlein configuration.

DVD Track 37: Stereo drum overhead recording using a single pair of condenser figure-8 mics in Blumlein position in front of the drum set.

Figure 1.52: The Blumlein mic technique.

The Mid-Side (M-S) Mic Technique

The mid-side technique is quite complicated because you will need to actually encode and decode the signal to achieve a true stereo field. M-S recording involves combining a cardioid mic pointing towards the source and a figure-8 mic pointing to the left and right of the source. The idea is that the mid signal (the cardioid) is shared between each of the figure-8 sides. For example, one side of the stereo image is created by adding the M signal onto half of the figure-8, let's say the left. The other side of the stereo image is created by subtracting the right side of the figure-8 from the M signal. Additionally, M-S encoders often come with a balance knob that allows you to choose how much of the M is used in the signal. This results in an increase or decrease of the front sound—usually more of the direct signal. M-S is very useful when you want a stereo signal that you can control without moving the mics around! **Figure 1.53** shows a cardioid condenser mic and a figure-8 ribbon in an M-S configuration.

DVD Track 38: Stereo drum recording, decoded from a figure-8 and a cardioid mic in the M-S configuration.

Figure 1.53: The M-S miking technique.

RECAP

Great care should be taken when using mics, as they are often delicate and prone to damage. Repairs are expensive and replacing them is even worse! Be sure to secure the mic to the clip after the clip is secured to the stand. This ensures that you have two hands free to handle the mic when attaching it to the stand—the time when most damage occurs. Handle your cables with care, as they often fail from misuse. Wrap (coil) them gently and avoid bending them unnecessarily to avoid breaking the wired connections inside the cable. Also, run the cable along the stand and keep all slack out of walking paths to ensure that no one accidentally trips on the wires and pulls your mic stands down.

Mic placement is an art form that's rooted in a producer's ability to hear the difference between the sound of the instrument in the room and the sound coming through the mic. It can take years of experience to develop a miking style that produces the sound you are looking for in a recording. During the recording process, you will decide whether you're looking for an accurate (colorless) replication of the original sound or a unique and personally pleasing sound that suits the song's needs (colored).

Here are some basic guidelines to help speed the process of developing "your" sound:

☞ Start with one mic up close. This presents a big and very dry, present sound with cardioids and a bit more of the room sound in figure-8s and omnis.

☞ Move the mic away from the source to get a better blend of room-to-direct sound. This has a dramatic effect with cardioids but less so with omnis and figure-8s, as they inherently capture some of the room sound.

☞ Move the mic to a far position to capture mostly room sound with little direct sound. As you move the mic further back, you should expect a smaller dynamic range in the recording.

☞ If you can't get the sound you're looking for, try blending two different mics together. Place them very close to each other (coincident) to minimize phase shift.

☞ When using two mics, experiment with mis-directing one of them to introduce some phase shift. You might enjoy the sound as the phase shift can remove some of the edge of an overly direct sound.

☞ Try putting the two mics in different places so each can capture a unique tonal quality. Phase shift can be of concern here, so you'll likely need to play with the positions to get a good sound.

☞ If you have access to two models of the same mic, try using a standard stereo technique (assuming the source is stereo).

"computers are the heart and soul of a digital music production studio, and when building your facility, finding the right computer for your particular needs is one of the most important considerations . . ."

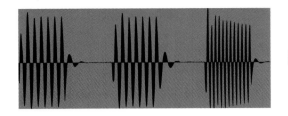

Computer-Based Audio

The Computer

Computers are the heart and soul of a digital music production studio. When equipping your facility, finding the right computer for your particular needs is one of the most important considerations. The technologies involved in making music are constantly changing, meaning that the software and hardware running your studio are changing as well. It's hard to tell whether the advances in software push the hardware to be more powerful or vice-versa, but manufacturers on both sides of the equation are perpetually releasing newer, faster and more powerful products.

Note: For convenience, we've abbreviated "Mac" for all Apple computers and "PC" for all others.

If you want to run the latest and greatest virtual instruments or software synthesizers, you'll need powerful hardware—virtual instruments (VIs) require *lots* of processor power. Cutting-edge hardware typically only works with the latest versions of software—applications written for an older computer chipset rarely make the transition to the new chipset. When the time comes to upgrade or purchase a new computer for your studio, you have a number of jobs to do.

The first task is to figure out what your system will be asked to do. There is a big difference between calculating the path of a rogue asteroid on its way to destroy Earth and posting a picture on Facebook. There's also a difference between recording (or emulating with VIs) a 114-piece orchestra and producing a simple hip-hop beat. Will you need to record a choir, a 4-piece rock band or maybe just a singer? Will you need to run every virtual instrument ever made or will your system just be a sketchpad? Do you produce hip-hop, electronic music or score video games with a virtual orchestra? Each of these production scenarios has a different impact on your resources.

Secondly, you'll need to determine whether your studio is going to be for personal fulfillment (hobby) or professional work (I want to get paid!). There is a significant difference between the home and professional studio, although that line has blurred over the last few years. Computer power and affordability have leveled the playing field, especially for electronic musicians who don't record large numbers of live instruments. You may not have the preamps, microphones or speakers that a big studio has, but you can have the computer!

With the right computer, you can run as many VIs in a session as any top film composer can—you'll find the same computers in many home studios that you would find in major production companies. Home studios tend to have more flexibility in choosing a computer. While the bigger studios *must* have the most powerful systems to handle whatever project comes through the door, home studios can find just the right computer to fit their needs and budget.

COACH'S CORNER

There was a day when the phrase "home studio" had some very negative connotations. It conjured up images of 4-track cassette decks, beat-up mics, and egg-carton soundproofing (a bad idea; read about this later in the section on monitors), along with ripped up couches or worse. Over the past decade, the concept of the home studio has evolved to something much more commonplace. Hit records are being made in all kinds of places—from remote barns, to rehearsal spaces—all due to the availability and affordability of powerful computer-based production studios. Nowadays, a "home" studio is usually reserved for hobbyists—folks just having fun. However, an affordable and even portable studio that's computer-based is a very viable production solution. We refer to these as "project" studios. Even in someone's home, the name basically refers to a studio that earns money at a cost below the professionals.

After deciding what you need to do with your system—the type of work and the level of service (home, project or pro)—you'll need a basic understanding of how computer-based production works. In most home and project studios, your computer will do all of the heavy lifting, meaning that it serves as the recording device, the synths, the mixer and the storage device. This type of system is called a host-based system since the computer—aka host—does the work.

Your computer will power your track counts (how many tracks you can/will record in one piece of music), VIs and plug-ins. If you need large track counts, you will definitely need a powerful computer. If you use a lot of plug-ins, you will need a powerful computer. If you run a lot of virtual instruments you will need a very powerful computer. If you use all of these together, well . . . you get the idea.

A common misconception is that your audio interface helps with your processing needs. Your audio interface works as your I/O (input/output) and also handles the AD/DA conversions that is, it converts incoming analog signals to digital, thus A/D converter. Your interface brings analog electrical audio in to your computer and then takes it back out to your speakers. An A/D (analog-to-digital) converter takes in the analog signal and converts it to a digital word—ones and zeros (or binary code)—which is the universal language of computers. During playback, the D/A (digital-to-analog) converter takes the ones and zeros and converts them back to analog sound waves. There's more on this in the section "Digital Audio Basics."

Your software will often dictate which types of VIs can be used, how many tracks you can run and the number of plug-ins that can be accessed in a session. VIs come in many forms—one for each of the competing DAWs out there. No matter the DAW, running lots of VIs, tracks and plug-ins is always reliant on compatibility with your brand of processor, the available processing power and the amount of RAM you have. Stable combinations of software and hardware are vital in a studio, so taking time to research which software works with which hardware is a must! Compatibility issues can (and do, every day) stop a studio dead in its tracks, turning away creativity and—even worse—customers.

If your needs are primarily recording and mixing a basic band setup (10 or so tracks only, with minimal processing for demos or quick ideas), then you can get away with a smaller system like an all-in-one or a laptop. Small track counts with fewer plug-ins mean less of a hit on your system resources, so you can scale down your computer choice intelligently. If you need to track and mix a larger configuration of instruments (20 to 30 tracks, with significant processing) then you will require a higher-end system to handle the load. Usually, more tracks means more processing (plug-in DSP, etc.) which in turn means more processing power, and lots of RAM is necessary. Studios that record mostly live music tax their processors far less than productions running dozens of VIs, but this advantage is lost if you then turn around and load up every track with plug-ins! If that describes your situation, consider investing in less computing and buy better mics—you'll have to process a whole lot less and you'll get better tracks, anyway!

The hardware system requirements listed with software documentation will help you with your choices. If you're an electronic musician and your needs are mostly VI and effects-driven, you will require significant processing power and lots of RAM. It takes as much processing to run a session with a half-dozen VIs as it does to run a much larger session containing solely audio tracks. Unfortunately, the needs of most production isn't as cut and dry as simply working on one type of project (all-audio or all-VI) and here, the choice of which computer to buy can get a little fuzzy. Most studios do a little bit of everything—recording vocals and acoustic instruments, composing with virtual instruments and of course putting plug-ins on everything.

To this end, both project and pro studios tend to require lots of power, RAM and software choices. DAWs are like cars—they'll all get you where you have to go, but some drive much better than others. When you work with clients, there's just no telling which DAW they're working with, and you'll need to be flexible with your system. Many studios invest in external hardware than can run the plug-ins and VIs *outside* of the computer, freeing up more resources for the different types of clients and jobs that come in the door. These systems utilize additional processing power in the form of DSP (digital signal processing) chips on expansion cards or hardware boxes. This external processing can take a substantial load off of your computer and increase your overall capabilities.

The downside to these systems is they'll increase the cost of your computer system. Price these carefully, though—you might buy a middle-of-the-road computer and save hundreds of dollars, and then have to reinvest that savings into an external DSP box. On the upside, you can keep the DSP box in this situation and upgrade your computer in a few years, when your power needs grow even larger!

Computers tend to have a fairly short life span of usefulness—in software years, computers become outdated every 18 months. The best computer shopping strategy is to buy the most powerful system available *today* without breaking the bank. It's never a good idea to go on the cheap for a system, as you'll need to upgrade sooner than you like. If your needs are simple, you can go for a less powerful, less expandable system, but keep in mind that the shelf life of your system is ticking away as soon as you buy it. They're just like cars—drive one off the lot and it's already worth less than you paid for it!

In an attempt to save money, some users purchase less powerful, less expensive used computers. However, most manufacturers don't support older machines once they release their new operating systems. If you buy used (dead) technology, you are locked into the past—you can't upgrade the computer or your DAW to the latest versions of software.

On the other hand, if you have major computing needs for your rig (big track counts, lots of VIs, lots of plug-ins or even video), then get as much computer as you can afford. The reason is that high-end models of any manufacturer have the longest staying power, which results in the need to buy a new system less often. When the costs run in the thousands of dollars, this does indeed matter. So pay more now, and save a lot more later—easy math!

COACH'S CORNER

We have lots of fun phrases around Pyramind, but two come to mind when discussing purchasing tools, or the computer, in this case. The first is, "The poor man pays twice." Basically, this predicts that going cheap usually means under-purchasing—you'll buy the computer then realize you have to buy it again to get the power you really need. The second is, "Good, fast and cheap—pick two." In other words, going cheap either means your computer won't be fast, or it won't be good. Buying speed and quality means it ain't gonna be cheap!

Once you determine your needs, budget and expected time-to-upgrade, you'll need to actually go buy the computer! It's hard enough to determine what your budget range, compatibility and production needs will be, but *now* you've got to find the computer that *fits* those needs. The choice of DAW is a big part of your decision—some DAWs simply don't work on all computers, while others are ubiquitous. You can either buy the computer then find the DAW that fits, or buy the DAW then find the computer that fits.

COACH'S CORNER

Choosing a DAW is a serious matter. Most DAWs can "get the job done" with excellent results—and results always matter—but how you get there can make all the difference in the world. Each DAW comes with a complement of similar tools—the ability to record audio, MIDI, plug-ins and VIs—but their workflows can be radically different. Some tools are based on traditional audio production processes and as such, concentrate their power into recording, editing, and mixing. MIDI and VIs are secondary considerations. These DAWs are great for instrumentalists who will be concentrating on recording their performances, perfecting them with editing and mixing them to professional standards. Others focus on piano and MIDI-based compositions, and recording audio is a secondary consideration.

Choosing a DAW

In the earlier days of DAWs, the delineation was much clearer—sequencers and composition tools were horrible at audio production. The time and effort required to record, edit and composite a selection of "takes" took more time than simply recording it again and again until you nailed it. In other words, you'd spend less time practicing your instrument and becoming a better player than you would recording and editing! Working with MIDI, synths and odd time signatures, however, was a breeze. Some familiar names of tools back then include: Studio Vision from Opcode (now defunct), Digital Performer from MOTU (Mark of the Unicorn, still active), Logic from E-magic (now owned by Apple and still active) and Cubase from Steinberg (still active).

Audio production tools, however, were primarily recording, editing and mixing tools. You were lucky if MIDI was even supported! Most of the time, if you needed MIDI work done, you'd have to connect two DAWs together—one for audio and one for MIDI—and get them to sync so the music played together. The level of technical knowledge at this stage was intense—there were support issues, timing issues, and memory issues, and if you were lucky, you could almost finish a piece of music! Pro Tools by Digidesign (now owned by Avid, still active) and Deck II by OSC (then bought and destroyed by Macromedia, Inc.) were the biggest competing products out there.

Back then (mind you, this is barely a dozen years ago—a lifetime in dog years!), users clearly fell into one group or another—a MIDI composer or an audio producer. Over time, each camp began to grow into the other camp's skillsets to the point where a MIDI composer's DAW began to excel at audio production and the audio tools got hip to MIDI. MIDI and audio were merging the tools, becoming more similar than dissimilar.

Not long after the millennium, several tools debuted that merged all of these skills into a single application, including built-in synths. Tools like Reason by Propellerheads (very active) and ACID by Sonic Foundry (now owned by Sony Creative Software, still active) were revolutionizing the DAW scene—everything you needed was already built into the tool! There were serious limitations, however. Reason could not record audio at all, but seriously streamlined the MIDI composer's world by hosting a wide assortment of decent VIs built into the tool. ACID made recording and loop manipulation (all the rage in production at the time) a breeze, but was limited in MIDI work and VIs. The biggest advantage of these apps was that they were both inexpensive!

Arguably, Reason made the biggest impact in the DAW world. Intelligently, the company, Propellerhead Software, co-developed a protocol with Steinberg called ReWire that allowed Cubase and Reason to work together seamlessly. ReWire lets the MIDI from Cubase flow easily into Reason and the audio output from its VIs to flow easily into Cubase. ReWire was an open protocol—DAWs required very little coding to use it. Soon after, Reason (the light version) was bundled with other DAWs as a giveaway, allowing audio DAWs to take advantage of this easy-to-use, sounds-great-out-of-the-box format and giving new DAW customers sounds they could play with immediately.

Propellerhead quickly developed a huge market as a result. Several DAW manufacturers saw a downturn in their market share and began developing VIs of their own. Or, they partnered with companies like Native Instruments, IK Multimedia, and Spectrasonics, which all make dedicated VIs (among other tools). And the line between the audio production DAW and the MIDI production DAW blurred and thinned.

New tools like Ableton's LIVE have re-invented the DAW, as it's a fully interactive performance tool *and* DAW. You can use LIVE like a traditional DAW (record, edit, arrange, mix, etc.), you can use it like a loop editor (like ACID was at first) *or* you can use it like a DJ performance tool. This makes it unique among the others!

Today, choosing a DAW is much easier, but it is still a serious matter. The heart of each system is not unchanged from the early days—Pro Tools is still an audio production tool first and Logic is still a MIDI production tool first. Reason still cannot record audio, but Propellerheads has solved that by releasing Record, an audio recorder designed to work with Reason. LIVE is a full-featured DAW, but is certainly more apt at producing like a DJ than a composer.

When choosing a DAW, try to envision your workflow: Are you a MIDI composer aiming to produce complex musical pieces? Film scoring or orchestration work? Intricate VI work and sound design? Consider Logic as your tool. Keep in mind that it only works on the Mac platform. (And the latest version only operates on the newer Intel-based Macs!) If you already own a Windows-based PC, look to alternatives—SONAR and Cubase are two good ones.

If you're a DJ seeking to produce high-quality electronica or dance music, consider Logic or LIVE. LIVE is supported on both Mac and PC, while Logic is a Mac-only tool. If you're a beat maker or working with MIDI only *and* you like to keep it simple, using mostly loops and simple sounds, consider ACID, Reason, or LIVE. All three are easy to get into and can give you great results fast. Plus, you don't need super deep music chops to use any of them, and they're mostly supported on both Mac or PC (ACID is PC only).

COACH'S CORNER

Pyramind's workflow is dedicated to the Macintosh platform. We have found that the tools available for the Mac are more industry standardized and the support is much easier. Our four main tools are Pro Tools, Logic, Reason, and LIVE. Both Reason and LIVE let you send audio via ReWire into both Pro Tools and Logic (LIVE can be both a ReWire host or slave), and we usually cluster tools together in intelligent workflows. For example, Pro Tools and Reason are a great combination for rock and hip hop, while Logic and LIVE are a great combination for dance and electronica. These are suggested pairings—like a good wine with a meal at a nice restaurant, you can mix and match if you like, but why not trust the chef?

And finally, for the audio producer, consider Pro Tools or Logic as your primary tool. Pro Tools is the industry standard for audio producers, with over 80% of studios worldwide using Pro Tools at some level. Sessions are often standardized to Pro Tools format from all other formats as it is a most common denominator—just about everyone has a Pro Tools system of some size. (Prices range from about $200 to about $75,000 or more, depending on hardware and software configurations!)

The Mac Versus PC Question

You've probably seen the ads comparing Macs to PCs , talking about which one is better and why. The truth is, each platform has something significant to offer the user and each one has its challenges, and for certain, there is no one-computer-fits-all solution. The difference between platforms—including price—has diminished considerably in recent years and most likely will continue to do so. Both have tremendous power , RAM expandability, a wide assortment of software tools on the market and a wide range of prices. So what's the real difference between them—other than what the ads tell you?

The biggest difference between them is the user interface—it's a personal preference, but a significant one. The graphical user interface, or GUI, of a system dictates how you interact with your computer. The GUI is the portal into your machine, and feeling comfortable (or not) with that interface can make or break a relationship. Would you be comfortable working in a chair that was hurting your back or using a mouse that strained your wrist? While those are physical concerns, the GUI interaction is more of a mental, organizational issue. For some, it's even emotional!

If you aren't comfortable with the way *you* interface with your computer, then odds are you won't be very productive with your work. Don't just grin and bear it; get a system that you vibe with. It sounds a little "new age," but it really matters.

Traditionally, Macs have had fewer models to choose from, but each model has several options, widening the range of overall choices. With all of the hardware choices on the PC side, you have to put a little more time into your research—there are numerous manufacturers making PCs but even more that just make parts for PCs, and you can always build your own! Not all chipsets are compatible with all software, so if you know which software apps you'll be using, hit the websites of the manufacturers and your favorite, trusted support community.

COACH'S CORNER

Odds are, you've already been working with one system or another, and you may have become accustomed to that system. Familiarity is not comfort—you may not even know how hard your work is until you try the other side! Have you ever spent a long time on an uncomfortable chair but not realized that your back was hurting? Computing can be the same—knowing how to engage twelve workarounds to get a job done is not the same as working efficiently!

The OS Conundrum

While not all DAWs work with all platforms, not all platforms work with themselves! Each platform requires an operating system to run—with PCs, it's usually some form of Windows, and with Macs it's some form of Mac OS. PCs can run other operating systems like Linux and Unix, but there just aren't a lot of DAW apps for them. And even if you narrow your OS choices to the main two, there's no guarantee that the DAW you want to use will even work on the OS on the computer! Again, the latest hardware usually requires the latest OS. With PCs, the OS choices are increased—XP Home, XP Pro, Vista, and Windows 7 are all in use as of this writing—but that doesn't help the situation. Your DAW may be compatible with, say, XP, but XP may have an incompatibility with a particular set of hardware chips, making it virtually impossible to run smoothly.

With Mac OS, there are more options. As of this writing, there are two operating systems: 10.5 (Leopard) and 10.6 (Snow Leopard). Each, however, has updates—the computer I am using to do this writing is running version 10.5.7, which should tell you that there were at least six other updates to 10.5 before this one! Keeping up with the OS in the Mac world is dicey work—upgrading is easy, back-grading is not. Again, be *very* careful to do your homework before buying a computer, and know which OS will come with it and whether or not it will even work for you and your DAW.

After you decide what your needs are and which platform you want to run, it's time to start thinking about the computer itself. Computer systems come in three basic configurations, regardless of the platform: all-in-one systems, laptops, and desktops. Performance, price, and expandability are dictated by your choice of configuration, and each of these systems gives the user tier-based choices in processor speed, number of processors, amount of RAM, and hard-drive size.

The All-in-One Computer

The first system we'll look at is the all-in-one computer—named as such because the monitor is built right into the computer. The first Macs and PCs produced in the late '70s and early '80s were this kind of system—they were very basic by today's standards ,and the only upgradable component was the RAM, if that. Computer manufacturers adopted a modular design in the late '80s to accommodate different components and allow the computer to be upgraded and expanded. In the late '90s, the all-in-one computer made a comeback with the introduction of the eMac. When eMacs were introduced, they changed the landscape of home computing by offering solid performance bundled with a small price tag and an even smaller footprint than desktop systems—a computing trifecta!

Included in anAll-In-One System:

- ☞ CPU
- ☞ Monitor
- ☞ Keyboard
- ☞ Mouse
- ☞ Various software apps, depending on the system

One advantage to the all-in-one approach is that you get everything you need in one box at a less expensive price than its equivalent laptop counterparts (which also provide everything in one box). Although not as portable as a laptop or powerful as a desktop, all-in-one systems are a great price-point compromise between the two. Another advantage is space, an all-in-one computer takes up the same desk space as the monitor and keyboard for a desktop—without the desktop!

The downside of all-in-one systems is their lack of expandability. Because all-in-one systems are built into the smallest box possible with no unused space, you lose the ability to add additional hard drives, optical drives or expansion cards. The one component you can upgrade in an all-in-one system is usually RAM, although such machines often have severe limits on the amount of available RAM that can be installed.

COACH'S CORNER

The eMac was a very popular computer for Apple as it was one of the first truly affordable Macs. For a brief time, long-time CEO and guru Steve Jobs had left the company and the Mac hardware had been licensed and cloned into copycat Macs. It was a horrible business move and nearly bankrupted the company. Jobs returned to Apple and unleashed the eMac to wide praise amongst the public and Wall Street.

Pros: All-in-One System
- ☞ Everything you need to get up and running is included
- ☞ Inexpensive
- ☞ Small footprint

Cons: All-in-One System
- ☞ Limited expandability
- ☞ Higher-priced components
- ☞ Not as powerful as a desktop computer

Laptops

Formerly the exclusive territory for well-heeled business executives, laptops are powerful, portable computers that are perfect for on-the-go creativity. Smaller than desktops and all-in-ones, the laptop used to suffer from power versus space compromises—manufacturers couldn't build them small *and* powerful. As available power became smaller, the laptop got the biggest boost in performance, allowing today's models to rival the bigger boys in power and performance.

What's In the Box:
- ☞ CPU
- ☞ Monitor
- ☞ Keyboard
- ☞ Trackpad
- ☞ Various software, depending on the system

When the first laptop debuted in the '80s, it was mostly a novelty item because it offered little power in a very heavy package. (Think 18 pounds.) The screens were monochromatic, the RAM was minimal, and the processors were weak, but these were indeed portable—and what a deal at only $12,000! Modern laptops offer amazing power and rugged durability, as long as you're willing to pay for it.

The main advantage of a laptop is obvious—portability. You can work at home (perhaps in a nice, comfortable chair) and then take your work to the office and pick up right where you left off. In a musical environment, the laptop is the ultimate traveling solution—work on your DJ set in your home studio, and then take it to the club to perform it. Make a beat at home, and then take it to your buddy's studio to collaborate on the track. Moving data between different studios is done all of the time, but it's certainly easier to just take your whole studio with you wherever you go. Touring is another consideration for your purchase. As a laptop contains basically everything you need to work in one neat little package, it's the easiest to travel with.

The laptop's downside is two-fold. The first is expense. Because the components in a laptop have to be miniaturized to fit in such a small space, they will cost you more than a desktop or an all-in-one with the same specs. The other potential problem with a laptop is the lack of expandability. Just like with an all-in-one system, laptops come in very tight little packages, with little room left to add any peripherals.

RAM is another issue. Laptops ship with differing amounts of RAM depending on the model you buy (just like any other computer), but the total amount of RAM you can install is considerably less than what you can put in a desktop model. It's also not as easy or as cheap to install additional RAM in a laptop as it is in a desktop system. You will pay a premium for laptop RAM and then struggle to install it.

The next concern is the hard drive. Internal hard drives in a laptop are scaled down to fit in that small footprint, so the capacity of most laptop drives is considerably smaller than a desktop or even an all-in-one system. Additionally, they tend to be slower drives, so they generate less heat while spinning— heat is a computer killer. The rule of thumb with *any* computer is to always keep at least 10% of your system drive free, or bad things will happen. These bad things include sluggishness, crashing and overall poor performance—not nice. And as laptops have fairly small drives to begin with, maintaining that 10% safety cushion can be a hardship—it's far less of a problem with a desktop machine running on a 1TB disk.

Overall, laptops offer amazing performance in a small package with (fairly) rugged portability. Even if you don't like using the built-in keyboard and trackpad, it's easy to hook up a mouse and USB external keyboard and even another LCD screen to either replace or complement the screen in the laptop. This gives you the best of both worlds—a mobile monster when needed to travel and a killer home system when you plug it into an external monitor, mouse and keyboard.

Pros: Laptop Computer
- ☞ Portable
- ☞ Rugged
- ☞ All you need in one box

Cons: Laptop Computer
- ☞ Expensive
- ☞ Limited expandability
- ☞ Not as powerful as a desktop computer

Desktop (aka Tower) Computers

The top of the line in personal computing is the desktop or tower system. Desktops are just boxes of computing power with lots of space—space to connect keyboards, mice, monitors (two or more), I/O cards, processing cards, graphics cards, gaming cards—you name it. Of course, you'll have to actually go buy these things *and* the desktop itself—which you'll pay a premium for, since it's the only one that's expandable. These factors can make this a pricey—although powerful—possibility.

What's In the Box:
- ☞ Tower computer
- ☞ Mouse
- ☞ Keyboard
- ☞ Various software, depending on the system

The main advantages of desktop systems are expandability and power. Professional applications often require this level of computer to do the heavy lifting. Tower computers are more expandable than laptops (there's more room inside the computer for additional components) or all-in-one systems, and they are much larger. Some tower models can hold up to four internal hard drives, giving the computer a massive amount of storage. This is an advantage, as internal drives are always less expensive than their external counterparts.

Large towers can have up to eight slots for RAM. The amount of RAM is one of the most important considerations when buying a computer—more RAM means less crashes and faster performance.

The second advantage of a desktop model is sheer, unadulterated power. Towers typically have more raw horsepower than any other system. Desktop models have few space constraints, so component design can focus on performance more than size. Modern computers utilize multiple processors, and the number and speed of those processors is a selling point. More processors equals more power and faster processors equals faster calculations. Running a DAW requires as much processing power as possible, so you'll find big tower systems powering pro studios for all kinds of production.

Desktop systems are well suited for pro applications and hold their value longer than entry-level systems. With more power and expandability, they have a longer shelf life and keep you from buying as often. In the long run, it's a good idea to get as much computer as you can afford and maybe just a bit more, then enjoy the power for years to come.

Pros: Desktop Computer
- Expandable
- Multiple processors available
- Faster processors available
- Future-proof
- Modular design allows customization with peripherals, and selection of monitor(s), keyboard and mouse to suit specific needs.

Cons: Desktop Computer
- Can be the most expensive type of system
- Large footprint with multiple components
- Compatibility issues exist among components from different manufacturers

Upgrade Options

Having determined your power needs (home, project or pro), your platform of choice (Mac, PC, Linux, etc.) and which type of computer you want (all-in-one, laptop, desktop), it's time to get your shiny new baby and bring it home. One of the greatest things about a computer is the ability to customize it to your specific power and budgetary needs. You can add RAM, an external hard drive or even a second monitor to your system. Go ahead, pimp your rig! Just keep in mind that there will be limits. When building your computer, you're likely to run out of expandability—or money—at some point.

RAM

When customizing your computer, the first upgrade consideration should be RAM, but how much is enough? Some say there is no such thing as too much RAM, but the truth is, that while you do need a lot of RAM to really get the most out of a computer, your OS will dictate how much you can use per application. If you run multiple applications at once (surfing the web, writing a paper, editing audio and burning DVDs, etc.), then you'll need a lot. RAM is sold as a socketed chip containing individual memory modules that gets installed directly into the motherboard (the "plate" where all the devices on the computer are connected, including the CPU, or central processing unit). These days, RAM is very simple to install in a desktop system, but it still can be tricky to upgrade certain laptops and all-in-one computers because of the limited space.

Tech-Speak: *RAM*

RAM is short for random access memory. RAM is the kind of memory that applications, such as your DAW, use to access quick information. RAM processes GUI functions, VIs and many plug-ins, and provides temporary memory storage for the OS itself and all applications. More is better than less—much more.

RAM has increased in size from the days of the Commodore 64 machine in the 1980s, which had a paltry 64k of RAM. Most machines today can be expanded to 32 gigabytes and beyond—that's about 470,000 times the memory capacity! The amount of RAM you can install in your machine is limited by your computer's capacity, so check the specs to find the maximum it will hold. Laptops and all-in-one systems typically hold less RAM than tower models, so if your musical needs require massive quantities of RAM, that alone might dictate selecting a desktop system.

Hard Drives and Storage

Another important consideration is your hard drive. Most home computers that are only used for simple tasks like e-mail and web browsing can get away with a single internal hard drive, as there is no need for huge amounts of data storage. Of course, as you collect a music library, photo library, and a video collection, even your innocent home computer will need additional hard drive space—lots of it. Fortunately, hard drive capacities have become enormous and drives have become very inexpensive. In most tower computers, you can add internal drives to your system—drives that are enclosed within the tower itself. Internal drives are usually cheaper than external drives, though not all drives are made equally. There are many different types and speeds of drives available, so check your computer specs for compatibility. (By now, this should be a recurring theme in your head!) Some towers have up to four internal drive bays, allowing massive storage capacity inside your computer.

The internal components in an all-in-one system or a laptop occupy *all* of the available space, so if you need additional storage capacity, you have to add an external drive. This is a storage device that lives outside your computer and connects to it via some digital cable. There are two main connections types: USB (universal serial bus) and FireWire (known technically as IEEE 1394). Each has its advantages and disadvantages. USB is fast and stable, but data is transferred serially, one chunk of data after the next. FireWire is faster, as the data is transferred in parallel, not series, but it's not available on all computers. Macs usually carry both connections, while PCs tend not to have FireWire connections without buying a dedicated interface card.

The hard drive needs of a computer used for music applications are much greater than those of a *non*-media based system. If you are recording live music, you will need a lot of space for all of those tracks—and four times as much if you're also working with video! Recording audio and video to your system drive unnecessarily taxes your resources, which is another reason why people opt for dedicated external drives. All of your media and productions can live on the external drive while the OS and DAW applications will live on the internal drive (referred to as the system drive).

Most electronic music producers have huge sound libraries, which require a lot of drive space. It's common to have a few external hard drives to accommodate these sounds, but external drives are also used as backups. Storing data is one thing, but securing that data is another. What would you do if you lost all the data on your drive and all of your music?

Having multiple drives and duplicating your most sensitive data is a necessity for *all* producers.

There are many backup options, and as you might guess, each has ups and downs. Backing up a terabyte (1,000 GB) drive to DVD, for example, would require some 200 discs. The media is cheap, but it's expensive in terms of time and organization. You can back up to another drive, but drives can build up cost over time and they do fail on occasion.

Another type of hard drive is the pocket drive. These are portable drives that are great for moving sessions between studios and are fairly rugged in construction, so they travel well. They're typically smaller in both size and capacity (up to 160GB or so) than desktop-style external drives or internal drives, and cost more per gigabyte or terabyte.

You can also perform network backups. This is great for the cost-conscious, in that you don't need to buy anything—you simply upload your data to a remote web server and—*voila!* You can retrieve your data at any time from any place with an Internet connection too, but you'll pay a monthly fee and if you have a slow Internet connection, this will take time. Lots of time.

Computer Displays

The last choice for your computer rig is the video display. Regardless of your system, bigger is really better when it comes to monitors—constantly switching between open windows takes time that you could use for something productive, like being inspired! DAWs often have several windows that display different information, and producers like to see all of them at once, so having more screen real estate available can help you develop a quicker workflow. If you have an all-in-one system or a laptop, this is decided by which model you choose—they come with fixed screens ranging from 13 to 20 inches.

If you want a bigger screen in a laptop, odds are you'll pay dearly. In an all-in-one system, you can get a substantially bigger screen than you can get in a laptop and still not pay as much for the computer overall. Most systems allow you to connect an additional display, getting the best of both worlds—smaller budgetary needs and a huge screen.

For a desktop model, this is a more complex decision. With laptops and all-in-one systems, the screen is often selected for you once you settle on the model. With desktops, you can connect to nearly any monitor as your primary or secondary monitor. If you're going to get a large display, you'll likely only need one, but if you're going for two displays, don't go overboard. Twin 30-inch monitors may seem cool, but they're expensive and take up a *lot* of desk space. You'll also have to put them further away as they'll hurt your eyes (and give you headaches) if you stare at them for too long!

The days of bulky CRT (cathode ray tube) monitors are thankfully gone, so your choice of monitor will be based on LCD (liquid crystal display) technology instead. LCDs are better in almost every way for making music. LCDs are cheaper, require less energy, less space, are better for your eyes, and offer substantially larger screen sizes than their old CRT counterparts. As an added bonus, LCD monitors are immune to visual distortion caused by placing studio speakers (with their large magnets) adjacent to the picture display, which was frequently a problem with CRT displays. The main downside of LCD displays is the way they handle colors and the angle at which you can view the screen—they're meant for direct viewing, so if you look at LCD screens from the side, the picture may be dim and/or color-shifted.

With the affordability of LCD displays, having two monitors makes even more sense—and cents. For example, you can dedicate one monitor for your audio tracks and one to your VIs or mixer window. Be warned though, once you work with a dual-monitor setup, its hard to go back to a single display! Displays and computers usually come with VGA (video graphics array) or SVGA (super video graphics array) analog connections and digital connections, called DVI (digital video interface).

Keep in mind that monitors don't like to be too far away from the computer—there's often a cable limitation of five feet or so. In home and project studios, this is less of an issue as the computer is often located next to the workdesk, but as you grow into pro status, you'll need cable extenders, especially if the computer is located in a separate machine room to reduce noise in the control room.

Digital Audio Basics

Every digital audio workstation works by capturing, manipulating and playing back digital audio. Audio converts to digital though a process that measures electrical voltages (which represent frequency, amplitude and time) and transcribes them into a binary code of ones and zeros. In some ways, this can be thought of as a type of transducer that converts analog voltage energy to digital energy. The process is called A/D (analog-to-digital) conversion. The reverse is called D/A conversion, where digital audio is reconverted back to an analog voltage that's then sent on to an audio monitor (back to free sound).

Digital audio was released to the music buying public in the early 1980s, but has actually been around since long before then—originating from Bell Labs in the early 1950s. The father of digital audio is Harry Nyquist, and his work, which remains the underpinning of digital audio, is known as the *Nyquist theorem*.

Digital audio is stored in binary form—a language of code consisting of only ones and zeros. If you think of them as the only two letters of the alphabet, then when the ones and zeros are strung together, they form words. Some words use only 4 letters, like 1111 or 0000. CD's, for example, use 16 letters like 1111000011110000 or 0000000011111111. The number of "letters" used in a binary word is known as the *bit depth*: on a CD the bit depth represents the dynamic range of all the audio on the CD. The amount of words captured per second is known as the *sampling rate*, and determines the frequency range available in the digital audio system. In short, the bit depth refers to the dynamics, and the sampling rate refers to the frequency range.

Sampling Rate

The Nyquist theorem is built on simple sampling techniques, where a sound is studied in a moment of time, analyzed, then codified. The trick is in both the coding and the amount of samples taken within a given time period—per one second, in the case of digital audio. Once the sound is sampled at one moment and coded into binary, the process repeats over time and the words are strung together to replicate the original audio. In digital audio, samples are taken thousands of times per second, every second, until the conversion is done. As you might guess, the number of samples in a four-minute song can be huge.

Audio is sampled by having a "picture" taken of the sound at any given moment in time, then assigning a code to represent the value of the picture. However, a single picture cannot tell you what the sound does over time—it's just a captured moment. Much like film or video, if you string together a series of these pictures, you can begin to piece together the movement, or the change in the scene you're taking pictures of. Sampling works in this way—several pictures are taken over the course of time and then strung together to emulate the motion of the sound.

Nyquist's theorem holds true to this concept: the more samples you take in a given period of time, the more realistic the picture being strung together. This is the *sampling rate*—how fast the audio is sampled as it flies by, or, how many samples are taken in a given time period. Keep in mind that these samples are only half of the story—the other half is that there is an equal amount of time in between the samples where the sampler isn't capturing data. It's the same in a motion picture camera—the shutter is either open during a picture, or closed as it finishes one picture and begins the next one.

COACH'S CORNER

Sampling is not unlike the trick of drawing a stick figure on a pad of paper, and changing it slightly on each consecutive page. As you flip through the papers, the stick figure comes to life. The faster you flip, the smaller the changes and the more pages you use, the more realistic the motion becomes to your eye. Similarly, imagine being in a dark room, then having a strobe light turn on every second. Over time, movement that you see becomes a series of still frames. As you increase the speed of the strobe, the movement around you starts to piece together into fluid motion. When sampling digital audio, every sample has an "off" moment between the moments of capture and the set-up for the next capture.

Understanding this concept is key to understanding how sampling rate affects sound quality. Let's say that the sampling rate is 1,000 Hz, meaning 1,000 samples are taken during one second of audio. This means that the sampler "opens" 1,000 times in that second, but is also closed 1,000 times during that second. Any frequency moving faster than 1,000 Hz—say 1,500 Hz—is likely to be missed, as the sampler simply can't keep up. To compensate, Nyquist's theorem states that the sampler must operate at twice (2x) the speed of the highest frequency captured in order to properly represent that frequency range. Since human hearing has an optimal range of 20 Hz to 20,000 Hz, it stands to reason that the sampling rate should operate at 40,000 Hz in order to capture the full frequency range. This is true—at least in theory . . .

One of the unfortunate by-products of sampling this way is known as *aliasing*. Looking back at the case of 1,500 Hz trying to be captured by a 1 kHz sampling rate system, we know that the frequency will not be captured—at least, not how we want it to be. As the 1.5 kHz tone plays, a picture of it gets taken, but not as quickly as the tone is moving. However, a piece of the tone is captured, since some of the time the tone will be in the sampling picture and sometimes it won't be. The instances where the tone gets captured get strung together just like all the other pictures, but as there are big gaps in the picture of that tone, it ends up being perceived as a much lower-frequency tone—a sort of ghost image of the tone. This is its alias. The higher tone in this example is 500 Hz faster than the sampling rate, so the aliased sound will be audible at 500 Hz.

COACH'S CORNER

Picture yourself sitting in the back seat of a car on the highway, driving just a few mph slower than the car on your right. If you look long enough at the hubcap of the car to your right, you can pick out its pattern moving very slowly forward. Your eye is capable of recognizing that the other car is moving faster by, say 2 mph, and it pieces together the image of the hubcap rolling forward at 2 mph! The car is clearly moving too fast to see the pattern, but the change in its speed versus your speed is enough for your eye to catch the difference. Now, if the other car slows to 2 mph slower than you, the hubcap image appears to stop spinning, then begins to spin backwards at 2 mph! This is the essence of aliasing—the image of the sound playing higher than the sampling rate is still perceived, only at the frequency of the difference between the sampling rate and the frequency!

COACH'S CORNER

As of this writing, the highest sampling rate available is 192 kHz, which is capable of capturing frequencies up to 96 kHz, well beyond the hearing range of just about everyone. While we can't necessarily hear the difference directly, many people have been able to perceive an "open" sound and a realism unattainable at 44.1 kHz. This is subjective, of course, but reasonable to believe. After all, we do hear with more than our ears—the whole body is a resonator of sorts. You can sometimes feel the low end before you hear it, as in the case of a truck driving past. Why can't the same be true of high frequencies? It can. In fact, if you've ever felt your teeth rattle when a fork scrapes on a ceramic bowl, you understand this concept. Your bones "hear" the ultra-high frequencies of the ceramic and resonate too, making your mouth hurt . . . badly!

To avoid capturing aliased sounds, anti-aliasing filters are employed to remove any sound above the sampling-rate frequency. Filters are imperfect devices, though, and no filter removes sound exactly at the frequency it's set to. (More on filters later under the DSP section.) Think of it as having to apply car brakes—the car will stop, but it will take a little time. In the case of CD-quality audio, the range we want to capture is 20 Hz to 20 kHz, necessitating a sampling rate of at least 40 kHz—two times 20 kHz, as dictated by the Nyquist theorem. Thus, the sampling rate for standard CDs is 44,100 kHz (44.1 kHz), which allows for a theoretical maximum frequency response of 22,050 kHz, but given the realities of filter design, equates to a real-world response that's slightly less than that but still covers the 20 kHz range of human hearing.

Figure 1.54 shows a 1 Hz sine wave and the result of a sampling rate of 4 Hz—that is, four samples are taken per second. Notice that the result is a very blocky square wave, resembling stairs. Now, notice how the 4 Hz sampler tries to sample an 8 Hz wave in **Figure 1.55**. Notice how the resulting square wave misses the real shape of the wave? That's because there are simply not enough samples taken to capture the real shape of the 8 Hz wave.

Figure 1.54: 1 Hz sine wave, sampled at 4 Hz.

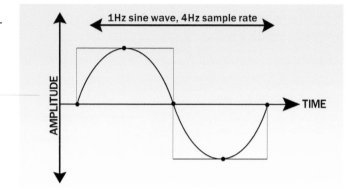

Figure 1.55: 8 Hz sine wave, sampled at 4 Hz.

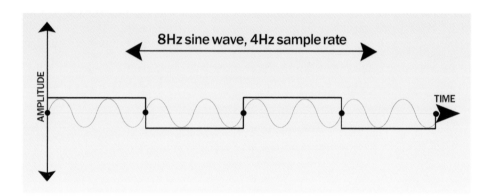

Now, lets go back to the 1 Hz wave, and sample it with 16 samples as seen in **Figure 1.56**. Notice how much closer to the original wave the digital wave looks? As you can see, even though the sampling rate is much higher than the frequency being captured, having more samples makes the shape of the square wave much more "curved," as in the original wave.

Figure 1.56: 1 Hz sine wave, sampled at 16 Hz.

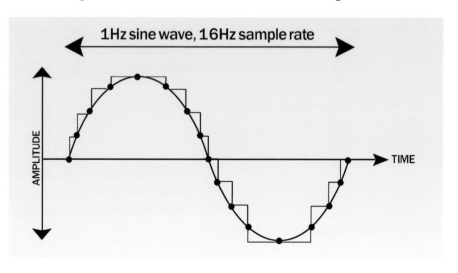

COACH'S CORNER

Our ears can hear the shape of a digital representation of an audio wave very clearly. In fact, many studio professionals shied away from the early digital audio recorders that employed a 44.1 kHz sampling rate claiming the quality was "harsh" or "brittle." This is a result of the amount and size of the square edges on the sampled wave. As sampling rates have increased and the quality of anti-aliasing filters and A/D converters have improved, the sound has gotten much closer to the shape of the original analog waves being captured, and as such, many of these professionals now use digital audio in their studios. Even more have dumped their tape machines in preference of the digital sound!

Bit Depth

The sampling rate of an A/D converter is directly responsible for the range of frequencies that can be captured in digital audio. The amplitude information of audio is stored in the *bit depth* of the digital word. Digital words can be of just about any length, depending on the need—the more bits, the more range of expression available. The math is based on permutations—i.e., how many configurations of the numbers are possible? This defines the range of dynamic expression in a digital system.

In the example of a 1-bit word, there are only two possibilities—1 and 0. If this were to translate to volume, a 1-bit system would either be screamingly loud (1) or dead quiet (0). Not much range. If we looked at a 2-bit system, there are four possibilities—00, 01, 10 and 11. That could mean dead quiet (00), kind of quiet (01), getting loud (10) and screamingly loud (11). Thus, a 2-bit word offers four states of dynamic range—more, but still not even close to musical. This goes onward in the form of 2^x (two to the power of x).

If you continue up the scale, at 16 bits (CD standard), you achieve over 65,000 combinations of values, representing over 65,000 points of volume, which is equivalent to 96 dB in dynamic range. A 24-bit system can represent over 16 million dynamic possibilities—now *that's* more like it! As a general rule of thumb, every bit added to the A/D process adds about 6 dB of dynamic range, so in a 24-bit system (DVD-A standard), a dynamic range of 144 dB is possible. See **Figure 1.57** for a chart comparing permutations and dynamic range at various bit depths.

These figures are based on theoretical math, however, and as of this writing, few devices are even capable of actually reproducing anything over 120 dB dynamic range. Keep in mind that 120 dB SPL is at the threshold of pain—loud enough for just about anyone and too loud for most. That means that in an A/D converter that can handle 120 dB dynamic range, you couldn't even hear the quietest sound in the recording unless you were listening at 120 dB SPL!

Figure 1.57: The number of permutations possible as bit depth is increased, and corresponding dB.

Bit Depth	Permutations	Dynamic Range
1	2	6 dB
2	4	12 dB
3	8	18 dB
4	16	24 dB
8	256 (MIDI bit depth)	48 dB
16	65,536 (Redbook Audio CD bit depth)	96 dB
24	16,777,216 (HD Audio bit depth)	144 dB
48	$2.81474977 \cdot 10^{14}$ (Pro Tools HD internal mixer)	288 dB

Most A/D converters claim to support sampling rates up to 96k or higher and capture audio at 24 bits. However, just because they are capable of capturing sound to those specs doesn't mean that all of your audio is actually using all of that bandwidth. For example, we know that the dynamic range is represented by digital audio's bit depth and runs at a rate of 6 dB per bit in the system. We also know that 0 dBfs is the highest signal possible in digital audio. However, it should be noted that unless you're actually capturing audio between -6 dBfs and 0 dBfs, you're not necessarily using all 24 bits! This isn't a bad thing, per se, but something to note. In practice, it is advisable to record your audio so the highest peak falls somewhere between -6 and 0 dBfs so that you can maximize your bits, keep the noise low and maintain the widest possible dynamic range of expressiveness for the artist.

No matter how careful you are about setting your levels to DAW, invariably, some sounds will peak beyond the capabilites of the system, meaning that the recording level gets too hot for the DAW. Digital audio is completely unforgiving in this manner—it simply does not like to be overloaded. The results of a signal that is recorded too hot is called *clipping*, and it does not sound very good, unless you like the sound of awful distortion—and some folks do!

COACH'S CORNER

When recording an artist—especially one that can get loud—always have the talent play a test pass of the recording. This will help you determine what the dynamic range of the performance will be—or at least what you think it will be. While the test performance is happening, you can fine-tune your recording levels and set your mics and preamps to capture the widest range being performed with the peaks between -6 dB and 0 dBfs. You can bet on two things during this test: the test pass will be a great performance (the first one always is, so record it anyway!), and the second and "real" pass will play harder than the test—sometimes by as much as 12 dB! In many cases, the talent doesn't take the "test" seriously (drummers are notorious for this, while vocalists are more likely to give you a good test) so they're much more relaxed, which often makes for a better performance! When the "real thing" happens, they typically stiffen up and play harder, defeating the purpose of the test! Be sure to tell the talent to play hard during the test to avoid the false reading of the SPL tests. If you want to be safe, set the levels right during the test, then turn it down 6 dB to be safe. No one is going to miss the 24th bit anyway, and more often than not, your talent will play harder and give it back to you!

Figure 1.58: DAW meter with clipping indicator lit, meaning the signal is too loud.

In this case of clipping, the A/D converter still tries to capture an authentic representation of the audio, but if it goes louder than 0 dBfs, there's just no place to put it. Again, 0 dBfs is the loudest signal possible in DAWs, and anything that tries to go above it is just written as if it were at 0 dBfs. Since the computer and the A/D converter are not "smart" enough to know how to change the sound pleasingly (in truth, they just don't care!), the result is a heavy distortion of the sound. The shape of the resulting wave has a flat top to it, as if the top portion of the curve was clipped off, or smashed down. DAWs tend to represent this with a red LED at the top of the track's meter, indicating that the file has been clipped, as seen in **Figure 1.58**.

Minor clipping on this peak or that peak may not matter—in fact, it may not even be noticeable, so don't panic every time you see red. **Figure 1.59** shows both an audio file zoomed out so you can't see the individual clip, and the moment of clip zoomed in to the sample level. Notice how the normally smooth curve is cut off or flattened at the top? The levels above 0 dBfs are cut off, or clipped, resulting in all of those samples being written at 0 dBfs.

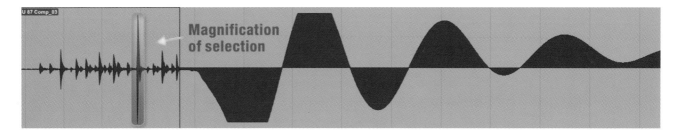

Figure 1.59: Clipped audio waveform, zoomed out and zoomed in.

Listen to your audio carefully for a clipping sound or a fuzziness. If clipping happens over several consecutive samples, you may have a problem. Clipping cannot be undone (at least, not well) and you should take extra care to avoid it if you are trying to capture a clean sound. Industrial music, noise rock and many kinds of electronic music rely on the sound of clipping to create the aggressive sound sought after. The sound is unique and worth exploring if you want your sound to be "angry."

If not, just stay away from the dreaded "red" by recording at a slightly lower level—just a bit quieter. Get it? A *bit* quieter?

I never said the jokes would be good . . .

RECAP

Choosing the right computer for your studio can be difficult there are many choices, at a wide variety of prices. Consider the need for power, RAM, and expandability versus the need for portability, as well as your application—recording lots of tracks or using lots of VIs.

Hard drive space is a major requirement for digital audio. Remember that the quality of the digital audio recording is independent of the computer's power or RAM—it is dependent on the quality of the I/O or the analog-to-digital converter. When referring to this quality, remember that the sample rate needs to be twice as high as the highest frequency recorded to represent the entire spectrum accurately. The bit depth relates to the dynamic range quality (how loud and how accurate the range is).

Avoid clipping the recording by building in headroom. Once a sound is clipped, its distortion is likely to be very noticeable and un-fixable.

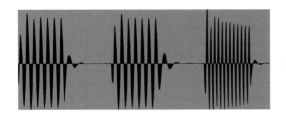

MIDI and Synthesis

A Brief History of MIDI

Synthesizers have been a part of the popular musical landscape for decades, and they have become more entrenched in our culture every year. Today's pop, dance, and hip hop hits are almost entirely driven by the sounds and technology born out of the earliest days of audio synthesis almost 50 years ago. The first synthesizers were electrical engineering endeavors—the designers had little idea of what kinds of sounds would come out, and even less of an idea of how to build them. It was a brave new world with no frontiers.

Early synths were born out of parts found in old telephone patching equipment and sitting around the electronics departments of schools and research facilities such as Bell Laboratories. These instruments consisted of parts, or modules, that were controlled by pads—pressing the pad sent a controlling voltage to the module, which generated different tones. Each pad controlled a different sound and was laid out much like a keyboard. As construction techniques improved, plastic piano keys were integrated into the designs and the modules began to condense for ease of use. A pioneering synthesizer that offered great sounds and ease of use in an affordable, compact system became what is arguably the most influential of them—the Minimoog. This was created by synth legend Robert Moog, whose designs led to dozens of other synths, all of which were new and exciting, offering seemingly endless sound creation possibilities!

Figure 1.60: The late synthesis pioneer Robert Moog with one of his original Minimoog synthesizers

In the '60s and '70s, keyboards and synthesizers were analog instruments, played, recorded, and edited just like any other instruments. Players would manipulate their instruments and play along with the band, with the analog outputs of their keyboards being fed into the record just like all the other players. Mistakes in the performance were captured, just like everyone else's. Unlike guitarists, drummers, vocalists, and horn players, the keyboardist had two hands free to play multiple parts on multiple keyboards, expanding their tonal range significantly.

Many keyboard players toured with as many as six keyboards—all at the ready on-stage should the song call for a different sound. Other than organs and electric pianos, most of these keyboards were just big, fat (literally) analog synths that couldn't "talk" to each other, share information, or even save patches (pre-programmed sounds). Sounds had to be created from scratch every time (no presets!) and there was no guarantee that each keyboard would sound the same night to night. These analog designs required constant tweaking, re-setting and re-conditioning. The electronics were all fairly sensitive and prone to damage—especially given the rigors of hard-core touring in the '60s and '70s.

Over time, the concept of touring with a half-dozen key- boards, and spares that were on hand for parts, became tiresome. Additionally, having to jump from one instrument to another just to get a different sound was also tiresome. Players were frustrated with the inability to hold one position and simply play all of their sounds from one "master" keyboard. This necessitated a method of controlling *other* keyboards from one.

One of the first technologies to broach the inter-keyboard communication problem was the use of *control voltage* (CV), a keyboard-triggered voltage that defines the pitch of the sound created by the sound module. By changing voltage, the user could changed the pitch. This technology left a lot to be desired, however—if the AC (alternating current) power from your local electric company fluctuated, your synth went out of tune!

Another part of the CV control equation was a gate (CV/Gate) that turned the note on and off. Between these two components, you could control both pitch and duration, which allowed for control over synths by keyboards. CV was used as a means of triggering sounds within the keyboard, but had been modified to send from one keyboard to another, alleviating the control issue, at least, for some. Not all keyboards worked with each other via CV/Gate—just because one keyboard sent it didn't mean that the other would receive it.

Tech-Speak: *Control Voltage (CV)*

CV, *or control voltage, is a means of controlling synthesizer sound modules from keyboard controllers. Using this early control system, each key on a keyboard sent a voltage whose value represented a musical note, or pitch.*

Tech-Speak: *CV/Gate*

CV/Gate is the combination of a control voltage, which sends musical note information to a sound creation module, and a gate signal, which triggers the creation module to turn on and off.

Concurrently, a new idea was brewing among synth enthusiasts—storing and repeating patterns of CV/Gate information for playback at any time. By setting up the CV/Gate information sequentially, notes could be triggered to play back in sequence on demand. This was the first sequencer. Many companies manufactured synths and sequencers with variations of this technology, including Roland, Oberheim, Arp, Sequential Circuits, Korg, Moog, and others. CV had—and still has—its devotees, and when you hear some of the music created using CV technology (such as Pink Floyd's *Dark Side of the Moon*), you'll note it has a certain flavor that many listeners found new and exciting. Technology has a way of dictating or creating styles of music for those who use it, and indeed, CV control had this effect. CV and electronic music go hand in hand, and it is still seen today in some retro style keyboards. It is also used in a virtual form in Propellerheads' Reason application as a source of modulation.

Roland's DCB-8 was another form of keyboard control and sequencing. Developed in the early 1980s, DCB-8 technology allowed Roland synths such as the Juno 60 to communicate with a Roland sequencer like the MSQ-700. DCB-8 technology allowed you to send note-on and note-off data from the synth to the sequencer and change patches. Meanwhile, Oberheim developed its own system (called the Oberheim System), which let some of its synths and drum machines synchronize with an Oberheim hardware sequencer, but not with gear from other manfacturers. Because these and similar technologies were limited in scope and capability, they never really caught on and thus had a very short shelf lives.

The biggest problem with both CV/Gate and DCB-8 technology was that they were proprietary systems. Communication had to be brand-to-brand. A Yamaha keyboard couldn't trigger the sounds from a Korg synth. A Roland synth couldn't sequence to an Oberheim sequencer.

Herbie Hancock, the legendary jazz keyboardist, composer, and producer, was among the frustrated players who lamented the fact that he couldn't control his arsenal from one location. The story goes that in the early '80s he spent vast amounts of money to have his arsenal of synthesizers modified so they could communicate with each other, allowing sound layering and combinations never before heard of. As news of this idea made its way to other well-known and respected keyboardists and industry leaders, interest in developing a language common to all manufacturers began to grow by leaps and bounds.

Engineers from many different companies started thinking of ways to implement this idea on a viable commercial level. In particular, engineers from leaders like Roland, Oberheim, and Sequential Circuits began to discuss a joint effort to develop this technology. These manufacturers began to develop a digital language code and implement a means of musical expression that would become a standard for decades. All of this was inspired by Herbie, which earned him the title "The Godfather of MIDI."

On the cutting edge of this movement was Dave Smith of Sequential Circuits. Sequential Circuits was a well-known company, manufacturing some of the most famous and beloved synthesizers of all time, including the Prophet 5. In addition to sounding great, the Prophet 5 was the world's first commercially produced microchip-controlled synthesizer, which gave it the ability to save a patch!

After successfully garnering support from the industry at large, Smith (with some input and help from other companies) developed what eventually became MIDI, which stands for musical instrument digital interface.

The first developments were tested rigorously by Smith, who gave the first demonstration of MIDI to the world at a NAMM (National Association of Music Merchants) conference in January 1983. In this demonstration (shown in **Figure 1.61**), Smith connected a Sequential Circuits Prophet-600 to a Roland Jupiter-6 and for the first time displayed interconnectivity and communication between synthesizers of different manufacturers. The rest, as they say, is history.

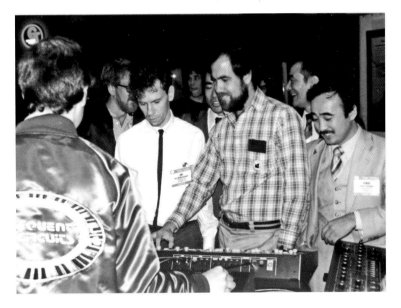

Figure 1.61: MIDI developer Dave Smith (in plaid shirt) demonstrates MIDI communication between a Sequential Circuits Prophet-600 and a Roland Jupiter-6 at the NAMM show in 1983.

Tech-Speak: *MIDI*

Known as the Musical Instrument Digital Interface, *this digital language specifies a range of information used to allow synthesizers to communicate to each other. Information stored in MIDI transmissions includes pitch, note on/off timing, controller data, and patch settings and names.*

As simple as this may seem now, this demonstration provided a glimpse into the future of making music. The idea of MIDI and how it worked was revolutionary because it went against the grain of traditional analog thinking—instead of manufacturers fighting for control over keyboard control, they banded together to create a universal standard!

No one in 1983 (except perhaps Smith and Herbie Hancock) foresaw the huge impact MIDI would have on the industry at large. MIDI has endured to this day because it was designed to be open-ended: as new ideas and new technologies come into existence, they are integrated into the existing code. Technological years are like dog years, so it's remarkable for any protocol to be in place this long! By the late '80s, MIDI was gathering steam and saw more use and acceptance by the traditional music community.

Keep in mind that the computer was having its coming out party at the same time. Early computers could be networked together to communicate with each other—NASA did this with tape-based mainframes and reels of tape. (I suspect they were powered by space gerbils.) So, if networked computers can send ones and zeros to each other, does it matter what they represent?

Since the early keyboard manufacturers were all technically savvy, they began to see the computer as a means of storing MIDI information and replacing the on-board sequencers that were being built into keyboards. Computers became faster, and as studio owners and engineers began to understand the potential of digital information, MIDI began to play a larger role in music-making in the studio. Though it took years to become fully accepted, by the 1990s, MIDI had become a mainstream component of the industry.

Early MIDI sequencers did have timing issues—it couldn't swing a beat like a real player could, and many studio engineers and producers just didn't get the technology. Once they understood that some parts could be sequenced to a computer with a keyboard, the need for players came into question—although the feel of the human wasn't there, neither was the cost, the repeated takes, the egos and the inability to nail the part at all. There were great debates in the inner circles of professional studios about the use of MIDI as a result of these financial and ethical issues. Some studios were even blackballed by the union because they had adopted electronic keyboards and synthesizers! The first hardware and software samplers were met with this same resistance for many of the same reasons.

The power of MIDI continued to grow. Data, once sequenced, could be freely edited. With MIDI, an individual note or collection of notes can be transposed, moved in time, or deleted without affecting other notes—something impossible with recorded audio. Using MIDI, voices could be changed almost instantaneously—a performance originally "recorded" for piano as a MIDI sequence could become a harpsichord with a click of a switch. Such power gives MIDI incredible production flexibility. MIDI can also control the sounds of a synthesizer in real time, allowing musicians to create dynamic changes. Almost every aspect of a MIDI sound module can be manipulated. These manipulations can be recorded with automation (dynamic changes of MIDI parameters over time), allowing musical complexities never before possible!

Today's synthesizers come in two basic forms: hardware and software. Hardware synthesizers are more like the original keyboards, in that everything you need is built into the keyboard itself. Such a design contains its own key bed, (synths like this can take the form of a keyboard or rackmount unit, which has no key bed of its own), its own sound modules and controlling devices, its own set of preset sounds, audio effects, and an onboard sequencer to capture, edit, and perfect any performance played into it!

These hardware synthesizers generally have standalone capability and can be used independently of a digital audio workstation. Software synthesizers are internal to the DAW and rely on the processing power of the host computer. Thus, software synthesizers cannot function independently of the DAW. Regardless of whether a synthesizer is hardware or software, it will probably still use MIDI to perform these functions. With the popularity of keyboard-driven music staying on the rise, a solid knowledge of MIDI is beneficial to any musician, engineer, or producer.

Since the turn of the century, hardware sound modules have gradually given way to more and more software-based sound makers. Hardware synths still exist and are often lauded as sounding better than their software counterparts, but that's a subjective debate. In either case, the rise of the personal supercomputer has been a key player in the growth of software-based synthesis. Software-based synthesizers give a musician access to virtually unlimited sounds using only a computer and some software. This new power of a composer with a computer, a MIDI controller, and a DAW has changed the very fabric of the music industry. One producer can now do the work of an entire studio staff *and* the orchestra. Thus, a modern production facility is often no more than a laptop in a bedroom with a MIDI controller.

Over the years, the original MIDI spec was enhanced with features such as MIDI sample dump, MIDI time code, MIDI show control, MIDI machine control, general MIDI, and the incorporation of MIDI sequencing into the DAW environment.

Now, with computing power being driven by smaller and smaller devices, over wireless Internet and touch-sensitive screens, it won't be long until we're all making music with computer monitor sunglasses, MIDI gloves, and portable computer-phone-credit card-DAW machines—all from the beach.

Won't that be the day!

Until then, let's look back at the past to see why MIDI was born—the origins of synthesis and keyboards . . .

RECAP

MIDI—Musical Instrument Digital Interface—is a digital language that represents control of music pitch, timing, and multiple parameters of expression. MIDI was developed in the 1980s at the behest of many keyboardists, specifically Herbie Hancock, to allow keyboards and synths to connect to each other. MIDI data can be captured, edited, and replayed at will through a process known as *sequencing*—often performed at the keyboard, but primarily performed by DAWs on computers.

Fundamentals of Synthesis

Synthesizers as sound-making devices originated in the 1950s and '60s. Originally designed as a new form of musical expression, synths sought to manipulate sound electrically using the piano-styled interface as a means of musical input. In other words, a piano simulator, or keyboard, would trigger an electrical device that would play back a musical pitch. Think of it as a sort of musical robot—input the command, and it would respond in music. The earliest synth designs used three separate components to create sound: oscillators, filters, and amplifiers.

Oscillators

The central controlling device in synthesizers is called an *oscillator:* in the early days, it was an *oscillating unit*, or *module.* An oscillator is an electrical circuit that creates a fixed alternating vibration—a sine wave. Early oscillators let users twist a knob and raise or lower the pitch to values in between the standard musical pitches, which was fun, I'm sure—just not necessarily musical, although great for creating some sci-fi sound effects.

Later, oscillators were modified to receive a series of controller voltages—as this controller voltage arrived, the oscillator would then generate a fixed sine wave at a pre-determined pitch. As the voltage increased, so did the pitch. When paired with a keyboard, the oscillator would receive a set of fixed voltages corresponding to the notes on the keyboard and would play the appropriate pitch.

COACH'S CORNER

Every sound generated by oscillations (except a pure sine wave) has a series of overtones that relate to it. This includes piped instruments (like horns and woodwinds) and stringed instruments (like pianos and guitars). The overtone series is generated by taking the frequency of the main note (its fundamental) and multiplying it by 2, 3, 4, etc. The resulting pitches, while mathematical octaves, were not musical octaves. The series plays out as such:

- Fundamental
- Octave
- Perfect fifth
- Octave
- Major 3rd
- Perfect fifth
- Flat 7th
- Octave

The series continues beyond this point, but the pitches begin to fall off of the musical spectrum and become slightly dissonant—in other words, they don't necessarily relate well back to the fundamental.

Simple sine waves, however, lack tonal complexity—they only resonate at one pitch with no overtones. Therefore, early synth designers set out to create oscillators that could produce complex tones, ones that had richer timbres and could create more ranges of expression. After all, guitars, horns, flutes, voices, and drums all had complex timbres—could they build a synth that emulated these instruments?

One of the first realizations in this process was the understanding of these other instruments themselves. Even when both instruments played the same note, why did a flute sound like a flute and not a clarinet? The answer is that each instrument generates a series of overtones along with the fundamental that are unique to it. A clarinet *couldn't* be a flute, as the length and construction of the instrument predetermines the set of harmonics it generates. Synths, however, had no such limitations—these were electrical devices and as such, were not fixed by the same physical constraints!

Experimentation began on creating complex waves. Oscillators were modified to start messing with the harmonic series and the waves being created started taking on interesting shapes. Some of the first experiments on complex waves were based on simple additions. What happens if you add in all of the harmonics at even levels, for example?

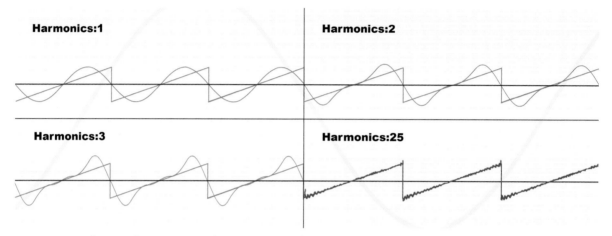

Figure 1.62: A series of waves, beginning with a sine wave. The next few images are the results of the sine wave after adding the first overtone (octave), but at a reduced level—one-half, in fact. The next image is the first and second (octave and fifth) overtones added, each at the respective levels of one-half and one-third—the pattern being that as a harmonic is added, its volume is reduced to a level of 1/harmonic number. Thus, the fourth harmonic would be added at one-quarter of the volume, etc. After many are added, the resulting waves starts to take shape. Notice how the wave resembles a saw blade? The resulting wave is called a sawtooth wave.

Tech-Speak: *Sawtooth Wave*

The sawtooth wave *is a combination of a sine wave and its harmonics. Each harmonic is added at a volume of 1/n where n=the count in the harmonic series—first, second, third, etc. The structure of a sawtooth wave is demonstrated in* **Figure 1.62.**

Further experimentation settled on two other important and well-used waves in early synths: the *square wave* and the *triangle wave*. Each of these waves consists of only the odd numbered harmonics, but the difference is in the volume reduction levels. The square wave, for example, has all the odd harmonics but each harmonic is quieter than the fundamental. The volume of each harmonic is reduced to an inverted number that reflects the harmonic "position" in the spectrum. For example, the fundamental is at full volume and the 3rd harmonic is at a volume of ⅓ the fundamental, -9 dB. Remember that each doubling is 6 dB and each halving is -6 dB. Therefore, ½ the volume is -6 dB, ¼ the volume is -12 dB, and ⅓ the volume is in-between, at a level of -9 dB. The 5th harmonic is at ⅕ the fundamental volume, or -15 dB.

With triangle waves, the odd harmonics are added in inverse squares—each harmonic is first squared, then inverted. For example, the third harmonic is first squared ($3 \times 3 = 9$), then inverted $1/(3 \times 3)$ or ⅑. So the harmonics are then added, with the 1st at 0 dB (fundamental, full volume), 3rd at ⅑, 5th at 1/25, etc.

Figure 1.63: The triangle wave and the square wave.

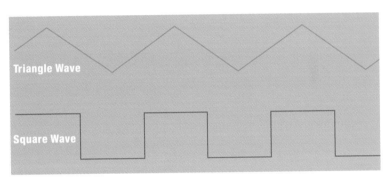

Triangle Wave

Square Wave

Tech-Speak: *Square Wave*

. . . .

The square wave is the sum of a fundamental sine wave and its odd harmonics when they are added at 1/nth the volume of the fundamental and n is the number of the harmonic.

Tech-Speak: *Triangle Wave*

. . . .

The triangle wave is the sum of a fundamental sine wave and its odd harmonics when added at at 1/nth the volume of the fundamental and n is the number of the harmonic squared.

DVD Track 39: A musical phrase, played using sine, saw, square and triangle waves.

Remember, these are the four basic waves in oscillators and synthesis. Early synths were single-oscillator synths but even early in synth history, products were being introduced that had two oscillators and the ability to mix them together. A single

MIDI key would trigger both synths simultaneously, although each oscillator could be set to a unique pitch—osc 1 could be at standard pitch, while osc 2 could be at an octave, 5th, etc. This added to the complexity of the overall sound, allowing many more permutations of sounds—sine and saw, sine and square, two sines, etc. They would then add together in some form—either additively or subtractively, to create the overall sound. This became the basis of modern synthesis, called *additive* and *subtractive* synthesis. Once these waves are added together, they would be then routed to the next module in synthesis—the *filter*.

Filters

Remember that synths are composed of three main sections: the oscillator, the filter, and the amplifier. While the oscillator creates the sound based on a fundamental pitch and selected overtones, the filter determines how many of those overtones actually get to play. Filters control the frequency by allowing selected frequencies to pass through, while attenuating the non-selected frequencies.

Similar to audio filters (seen in detail later in "DSP—EQ"), synth filters remove unwanted sounds either above a particular frequency or below a particular frequency; in other words, they remove the treble or the bass. Some synths add the waves together (or subtract—we'll use the word "add" here to mean the fact that the two waves interact in some way) and then send the combined sound to the filter. Others allow for independent filtering of each oscillator; for example, osc 1 might get the bass filtered out and osc 2 does not, or osc 1 has the bass filtered out and osc 2 has the treble filtered out. This allows for even more control over the sound as the waves first interact, then interact with the filters—together or independently.

Filters are categorized by the spectrum of the frequencies they control and the way they control them. The most common filter types in both software and hardware synthesizers are *low-pass*, *high-pass* and *band-pass*. All of these filters are controlled by *cutoff frequency*, *slope* and *resonance* parameters.

Low-Pass Filter

A low-pass filter attenuates the frequencies above a set point in the spectrum called the *cutoff*. Frequencies below the cutoff point are allowed to pass through unchanged. The result is a "darker" sound, as the low-pass basically removes treble. This means that sound passing through a low-pass filter can be *only* bass tones where a full spectrum signal was fed into it!

DVD Track 40: A big synth sound before and after a low-pass filter set at 220 Hz is engaged.

COACH'S CORNER

The low-pass filter hearkens back to the '50s, born out of Bell Laboratories, RCA, and some select universities. The roots of most low-pass filters found in today's synthesizers can be traced back to an analog voltage-controlled low-pass filter designed by Robert Moog in 1965. His low-pass ladder filter had a very warm and musical sound, which has spawned countless imitators over the years. It was called the low-pass ladder because of the ladder-like shape of his original circuit diagram.

Robert Moog is revered as one of the fathers of electronic music and was responsible for numerous advances in synthesis and synthesizer design. The company he founded decades ago still produces great sounding synthesizers today, after his sad passing in 2005. If you love synthesis and Moog's products, consider supporting his online foundation to carry on his ideals!

High-Pass Filter

A high-pass filter is the opposite of a low-pass filter in that a high-pass filter attenuates the frequencies *below* the cutoff point, allowing the frequencies above the cutoff point to pass unaffected. High-pass filters can be used to create brighter, thinner synth sounds by removing the fundamentals or lowest tones in the sound. Many synth patches are designed to be huge—lots of highs and lots of lows. When placed in a mix, they can be *too* huge and they can muddy the low end terribly. A high-pass filter can help by removing unnecessary bass from one of these huge patches, making room for the actual bass sound.

DVD Track 41: A big synth sound before and after a high-pass filter set at 220 Hz is engaged.

Band-Pass Filter

A band-pass filter acts like a combination of a high- and low-pass filter: It allows control over mid-range frequencies by cutting frequencies on both sides, leaving just the middle frequencies in a sound. A common use of a band-pass filter is for emulating AM radio or telephone sounds.

DVD Track 42: A big synth sound before and after a band-pass filter set at 220 Hz and 2,200 Hz is engaged.

Notch Filter

A notch filter is the opposite of a band-pass filter. Instead of leaving the mid-band intact, it leaves the highs and lows intact and cuts, or notches out, the mid-band. Notch filters are usually very narrow selections of frequencies and allow very precise reductions of a selected frequency.

DVD Track 43: A big synth sound before and after a notch filter is engaged at 2,200 Hz.

Comb Filter

A comb filter mixes a sound with a slightly delayed sound to produce a series of notch filters at a fundamental frequency and its harmonics. Note that comb filters can create notches or peaks, depending on how they're used. The resulting notches give its characteristic comb-like look, hence the name. Comb filters have adjustable feedback controls ("resonance" on most synths), which affect the shape and size of the peaks. In a synthesizer, comb filtering can induce phase, flange and give a swooshing sound when the frequency is swept by moving the resonance control.

DVD Track 44: A big synth sound before and after a comb filter is engaged, then swept.

Filter Parameters: Cutoff, Slope, and Resonance

In all of the filter types, the parameters are usually the same—*cutoff, slope,* and *resonance*.

By changing the cutoff frequency, you can dramatically alter the characteristic of the sound—a bright lead sound can become a deep bass sound by moving the cutoff frequency down using a low-pass, and a muddy sound can be cleaned up by removing some bass with a high-pass filter. Changing the slope can affect how much of these frequencies are removed and adding resonance can give a certain "bump" in the sound, accentuating a key tone in the sound.

The cutoff frequency in a low-pass filter defines where the filtering will begin. In actuality, the cutoff defines the point at which the filtering has already dropped the signal by -3 dB. Every filter has a cutoff frequency and some, like the band-pass, have two—one for the low-pass part and one for the high-pass part.

The amount of attenuation applied at the cutoff point is called the *slope*—it determines the degree of cutoff specified in dB per octave. Typical slopes are 6, 12, 24, and 36 dB per octave, and the greater the number of dB per octave, the more severe the angle of attenuation. A low-pass filter with a slope of 12, for example, would attenuate the audio above the cutoff point -12 dB per octave and each octave above that would then diminish another -12 dB, creating an angle of slope. A filter with a cutoff of 36 dB per octave would have a very sharp slope (think El Capitan in Yosemite), allowing only the frequencies close to the cutoff point to pass. A filter with a cutoff of 6 dB per octave on the other hand, would yield a much gentler slope, allowing more of the frequencies above the cutoff to pass.

COACH'S CORNER

Back in the early days of synthesis, filters with one resistor and capacitor produced a cutoff of 6 dB per octave. The combination of resistor and capacitor (RC) was called the slope. If you added more slopes, you could generate a stronger attenuation. A 2-pole filter would yield a slope of 12 dB per octave, a 4-pole filter would yield a slope of 24 dB per octave and so on, -6 dB per octave at a time. You still see this nomenclature in some modern software synthesizers today.

Resonance controls how much the frequency at the cutoff point will be boosted; adding resonance emphasizes the frequency *at* the cutoff point. Adding resonance can sometimes trick the ear into thinking that the filter isn't actually there! In high-pass filters, removing the bass makes the sound thinner, but by boosting the resonance at the cutoff, you re-introduce low end to the sound. Although the bass *below* the cutoff is gone, the bass *at* the cutoff is boosted, tricking the listener into thinking that the bass is still strong! Additionally, adding resonance and then sweeping the frequency down (low-pass filters) creates a very common sound in dance

Figure 1.64: Four low-pass filters set at 440 Hz, each with an increasing slope, one order at a time.

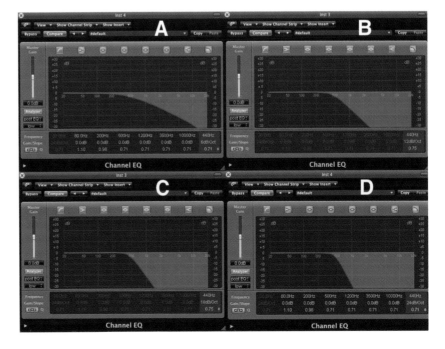

music—the filter sweep. Merely sweeping the cutoff lower doesn't do it—adding the resonance creates a spike at the cutoff, which allows the sweep to "stick out," creating a more dramatic effect. **Figure 1.65** shows a low-pass filter with a peak resonance of 6 dB added.

Figure 1.65: Low-pass filter with a peak resonance of 6 dB added.

DVD Track 45: A big synth sound, filtered at 550 Hz with a slope of -6dB/octave. Each consecutive pass increases the slope one order at a time until filtered at -36 dB/octave.

DVD Track 46: A big synth sound, before and after a low-pass filter engaged with a 6 dB peak resonance added.

DVD Track 47: A big synth sound with a low-pass filter and peak resonance of 6 dB added, then swept down from 20 kHz to 220 Hz.

Amplifiers and Envelopes

The final stage of synthesis is the *amplifier*—the point at which the sound gets louder. Synths are like microphones in that the actual electrical circuit puts out a small voltage. In order to connect to the "outside world," synths required an amplifier to push the voltage loud enough to connect to something (mixer, guitar amplifier, etc.) The amp is simple: turn up the volume, the sound gets louder: turn down the volume, the sound gets quieter. However, synth amps are different than traditional amps in one way—they are controlled over time by something called an *envelope*.

In synthesis, envelopes control parameters of sound over time. All sound conforms to an envelope. When you press a MIDI key on a synth, you trigger the start of the sound, and when you let go of the key you trigger the end of the sound. Once the sound is triggered, the envelope controls how the sound's volume behaves. Although controlling *volume* over time is the most common type of envelope, there are many different types found in modern synthesis—some that control the behavior of filters, and *not* volume, for example. *Envelope generators* (EGs) create these envelopes and determine a sound's temporal complexity, its overall performance over time. Envelopes are comprised of segments, each of which controls a different aspect of the sound. The most common version of an envelope in a synthesizer consists of four basic parameters: *attack*, *decay*, *sustain* and *release*, or the ADSR, shown in **Figure 1.66**.

Figure 1.66: A typical ADSR envelope.

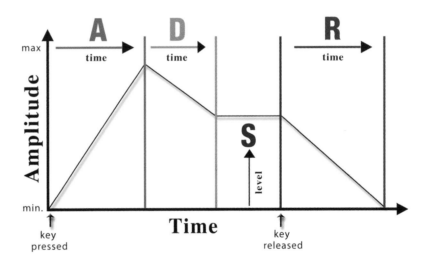

Attack

Attack is the amount of time it takes for a sound to develop from no volume to maximum amplitude. In synthesis, when you press a key, you trigger the envelope starting the attack. Since synths respond to MIDI triggers, envelopes are scaled in time to the MIDI range of data—128 values. This means that all values in MIDI must range from 0 to 127 (0 is a value in this scale).

An attack of zero is an instant attack, which means that the sound would hit its peak instantaneously. This can result in a Fourier click—an audio anomaly where an audible click is heard as sound turns on too quickly. Most sounds have at least *some* attack, even if it's very short. A snare drum is a good example of an instrument with a very short attack. You hit the drum, and almost immediately, it's at full volume.

An attack of 127 is a very long attack, which means that the sound could take several seconds (or longer) to reach its peak. You play a note and the sound develops very slowly to it peak. Some envelopes also contain break points in the attack section, enabling the sound to develop at different speeds (instead of just straight from nothing to full). This flexibility can create more complexity in a sound and can be used to mimic real instruments.

Decay

Decay is the amount of time it takes for the sound to drop from its maximum amplitude or peak to the sustained or held level. Some synth makers include a *hold* function before the decay section. This hold setting allows the sound to be held at the maximum amplitude for an adjustable amount of time before it starts to decay. More advanced envelopes offer a break point in the decay section as well as the attack, which allows the sound to decay at different speeds before it hits the sustain.

Sustain

After the period of decay, the volume will *sustain* at a certain volume as long as you hold the key down. Note that the sustain setting is a volume level and not a time period. With a sustain level above zero, you can hold a note and have it play infinitely until you release the key. The sustain level is not reached until the attack and decay times have run their course. A sustain level of zero and a very short decay will produce staccato-style sounds like plucked stringed instruments by turning off the volume after the decay.

Release

Release is the amount of time it takes for the sound to stop playing after you let go of the key. A release time of 127 will yield an infinite sustain (no release), while a setting of 0 will turn the sound off immediately after you stop depressing the key.

The combination of all four parameters—attack, decay, sustain, and release—can create unique "impulses" of sound, where the oscillators start to take on a certain life, as they grow and shrink with time. Some of these parameters can be set to full while others set to off—like decay off and sustain at full—to emulate the sound of real instruments. An organ, for example, tends to have a very short attack, giving it a percussive tone. It also stays loud (high sustain level) once it reaches its peak level and doesn't drop until you let go (no decay, attack goes right to sustain). It also turns off quickly (short release time).

Other sounds might behave in the opposite manner—pads and atmospheric sounds tend to have very long attacks and very long releases, making them linger for a while once they develop. **Figure 1.67** shows a few varieties of envelopes. The multiple examples found on **DVD Track 48** correlate to these images—you can hear what the envelopes look like.

Figure 1.67: A variety of envelopes. Continued on page 154.

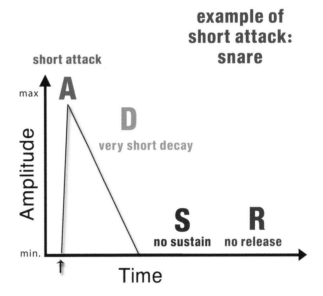

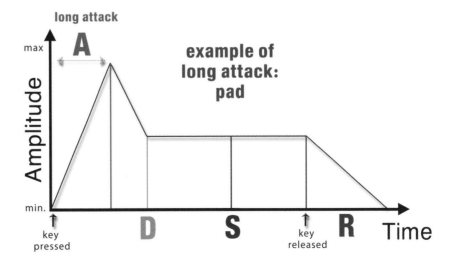

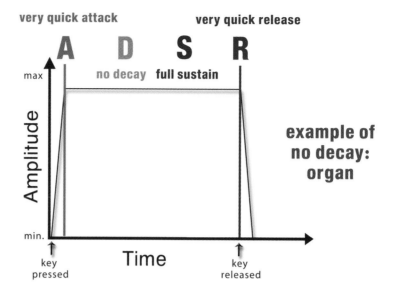

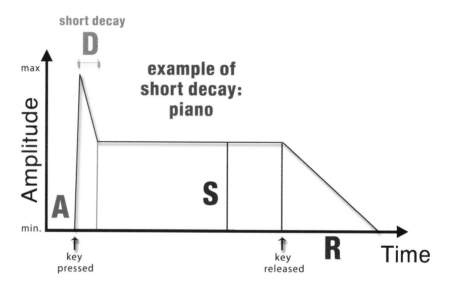

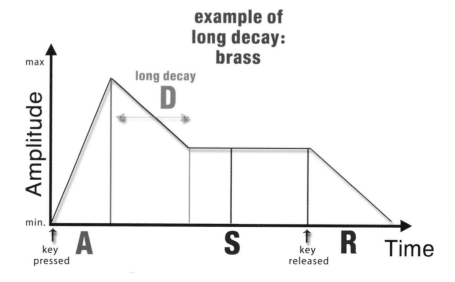

DVD Track 48:

Shorter attack: organ, snare drum, gunshot, lead synths

Longer attack: pad sounds, strings, brass

No decay: organ, some lead synths

Short decay: piano, strings

Long decay: brass, pads

Types of Envelopes

The *amplifier envelope* (amp env, for short) is a fundamental aspect in the creation of sound as it controls two of the most obvious functions—the time and the volume. There are, however, other uses for envelopes. These can be used to control the time of many other functions beyond volume. Two such functions are a synth's filters and modulation. Applying custom envelopes to parameters adds more complexity to the sound, even though the individual components (ADSR) are similar in all forms. And depending on the synth, users can create multiple envelopes to control the time behavior of multiple parameters, making for a very rich level of complexity of the sound over time.

COACH'S CORNER

An old trick from the '70s that works well on synth, guitar and bass is the envelope filter—known as filter envelope on synths. Envelope filters used then were low-pass filters, where the signal coming in would have the treble turned down over time. Funk bass players like Bootsy Collins were fond of the sound as every note had a sort of "wow" to it. Guitarists like Jerry Garcia also used the envelope filter liberally in this period. The envelope filter basically starts a filter (usually a low-pass) after the attack time has completed. The sound will play at full frequency at first, but as the filter envelope kicks in, the filter also kicks in, reducing the high frequencies. During the attack time, the sound develops an "aow" or "wow" sound to it—similar to what happens if you use your mouth to say the word. As the sound is played harder, the filter works more, making the effect even more pronounced.

The opposite is true in synths where filter envelopes are applied to a high-pass filter. In this case, the reverse sound is created—instead of darkening the sound, the sound brightens over time as the bass is removed. Classic synth sweeps like this have a sort of "whee" sound to them—they get brighter and sweeter "eee" sounds over time.

Amp Envelope

The amp envelope, which controls volume over time—the behavior of the amplifier section of a synthesizer—is a vital function in controlling sound. The ADSR of the amp envelope is what gives a sound its life cycle from the time you play the key, and continues as you hold the key and on to the point where you let it go.

Filter Envelope

The filter envelope controls how the filter section reacts over time. The filter envelope gives dynamic control over your filter, letting the user control tone or frequency over time. For example, if you have a high-pass filter engaged and hit a key, the sound will be filtered up to the cutoff frequency over the course of time set by the attack. A slower attack time in the filter envelope will cause the sound to sweep up to the cutoff point, creating a classic filter sweep sound.

Modulation Envelope

The modulation envelope is a wild card in most synthesizers. Unlike fixed-destination envelopes like those for the amp or filter, you can usually assign the mod envelope to different destinations, depending on the capabilities of your synth. A typical modulation envelope use is to control an oscillator. This lets you control pitch over time. With a slower attack time set on the mod envelope, the sound will rise in pitch over time as you hold down a note.

The attack setting is the ceiling for the pitch—once you hit the note, a lower tone will play (usually, you can set how low the starting pitch is) and the pitch will increase to meet the note being played. When targeting an oscillator, the decay setting controls the lowering of the pitch over time.

The LFO

The *low-frequency oscillator*, LFO, is independent of the audio oscillators. Essentially, it's a new, potentially third wave used in synthesis to modulate another parameter. LFOs are not really envelopes, but they do affect the way sounds play over time in that the LFO shapes the behavior of some other parameter on the oscillator, the filter, the envelopes, or the amp.

Tech-Speak: *Low-Frequency Oscillator (LFO)*

The LFO (Low Frequency Oscillator) is a special type of oscillator that generates waveforms to be used as modulation sources rather than audio sources.

LFOs usually generate waveforms at a rate slower than 20 cycles per second (20 Hz) and thus cannot be heard—not usually a problem since LFOs don't produce sound anyway;

they are used as *modulators*. In other words, they dynamically control a number of *other* parameters like pitch, envleopes or filters. Typical parameters in an LFO include (but aren't limited to) modulation rate, wave shape, amount and modulation destination.

The modulation rate can be either a freely assigned frequency or a time subdivision of a sequencer's BPM known as *clock sync*. Freely assigned rates are measured in Hertz (cycles per second), which may not have any relation to the music, while clocked rates are usually measured in musical increments such as quarter notes, eighth notes, sixteenth notes, etc. When assigned to modulate an amp, the effect is called tremolo, where the volume of the synth is raised and lowered in the shape of the LFO and at the LFO rate.

The waveshape of an LFO comes in the same four flavors—sine, saw, square and triangle. Each of these waves sets the shape of the modulation that the LFO will be applied to. If an LFO is set to sine, then the modulation will gradually increase and decrease smoothly in the shape of the sine wave. A square wave, however, sets the modulation between two states, the "on" and the "off," just like the up/down cycles of the square wave, etc.

The amount parameter tells you how much the LFO affects the sound. This can be measured in percentages or ranges—ranges might be good for pitch, where an LFO will vary the pitch by a major second, minor third, etc. Larger amounts increase and lower the amplitude of the LFO wave, which, in turn, raises and lowers the amount of modulation of the chosen parameter called the *modulation destination.*

When used to modulate pitch (pitch is the modulation destination in this case) it's called vibrato—the pitch of one or more oscillator, is raised and lowered in the shape of the LFO at the LFO rate. LFOs targeting a filter produce a *wah-wah* effect by opening and closing the filter at a speed determined by the rate and with a shape determined by the waveform. The shape of the waveform controls how the filter opens and closes. A square wave would move the filter back and forth directly, while a sine wave would move the filter gradually up and down. There is often an amount setting that controls how pronounced the effect will be. LFOs assigned to envelopes change the time behavior of the envelope—a popular technique in much of today's dance and electronica music.

COACH'S CORNER

One of the oldest LFO tricks in the world is the emulation of a police car. American sirens wail up and down smoothly while many European sirens flash back and forth between two pitches. Start with "default" synth with no other parameters set—a simple oscillator (square wave works well here), filter and amp setup. If an LFO is assigned to pitch with a sine wave with a medium rate and a small amount, a sound's pitch will vary up and down in pitch, emulating how sirens sound in America. Do the same thing, but vary the LFO from sine to square, and the result is a pitch that "jumps" between two notes, like a European siren. Vary the amount and the rate to taste, and you've made a police car sound!

RECAP

Synthesizers were born in the '50s and '60s out of laboratories and universities. The first ones were built out of leftover electronic parts! Triggered by a piano substitute, known as a keyboard, notes would be played and sounds would be output after being generated by electrical circuits known as oscillators, filters and amplifiers. The first oscillators generated only sine waves, but quickly developed into the four main waves still used today—sine, saw, square and triangle. Each wave is comprised of some grouping of a fundamental sine wave and its harmonics, creating rich and complex waves. The sawtooth wave has all harmonics added in diminishing amounts, the square wave is the odd harmonics in diminishing amounts and the triangle is also made of odd harmonics in inverse-square diminishing amounts.

Filters affect sounds by removing frequencies above or below a cutoff frequency. They come in various forms—high-pass, low-pass, band-pass, comb and notch—each of which affects different groups of frequencies. Filters change the tonal character of a synth sound; common parameters are cutoff frequency, slope and resonance. Lastly, an amplifier section changes the volume of the resulting sound through an envelope—a series of time and volume settings that shape the way the sound plays over time. Envelopes can be applied to the amplifier, the filter or to other parameters via modulation. Another form of modulation is called the LFO, or low-frequency oscillator, which creates a wave that is applied to alter another parameter.

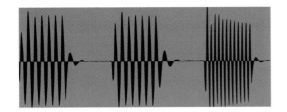

DSP

What to Do If You Captured It "Wrong"

Using microphones is an art form that takes a long time to develop. First recordings usually aren't very good because of many variables that are out of your control—the choice (and availability) of mics, the position on the instrument or talent, the connection and setting of the preamp as well as the level being recorded to the DAW. There are at least twice as many other things that can go wrong in the recording and while you my be happy that you got something recorded, it's not always good.

Once something is recorded to your DAW, you'll often find the need to manipulate it to your liking. If your recordings are captured well, this need is much less pressing—you can move directly on to blending those sounds together into a mix. For those who are first starting out, however, the need to correct poorly captured recordings far outweighs the desire to press on and mix anyway. For this, we have DSP, or digital signal processing.

Tech-Speak: *DSP*

DSP, short for Digital Signal Processing, is a large umbrella term covering any and all processes that manipulate sound in one form or another in the digital domain. DSP can refer to software or hardware that processes digital information—which is not necessarily audio. For example, DSP can refer to the processor chips that do the math behind a signal process, as well as the controlling software that drives the chips doing the math.

Audio DSP comes in two flavors—fixers and colorizers. Each of these work in two ways—ones that render a process to the file (destructively or *non*-destructively), thus "permanently" affecting the sound, and those that process the sound live, or in real-time. There are times to use each of them with advantages and disadvantages to each. As you might expect, the trick is to know what the sonic need is before attempting to employ one or the other. We'll work in reverse order and define real-time DSP versus process DSP first.

COACH'S CORNER

The concept of destructive versus non-destructive comes from the early days of DAWs and refers to audio editing. Early DAWs allowed you to cut parts from an audio file, but immediately re-rendered the file to reflect the edit. You could not undo this process. Non-destructive editing came from the ability to highlight regions of audio by positional markers (i.e., the start and end times of the regions selected) and list them in new orders. The newly ordered collection of regions could then be re-ordered at will, making the process non-destructive: the original file remained but the new order of the regions could be rendered to a new file. DSP can work this way where you often get choices of overwriting the file after a process or writing a new file so the unaltered original can always be referenced at some future point. **Figure 1.68** shows a DSP process where the option to choose destructive (overwrite files) or non-destructive (create new file) are available.

Figure 1.68: DSP process offering choice of destructive or non-destructive changes.

The recordings in a DAW end up as audio files on a hard disk. These are read off of the storage device and played through the DAW to the output of your digital converter/interface/sound card/etc. for playback on your monitors. The files on the disk remain exactly as they were when they were first recorded, for life—that is, until they are re-written as new files. A file that was recorded at far too low a recording level— say, -60 dBfs—can hardly be considered useful when compared to other files in the song that were recorded at roughly -6 dBfs. That -54 dBfs margin is so large a difference in volume that you'd really barely hear the quiet track if the two faders are set to the same level. In **Figure 1.69,** you can see a visual comparison between two files; one has a peak at -6 dBfs and the other has a peak at -60 dBfs.

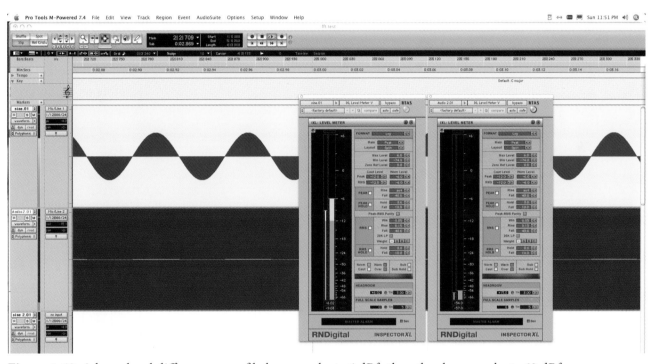

Figure 1.69: A huge level difference: one file has a peak at -6 dBfs the other has a peak at -60 dBfs.

If you don't have access to the talent to re-record the part (you won't, in many cases), the best course of action is to re-write the file after some sort of volume increase. In the example above, where an audio file is recorded at -60 dBfs, you might choose to do this (destructively in this case), as there is little reason to keep the original file. If you choose to do this non-destructively, the DAW will process the original into a new, second file, usually tagged with the name of the process in the name of the file (e.g., "Vocal-01" becomes "Vocal-01-gain"), as seen in **Figure 1.70**. Since you never know what's going to happen and you'd hate to do something wrong and lose the original, it's a good idea to work non-destructively for now. Once you get a handle on what the processes are and how they work, you can go ahead and choose the destructive one and commit to the decision.

Figure 1.70: With non-destructive processing, the DAW creates a new file with an alternative file name.

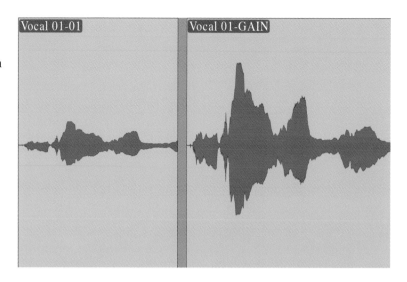

Most DAWs have DSP functions that will affect the volume of a track, and they usually come in two forms: *gain* and *normalization*. Gain is just what you might think—you pick a dB amount to add to a file and hit Process. Then, either the file is rewritten, or a new one is created at the higher volume. Keep in mind that whatever sounds are on that file—no matter how quiet they are—will also be increased. So if you have a quiet recording with lots of noise, the noise gets louder along with the signal, making your track louder, but not necessarily better.

When adding gain to a file, first take a look at its current volume. Leave the fader at 0 dB, hit Play and look at the volume meter to get a sense of how quiet the track is. Many DAWs allow you to read the peak of a file during playback; if possible, that would be best. If the peak reads, say, -15 dBfs, as in **Figure 1.71**, you're safe to add up to 15 dBfs of peak gain before you risk clipping the audio. You can add gain in 6 dB increments, as each gain of 6 dB represents the same doubling in dBfs as it does in dBu. This technique works well if you can't read the peak of the file or just don't know how much to add; try 6, 12, 18, etc., until you find a good resulting volume relative to the other files.

COACH'S CORNER

Once you know how quiet a file is, you can determine how much gain to add to it. Where a file peaks at -36 dB, you can go ahead and add 36 dB to the file, making the new peak 0 dB. A good idea is to leave some headroom, so the peak of the file is below 0 by some safe distance (-6 dB is a general standard, as every 6 dB down from 0 dBfs uses one less bit of information to store it). Your 24-bit recording is actually a 23-bit recording at recorded volumes between -12 dBfs and -6 dBfs.

Figure 1.71: A -15 dBfs meter reading.

Another common way to adjust the volume of a poorly recorded file is a process known as normalization. Unlike gain, the normalize function performs both a gain and a maximization process at once. The idea is that the peak of a file, the highest point in that file, is measured, then boosted to a user-defined maximum. You can set the maximum point in either dBfs or percentage of full scale. Many people normalize to some very high percentage, like 99%, which makes sense—why maximize a file to anything less than full? Of course, leaving some headroom is always a good idea, so adjust the percentage to some high point that leaves you a desired amount of headroom.

Tech-Speak: *Normalization*

Normalization is the process where a file is analyzed and its peak value is noted. Then, the peak point is gain adjusted to a user-defined percentage of full—often 99%.

When normalizing the file, the gain added to bring the peak of the file to 99% of 0 dBfs is then applied to the rest of the file, sample by sample. This results in a file with the same dynamic range as the original, just maximized to its peak level—the dynamics of the original performance are retained but the whole performance is louder. So if the highest peak in a file is -6 dBfs, and you set the maximum normalization level to -1 dBfs, then every sample in the file will be raised by exactly +5 dB (the difference between -6 and -1 dBfs) in the normalization process. With a long audio file recorded at a high sampling rate (say, 96 kHz), there are a lot of individual samples to be processed and the normalization procedure can take some time.

In **Figure 1.72** you can see a file before and after normalizing the peaks to 99%. Remember that the quiet sounds get louder too, so don't be surprised if your normalized file is louder but not better—just as with gain adjustments. This is a good reason to perform these processes in non-destructive form—just in case you don't really like the results and want to do it again with less gain added (or using a lower percentage).

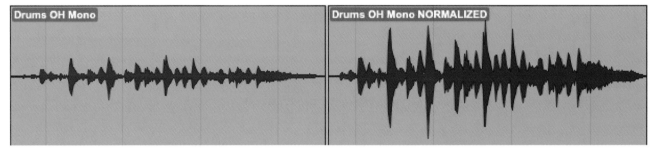

Figure 1.72: A file shown before normalizing, and after peak normalization to 99%.

Be careful with normalizing—some DAWs give you the choice to work in peak or RMS (short for Root, Mean, Square—an average) and others choose for you. When using the normalize function in RMS, setting the percentage to 99% or so takes the *average* volume of the track—not the peaks—and stretches it to full. That means that each of the peaks above the average (meaning all of the dynamic parts) have been gain adjusted to well over 0, resulting in nasty-sounding clipping distortion. Check out the results of RMS normalizing in **Figure 1.73.**

This can be a useful effect in industrial music and in sound design, but more often than not, it does not achieve the simple goal of making a quiet file louder—it destroys your sound. Again, choose the non-destructive method with all of the file-rendering processes until you've got a handle on their functions and results.

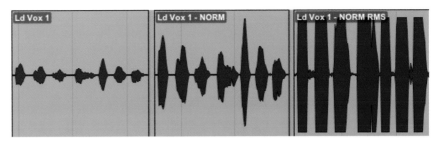

Figure 1.73: A file shown before normalizing, after peak normalization and then with RMS normalization.

Tech-Speak: *RMS*

RMS is an acronym for Root Mean Square, a common mathematical formula for a straight average. RMS is derived by squaring all the instantaneous voltages along a waveform, averaging the squared values and then taking the square root of that number.

File rendering processes don't have to be gain related—there are plenty of other processors that are very handy, like *reverse* and *invert*. Reverse does what it says—it renders a file that plays backwards, while invert flips the phase of the file. You won't hear the result of an invert process on a single file, though—by flipping the phase 180 degrees, you will hear the result only when you combine this file with another.

For example, let's say you chose to record a snare drum with a single mic on top and another on bottom (very common, by the way). The bottom mic hears a similar sound as the top mic, but as each are facing the opposite direction to the same source, the results of combining the two mic signals later can result in phase cancellation across many frequencies.

If you didn't catch this during the recording process by flipping the phase at the mic pre (or you used a preamp without phase flip), you can simply highlight one of the files (usually the bottom) and invert its phase. Whereas you won't hear the difference in the bottom track by itself, when you add it to the top mic, you'll hear a huge difference!

DVD Track 49: A snare drum recording demonstrating a bottom mic out of phase to the top, then the results after the bottom mic has been phase inverted to match the top mic. Notice how the low energy and "body" of the snare returns after the inversion.

Most DAWs offer users the option to run just about every DSP function as a file rendering process. You have the flexibility to process the file to your taste and then render it, removing the need to keep that process "open." One advantage to working this way is that once you finish a step, you won't have to think about it anymore—just "hit" the file with the process and it's done!

Another advantage occurs when you only want to process a small section of a file during a certain moment in the song. An example might be processing a vocal to sound like an AM radio or telephone in a breakdown. Dialing in the sound and then rendering the file to that sound locks in the decision without using any of the "expensive" real-time processing, and allows you to move on to other decisions in the mix.

There are disadvantages, however, especially if you choose to work destructively. With a rendered file, you can't go back and tweak the settings—they're baked into the file. You'd have to undo or re-import the original and re-apply the process with the same settings—as if you remembered them all! But don't worry—you can save them as you make them . . . *if* you remember to. If you rendered the file over the original—meaning you worked destructively—there's just no going back. You've committed to file all of your decisions—permanently. Hopefully, you can get the talent back to record again, but odds are, they're long gone and you just have to live with it or go back to a safety copy (you *always* back up your data, don't you?) and start over.

Real-time processing usually comes in the form of a plug-in—a software processor that sits "on top" of the track live. That means that the process is not rendered to the file—the file is still as it was when recorded. This means that the process and its parameters can be adjusted anytime and for any reason and the new setting will remain until adjusted again. This is a huge advantage over rendering files, as there's no render time at all—the plug-in just sits there doing its job, waiting for you to tweak it—and tweak it you will!

The trade-off here is that real-time plug-ins require some sort of computing horsepower to work. They dictate the controls of the processing, but the real math is still handled at the DSP hardware—usually a computer chip. There are many different kinds of plug-in DSP—some that work off of your CPU and others with dedicated hardware chips on a processor card(s) to do the heavy lifting. With the sort of computing power available today (and likely at any point in the future of computing), it is hard to conceive of the need to go beyond the CPU. Rest assured, if the power exists in any computer, someone will find a way to max it out and still need more!

COACH'S CORNER

Don't confuse "DSP, the audio processing" with "DSP, the power behind the processing." They're both called DSP and have the same name, but the same term can mean two different things. You have to use context clues to tell you whether someone means DSP, as in the audio processing (gain, normalize, phase invert, etc.), or DSP, the computing horsepower (Motorola, Intel, plug-in processing cards, etc.). DSP processing cards (whether in the form of actual cards or external boxes) can range in price from a few hundred dollars to tens of thousands of dollars. There are a few to choose from, but not all of them work with every DAW.

Introduction to DSP Tools
Chapter 2:
Introduction to Equalization

Check with the manufacturer specifications to see if your DAW is supported, then you should comb the Internet and the forums to verify that it will work as advertised. Many manufacturers say their cards/plug-ins work just fine but may still be prone to version conflicts in both operating systems and DAW software itself, where something may work with the new version but not the old, etc. Other snags lie in the form of poor-quality tech support. (Not all manufacturers are created equal in this regard.) Advance research on your part might help you avoid (or at least diminish) that chance that you'll have spent your money and bloodied your head on the wall just to find out that your hard-earned and recently-spent money bought a digital paperweight.

Equalization

One of the most popular real-time DSP functions is the equalizer, or EQ. Just about everyone that's ever messed with sound at any level knows what this is. On your home stereo, it's called bass and treble. iTunes has a few different ways to EQ the sound—from custom frequency sliders that you can adjust and save, to built-in presets for different listening experiences. The EQ is just what you think—it's tonal shaping, a way to adjust and balance the frequency content of any sound to your liking.

Remember that all complex sounds are a combination of individual sine waves, represented by the Fourier transform. That means that every sound has a custom and complex collection of frequencies within it. With an EQ, you can hunt them down and either boost or cut them until you've found the balance of the tones you like, meaning you can mess with the tones until you're blue in the face!

Just because you *can* equalize something doesn't mean that you should. The EQ is not a one-EQ-fixes-all problem solver—it works to balance frequencies in a sound, either to shape that sound or to adjust the balance of the one sound to others in the piece. Of course, EQ can be misused too. It can destroy a good sound, or it can shape a sound in creative (and sometimes very useful) ways. Before you go out and grab an EQ and start fiddling with the parameters, let's go through the kinds of EQs and what exactly the parameters mean.

The three main types of EQ used in the studio as DSP processing are filters, shelves and parametrics. A filter is just what it says—it filters the sound in a way where entire bands of frequencies are removed.

Filters

Filters come in three types:

☞   Low-pass: This is a filter that passes the low tones on, removing the high tones. Its other name is a high-cut filter. The result of a low-pass filter is a darkening of the sound. **Figure 1.74** shows a visual representation of a low-pass filter.

☞   High-pass: This is the opposite of a low-pass filter, in that it lets the highs pass unaffected, while removing the low tones. Its other name is a low-cut filter. The result of a high-pass filter is a "thinning" of the sound. **Figure 1.75** shows a visual representation of a high-pass filter.

☞   Band-pass: Usually created out of blending the two other filter types, a band pass filter removes the highs and lows, leaving the mid band. The result is both a "darkening" of the highs and a thinning of the lows, reminiscent of a telephone sound or AM radio. **Figure 1.76** shows a visual representation of a band-pass filter.

All three filters have one parameter in common—frequency. There are other parameters found on filters, but not every plug-in employs all of them. One of these parameters is the slope of the filter—how deeply does the filter remove the sound? The slope can be shallow, where the tones are removed less, or steep, where the tones are removed more. The slope is not a function of time, but of frequency and gain. The slope of a filter is measured in terms of dB per octave.

Figure 1.74: A -24 dB/ octave low-pass filter.

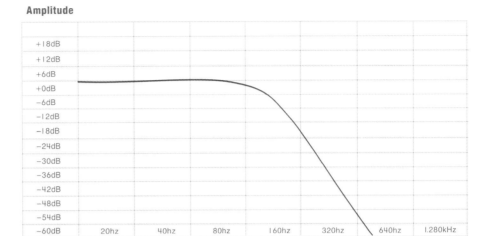

Figure 1.75: A -24 dB/ octave high-pass filter.

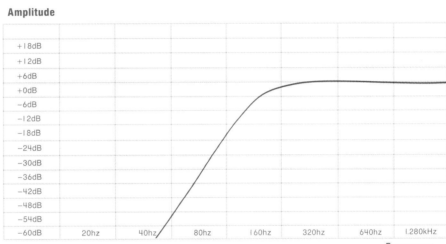

Figure 1.76: A band-pass filter.

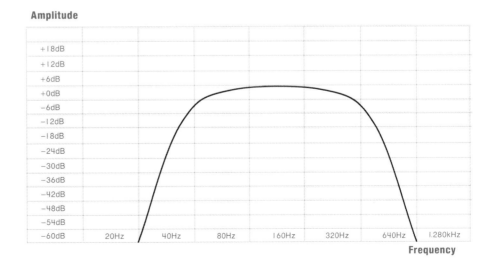

Let's consider a high-pass filter, where we're attempting to remove some unwanted low tones. The first parameter to set is the frequency. At what point does the cutting begin? This is known as the cutoff frequency. Interestingly enough, the cutting does not actually occur at the cutoff frequency—the cutoff is actually the frequency at which the cutting has already trimmed the sound by -3 dB (the cutoff is also known as the -3 dB down-point for this reason). The shallowest slope available is usually -6 dB per octave, meaning that at whatever frequency you choose, at the octave below, the sound will be diminished by 6 dB. If you set the frequency at 220 Hz, the lows will be reduced by 6 dB at 110 Hz. **Figure 1.77** shows a high-pass filter set at 220 Hz, sloping down at -6 dB/octave.

Figure 1.77: A -6 dB/octave high-pass filter set at 220 Hz.

As you increase the slope, the jumps tend to run in -6 dB increments, making the next setting -12 dB/octave, then -18, then -24 etc. Each 6 dB jump is called an order, so a -12 dB sloped filter is called a second-order filter. Many filters have the slope set this way, where you simply choose the –x dB per octave slope in -6 dB jumps, where as others give you a sliding scale of slope, allowing you to customize the slope at which the filtering is done. This gives you more control over how to set the filter and allows you to hone in on the cutting fairly well. **Figure 1.78** shows a high-pass filter at -12, -24 and -36 dB/octave.

Figure 1.78: A high-pass filter at -12, -24 and -36 dB/octave slopes.

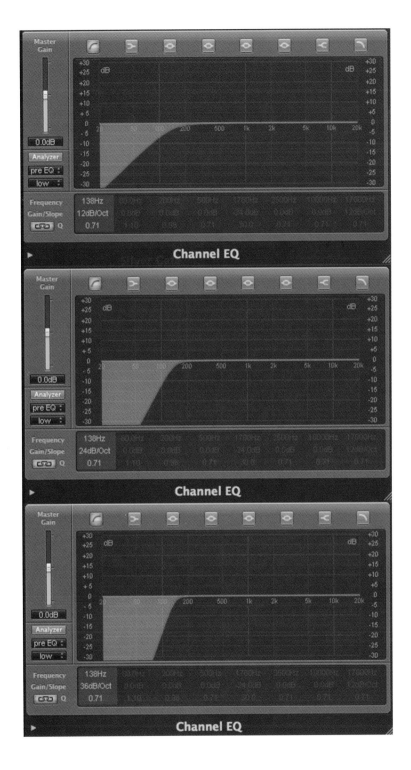

A third parameter offered by some filters is the peak resonance. In general audio terms, resonance refers to a vibration in sympathy with a particular tone or set of tones. In filters, the resonance allows you to add gain at the cutoff frequency while continuing to cut off the frequencies below it (the high-pass example still holding), as shown in **Figure 1.79** with a high-pass filter. The net result is removal of some tones, while boosting the cutoff tone, which tricks the ear into not noticing the reduction below (or above with a low-pass) the cutoff point.

Figure 1.79: A high-pass filter with a slight boost at the cutoff frequency.

COACH'S CORNER

In some original analog filter designs, there was a point at which the filter itself started to resonate with the cutoff frequency, resulting in a boost at that frequency. The tones below the cutoff were still being filtered, but at the cutoff, a gain had been introduced. Many people found this to be a very pleasing sound (and still do!), and many filters had a gain control introduced to allow the user to add resonance at the filter point. In electronic dance music, the filter and resonance controls are some of the oldest tricks in the book. Employ a low-pass filter, boost the resonance, sweep the frequency downward, and *voila*! Instant dance sound. Okay, it's a very rudimentary dance sound, but it still works!

DVD Track 50: A drum mix with the following filters:
High-pass at 440 Hz, slope of 24 dB/octave
Low-pass at 4,400 Hz, slope of 24 dB/octave
Band-pass at both 440 and 4,400 Hz—telephone EQ

DVD Track 51: A drum mix with a 440 Hz high-pass filter, then with -6, -12, -18, -24, -30 and -36 dB/octave filters.

Shelf-Type Equalization

Shelving EQs come in two forms, the high shelf and the low shelf. Where filters attempt to remove the sound above or below the cutoff, shelves attempt to raise or lower the frequencies to a fixed value above or below the cutoff. The idea is to create a general boosting or cutting up or down to a "shelf" level—i.e., drop the highs by, say -5 dB above 2 kHz (seen in **Figure 1.80**). In this case, you don't really want to remove 3k, 4k, 5k, etc.—you just want a little less of them. The shelving EQ allows you to set the cutoff frequency and the boost or cut amount. Some allow you to change the slope—how "fast" above or below the cutoff the shelf level stabilizes. Choosing the shelf point over the filter means you chose to keep all the frequencies in the sound—you just want more or less above or below the cutoff. This is very handy in areas where a sound is too strong in either the highs or lows. You can simply reduce the highs and lows without actually removing them, by lowering the shelf.

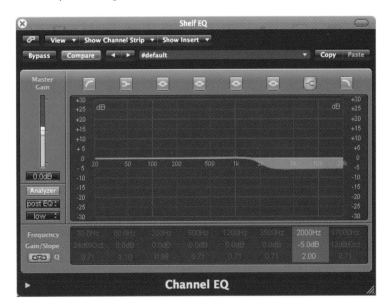

Figure 1.80: A shelf-style equalizer.

COACH'S CORNER

One of the simplest forms of equalization circuits, the shelving EQ is all around us—not only in DAWs, but in the form of treble and bass controls found on car and home stereos, electric guitars, guitar amps, etc. Although these don't seem as versatile as other forms of equalization such as parametric EQ—shelving filters are among the smoothest-sounding and most distortion-free means of tone manipulation, particularly in the analog domain—and for that reason, they're a popular choice with audio pros.

DVD Track 52: Drum mix with the following shelving filters:
Low-cut: -6 dB at 220 Hz
Low-boost: +6 dB at 220 Hz
High-cut: -6 dB at 8 kHz
High-boost: +6 dB at 8 kHz

Parametric Equalizers

Among the three equalizer designs mentioned here, the parametric EQ offers the most control over sonic tones. The parametric lets the user choose the frequency and the boost/cut amount and adjust how many frequencies around the chosen frequency get adjusted. Here, the frequency in question is called the *center frequency*, as the tones on either side of it are altered equally. The amount of frequencies adjusted on either side of the center frequency is controlled by a parameter called "Q," or bandwidth. Counter-intuitively, a high Q value means that there are very few tones adjusted on either side of the center frequency (meaning a very narrow band), while a low Q means a lot of frequencies are being affected at the same time (a wide band). **Figure 1.81** shows a parametric EQ with a +5 dB boost at 1k with a low and high Q setting.

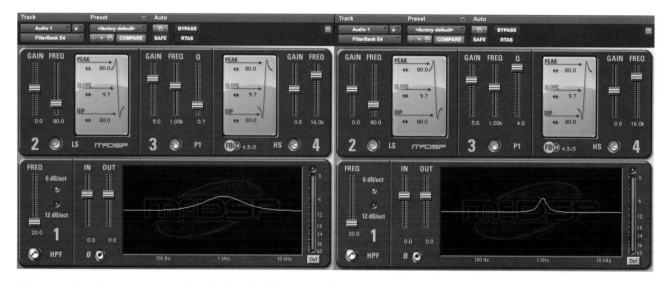

Figure 1.81: A parametric EQ with low (left) and and high (right) Q settings.

A parametric EQ is often referred to as a bell-curve EQ, as visually, its shape often resembles a bell, as seen in **Figure 1.81**. Parametrics are used every day in the studio, as they let users boost or cut tones in the mid band without employing a filter (removing the sound). They can pinpoint a singular frequency (or at least a potentially small range of frequencies) that needs either accentuation or reduction. Once you find the tone in question, you can then not only boost or cut the tone, you can adjust how much material around that tone also gets affected. If you cut a tone completely with a very high Q, the EQ is referred to as a notch filter—you've filtered out a thin slice (notch) of tones around a center frequency, shown in **Figure 1.82**. Equalizers specifically designed as notch filters often have gain reduction controls that go well beyond the -12/-15 dB cut range of most parametrics.

Figure 1.82: The high-Q, very narrow band effect of a notch filter with a 24 dB cut setting.

COACH'S CORNER

When using parametric EQs, it can be hard to find out where to set your center frequency. A good technique is one that we at Pyramind call the "boost, hunt, and kill" method. In this technique, first ask yourself this question: Is there too much of some tone or not enough of the other? If a particular tone is bothersome, such as a shrill (too-much high-end) electric guitar and you want to notch it out, start by boosting the EQ at a medium Q. By boosting and then sweeping the frequency (hunting), you will eventually run into the culprit—it happened to be 3.2k Hz in this case. Once you've emphasized the problem, simply change your boost to a cut (the kill) and adjust the Q accordingly. The idea here is to reduce the shrill high end, while keeping the treble intact. If your parametric won't cut deeply enough, mark your settings, change the parametric to a notch filter and enter in the values you liked. **Figure 1.83** on the following page shows the three-step boost/hunt/kill method.

Figure 1.83: The three-step boost/hunt/kill method of determining EQ center frequency points.

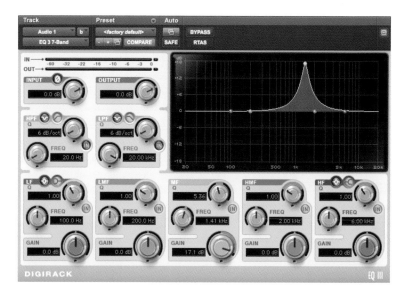

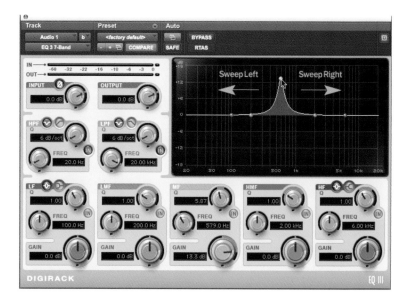

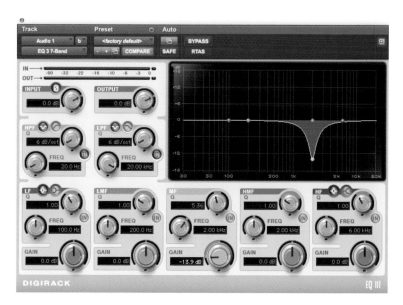

Before moving on, I'd like to make a plea to all producers using EQ—please go lightly at first! In my 300-level mixing class, songs always come in with tons of EQ and the end result is often a swirly, noisy mess. EQ is meant to fix problems and balance the tones you have. Many first-time producers think that they should EQ every part to be HUGE. However, it's the song that needs to be huge, not each sound, and sometimes, leaving sounds smaller allows room for the other, more important sounds to breathe.

So before you throw an EQ on every track, ask yourself this question again—is there too much of a sound, or not enough of a sound? We asked this question earlier when looking at one particular sound but now, you need to ask the question of the whole song. Start your EQ process from there and the song (and your listeners) will thank you.

DVD Track 53: Electric guitar with:
Wide mid boost, then narrow mid boost.
Boost at 1k wide—hunt down, then up, settling on 3.2k, and "kill" at a narrow EQ

Dynamics Processing

Processing the dynamic range is often desired when a part's range is too wide compared to the other parts in the mix. You'll know this is the case when you can't keep the volume of the part even over time. A wide dynamic range means that sometimes the sound is louder and other times the sound is softer. While dynamic range helps translate an emotional range as well, having a part like a lead vocal get softer than the sounds around it for a moment might take away from the listener's experience. The solution is dynamic range control.

Dynamic control, like EQ, comes in many forms—compression, limiting, multi-band compression (and multi-band limiting), gating and expansion. The first two shrink the dynamic range while gating and expansion increases the dynamic range. Like, EQ, there are times to choose between them and the differences can be subtle.

COACH'S CORNER

Dynamics are often difficult for beginner producers to hear—we're very accustomed to hearing in terms of tones, but not as accustomed to hearing in volume. Since the days of even the earliest recordings, dealing with dynamic range limitations has been an issue. Early recording meda did not achieve a wide dynamic range, and as a result, the music we've listened to for our entire lives already has a limited dynamic range.

COACH'S CORNER continued:

With the advent of the CD and the DVD, the hopes of audio manufacturers were that the public would enjoy hearing music in higher definition with wider dynamics and thus would re-purchase their entire catalog in the newer, "better" format. Sadly, convenience wins out over quality and the DVD-audio market never developed—it was eclipsed by the iPod and other portable, RAM-based players that employ data compression (not audio compression) to pack more data onto a smaller device. Data compression has the byproduct of a loss of dynamic range anyway, so as we, the producers were about to enter the world of wider dynamics, the audience began leaving for the world of greater portability, yet even narrower dynamics.

Thus, hearing dynamic range is a challenge for many, as it requires using your ears in a new way. Good news! Simply exercising your ears to hear dynamics will make them stronger and more attentive to dynamic range. If you listen to a lot of pop, rock, dance, hip-hop or other loud music, take a short break and audition some music with wide dynamic range. Try classical pieces or jazz pieces where the dynamics tell as much of the emotional story as the tones, even if it's not your listening cup of tea. Train your ears to hear the subtleties of volume change in recordings. After all, no one really likes to go to the gym, but everyone likes to look good, and sometimes, it actually feels good.

Introduction to DSP Tools
Chapter 3:
Introduction to Dynamics—
Compression

Compression

Compression is the process of shrinking audio's dynamic range based on the level of the audio. In this case, as the sound gets louder, the amount of compression, or shrinking, increases. There are a few different parameters involved in compression and they all work together to affect the sound. It should be noted that compression is sometimes difficult to hear, as the effect is based on volume, not frequency. The main parameters of compression are *threshold, ratio, attack/release,* and *make-up gain.* They all work together to create the amount of dynamic control and the resulting peak and RMS volume. Be aware, though, that compression's natural side effect is a change in the envelope of the sound—attacks and decays can get longer, while sustain levels tend to increase.

The *threshold* is the point at which the compression starts, measured in dB. It's similar to a trigger point—once the audio's volume crosses the threshold volume, the compression kicks in. Setting lower thresholds means that more audio gets compressed, because more audio will be above the threshold point. Higher thresholds usually mean that less audio gets compressed—usually only the very high peaks will cross a higher threshold level setting. **Figure 1.84** shows a software compressor's threshold.

Figure 1.84: Threshold setting in a software compressor. (Note yellow Threshold knob.)

Once the audio does cross that threshold, the amount of compression that kicks in is determined by the compression ratio setting. The ratio is a comparison value—how high the peaks are before compression versus how high they are after compression. Common ratio values are 2:1, 3:1, etc., which translates to ½, ⅓, etc., of the level of the original. **Figure 1.85** shows the same compressor, with the same threshold with ratio set at 3:1. Note how the resulting output curve bends lower above the threshold. This indicates that sounds crossing the threshold will come out quieter than they were before—they are compressed to ⅓ of their original peak value.

Figure 1.85: The same compressor, with a 3:1 ratio seting.

Attack and *release* are time measurements that define how fast the compression starts (attack) and how fast it lets go (release). The way you set the attack and release has a dramatic effect on both the threshold and the ratio—faster attacks tend to give the impression that there's more compression happening, as the ear can pick up the radical change in the envelope of the sound, while slower attacks tend to preserve a more natural sound. However, if the attack is set at a time that's too slow, the audio's peaks might come and go before the compression even kicks in. Some compressors have automatic (known as "program-dependent") settings that are based on the envelope of the incoming sound, making it easy to add just the right amount of dynamic control. If your compressor has one, and you're unfamiliar with compression, start by activating the auto mode and just concentrate on the threshold and ratio. The auto mode is also highly useful in live sound or broadcast situations, which sometimes leave the operator with little setup time in on-air or stage situations that require compression.

Lastly, *make-up gain* is the level of boost applied to the compressed signal. Remember that dynamic controls like compression have two effects at once—they lower the peaks, and they increase the noise floor, or the quietest sounds. After you apply compression, you'll notice a decrease in the peak volume, which gives the perception that the audio's getting quieter. This is not the end goal, however, so we need to take one additional step—raising the overall output to match the other levels in the song.

Remember why we're choosing compression? To shrink the audio's dynamic range in an effort to keep the volume of the part consistent (or at least, more consistent over time), so it doesn't get lost in other parts' volumes. So, if compression lowers the peaks, giving the impression that the part got quieter, doesn't that defeat the purpose? Quite likely, yes. To this end, you could simply turn up the make-up gain and bring the overall volume of the part up. This achieves the goal we want—a more consistent volume, where the audio plays at a volume where the part "stands up" over the others, or at least does not get lost in the mix of the tracks.

In **Figure 1.86**, note the resulting curve of a compressor with a threshold of -10 dB, ratio of 3:1 and make-up gain of 3.1. The make-up gain amount is determined by inspecting the amount of compression (*gain reduction*, or GR) and making up that amount. Therefore, if the compressor takes out 3 dB, then add 3 dB back in. Also, keep in mind that the ratio is only one half of the equation—a small ratio like 1.5:1 might yield a substantial amount of GR if the threshold is set -20dB below the peak, for example. When a 20 dB peak is crossing the threshold—even at 1.5:1—a lot of dynamic range is being siphoned away. Trust the meter if you are having trouble hearing compression and at first, keep it light—you might not be hearing it, but someone in your audience is.

Figure 1.86: Compression curve resulting from a threshold of -10 dB, ratio of 3:1 and makeup gain of 3.1.

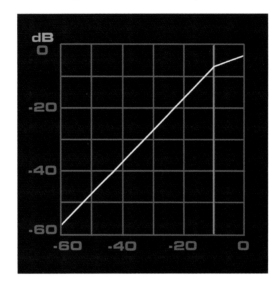

COACH'S CORNER

One of the measures of any compressor is a parameter simply called compression amount, or gain reduction. It's usually shown as a meter with the abbreviation GR. As you play with the threshold and ratio, watch the GR meter to see what the dB adjustment is—you might see the effect before you hear it as you start training your ears to hear compression. Small amounts of GR hover in the 3 to 5 dB range, while 7 to 10 dB (or more) in reduction is considered a lot—too much to be subtle!

The Math Behind the Compression

Let's say that we have a lead vocal that needs some compression. We've listened to it and determined that occasionally, the part gets too quiet and needs to be brought up in sections. Additionally, it gets too loud in other parts, so it needs to be brought down at those times. After watching the dB meter, we've also determined that the quiet parts happen when the audio plays at -14 dB and the loud parts happen when the audio plays at -4 dB. The sweet spot is somewhere in between—let's say halfway. This means that the dynamic range that we want to affect is between -14 dB and -4 dB: 10 dB.

Half of this 10 dB range is 5 dB, so setting the threshold at the half-way point between -4 and -14 puts it at -9 dB. With the ratio at a starting point of 2:1 (½), all the volume that crosses the threshold (-9 dB) gets cut in half. So, at the moment when the volume hits -4 dB (peak), the resulting level would be -6.5 dB, dropping the level by 2.5 dB. Looking at it another way, at the peak of -4 dB, the volume has crossed the threshold (-9 dB) by 5 dB—exactly half of the range we set out to compress. As the ratio is set to 2:1, or ½, the 5 dB range over the threshold gets cut in half, resulting in a 2.5 dB range. Add the 2.5 dB to the threshold of -9 and the result is -6.5 dB.

One More Time, for the Mathematically Disinclined . . .

- ☞ Threshold at -9 dB
- ☞ Peak at -4 dB
- ☞ Peak goes 5 dB over the threshold
- ☞ 5 dB gets compressed
- ☞ Compression is set to 2:1 or ½
- ☞ ½ of 5 dB is 2.5 dB
- ☞ 2.5 dB is added to the threshold value of -9 dB, resulting in -6.5 dB
- ☞ Old peak = -4 dB and new peak = -6.5 dB

If you know that the GR is 2.5 dB, it stands to reason that you can set the makeup gain at 2.5 dB and the overall signal will be increased by 2.5 dB. This makes the quiet section (-14 dB) now play at -11.5 dB. In fact, the overall volume of the track (including the now-compressed peaks) is now 2.5 dB louder, which in turn brings up the noise in the track 2.5 dB too!

That might be enough to make the quiet section loud enough to stop being buried by the other parts. Of course, this might not be the case. You can achieve your goal by either increasing the ratio, which will change the amount of volume getting through, or turning down the threshold, thus compressing more of the signal in the first place. Either method can get the job done, but you'll have to try one or the other to hear the results and see which works best in any particular situation.

DVD Track 54: Drum mix without compression, then compressed with -6 dB GR, then +6 dB GR added back in.

COACH'S CORNER

If you're having trouble hearing compression, remember that what you're listening for is a change in volume. You can sometimes hear the compression better by comparing the compressed sound to the uncompressed sound to hear whether or not the part continues to be buried at times. When working in a DAW, it's usually a good idea to leave compression as a real-time plug-in and not as a file-render plug-in. This is because the dynamics of a piece change a lot more than, say, EQ over the course of a song and you're likely to change your mind often. That's not to say that EQ should be usually be employed as a file-render plug-in—only that compression should not be used as a file-render plug-in if it can be avoided.

COACH'S CORNER

The leveling amplifier is a special type of compressor where the threshold and makeup gain settings are replaced with simple input and output gain knobs, as seen in **Figure 1.87**. In this case, adding more gain into the compressor, by turning up the input, works similarly to threshold. Turning up the input yields more compression. Turning up the output yields more gain. Ratio, attack and release are still available, but the parameters' names are changed. The result is still compression, although in this case, the peaks are leveled and then amplified—hence the title, "leveling amplifier".

Figure 1.87: Example of a leveling amplifier.

Limiting

In essence, a limiter is simply a compressor with a ratio fixed at 10:1. (This is true for many limiters but some limiters have the ratio fixed at 12:1 or higher. You'll have to consult the owner's manual of the plug-in to see, as limiters don't always give you the option to set the ratio.) Limiters function best as either peak reducers, for protection against clipping with very dynamic sounds, or for shrinking the dynamic range to practically nil. The latter example is often referred to a *brick-wall limiter* as a metaphor for the audio running into a brick wall—a suitably impassible object.

Compression has a certain amount of dynamic "give" to it: Loud sounds enter the compressor and come out quieter, but the overall sound still "breathes"—that is to say, the original dynamic range is still being emulated in that loud sounds are still louder than the average—they're just not as loud as they used to be. With limiting, the resulting audio doesn't really emulate the dynamic range—audio that crosses the threshold is effectively squashed, much like if a car actually ran into a brick wall. Peaks get reduced to $\frac{1}{10}$ of their original volume once they cross the threshold—serious gain reduction, for sure.

Many limiters come with the added feature of automatically matching the gain so while the peaks are reduced, the makeup gain is added in automatically! In many cases, this makes limiting a breeze—simply lower the threshold until the limiter gives you a blend of peak reduction and make-up. The audio should "stand up" against other tracks. In this way, the resulting audio prevents the part from being lost against the others.

Limiting often has another useful parameter called the ceiling. As its name implies, the ceiling is the maximum volume that the limiter will allow through. Remember that limiting is reducing the peaks and increasing the gain at once; it can be easy to get out of control with limiting by cranking down the threshold until the volume screams and calling it "done." This method can generate distortion due to too much output, so the ceiling protects the limiter from overdoing it. Note that the ceiling is always maxed out at 0 dBfs, and you can only lower it from there. **Figure 1.88** shows a limiter with the threshold and ceiling set to -0.1 dB. In this case, the limiter is simply protecting against the peaks—only peaks that approach clipping (-0.1 dB) are limited, and the resulting volume is no louder than -0.1 dB.

You can also use the ceiling and the limiter to "flatten" a performance. Similar to compression, limiting alone (without the auto gain-make-up) will lower the peaks and flatten the dynamics. After make-up gain is added, the overall volume is much louder, preventing unwanted drops in volume. Limiting with auto gain-make-up does it all in one step, but sometimes, this makes the resulting (louder) audio too loud. In this case, you can lower the ceiling to match the desired output level. You can raise the threshold to reduce the limiting, but the combination of limiting and heavy compression might not give you a desired effect. If the tone is right, but the output is too high, lower the output by lowering the ceiling to match.

Figure 1.88: Limiter with threshold and ceiling both set at -0.1 dB for maximum protection against overload peaking.

DVD Track 55: Drum mix with no limiting, then with limiting and gain make-up, then with limiting and lowered ceiling.

Multiband Compression

Most compressors and limiters affect the whole sound at once. But what if your dynamic problem only exists in one part of the frequency range, such as the low end? Sometimes, with low-frequency instruments in particular, a resonant frequency in the recording makes certain tones jump out more than others. Have you ever heard a piece of music where a single note makes your stereo shake? If so, you've identified the need for a special kind of compressor and limiter—the multiband.

With multiband compression, the signal coming into the DSP is first split into bands—usually lows, low-mids, mids and highs, as seen in **Figure 1.89**. Each band is then routed to its own compressor, each with a full complement of parameters. You can set the amount of compression individually on each band—compressing the low end, for example, while leaving the mid-band alone. The same works for high frequencies—some drum recordings have cymbals that are simply out of control and no amount of EQ can tame the high end effectively. Filtering it out darkens the sound too much and shelving it downward also results in a dull sound. Multiband compression can help out here by compressing the highs and keeping them in check, while still leaving the rest of the track present enough to keep the drums sounding bright.

Figure 1.89: A multiband compressor allows differing degrees of dynamic control in several frequency bands.

Multiband compressors are often difficult to manage and use—early adopters of them found the results to be extremely heavy-handed, with greatly over-compressed sounds. Like with compression alone, it's a good idea to start slowly and use lighter settings until you can hone in on what the processor is really doing to the sound. Luckily, most multibands give you the opportunity to *solo* (individually listen to) each band, so you hear only what's happening in that band. In the cymbal example, soloing the high band lets you hear the treble only and gauge whether the compressor is working hard enough or not.

DVD Track 56: A drum mix (shown in **Figure 1.90**) with no multiband compression, then with multiband compression, demonstrating multiband compression at various levels across the bands.

Figure 1.90: Settings used on the drum mix in DVD Track 46.

Expanders

Expanders are exactly what they sound like—they expand the dynamic range of a piece of audio. That means that while compressors, limiters and multibands are trying to reduce the dynamic range, the expander does the opposite. One might ask, why would you want to increase the dynamic range of a piece? In most cases, there is too much dynamic range for the overall blend of a set of tracks and compression makes more sense.

An expander tries to restore dynamic range that got compressed somehow. Remember that one of the side effects of compression is that the quiet sounds are increased while the peaks get reduced. In some cases, too much compression is added (intentionally or not), and can't be undone. This often happens when someone compresses a file in rendered fashion destructively, where the file was over-compressed and the original has been overwritten, never to come back. An expander might be able to help.

Expanders work much like a compressor in reverse: The threshold sets the point at which the expansion begins and the ratio determines how much expansion is used. For example, while compressors have ratios of 2:1 and 3:1, expanders have ratios of 1:2 and 1:3. (**Figure 1.91** shows a combination of a compressor and an expander, known as a compander.) That means that if 1 dB crosses the threshold at 1:3, 3 dB comes out. The expander adds gain to the signal during this process to increase the signal coming out.

Figure 1.83: A combo compressor/expander or "compander." As the ratio is brought up, it functions like a compressor; as the ratio goes down, it functions as an expander.

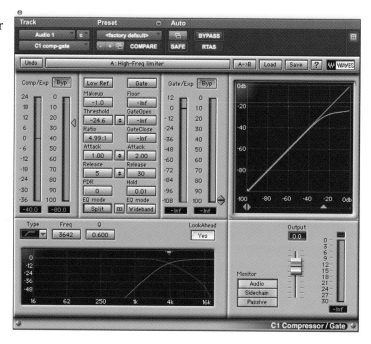

Another way to look at it is simply that sounds above the threshold are increased while sounds that are below the threshold are decreased. This is handy in poor recordings where it's hard to tell the source from the noise—expansion seeks to interpret what the source is and make it louder, while taking the noise and reducing it, thus creating a dynamic range where there wasn't one before!

One good example is a kick drum recording containing snare drum bleed. An expander can detect what is kick versus what is snare, based on the volume of the track; louder sounds above the threshold are kick and softer sounds are snare bleed. An expander will make the volume louder as the peaks cross the threshold (kicks get louder) and will lower the volume as the peaks fall below the threshold (snare bleed gets smaller).

DVD Track 57: A kick drum track with snare bleed, pre- and post-expansion.

COACH'S CORNER

In San Francisco, the staff at the District Attorney's office used to collect information about crimes by interviewing witnesses and victims with handheld cassette recorders. Many of the recordings were terrible and had more tape hiss than actual interview. Pyramind was brought in as the forensic audio team on one particular case that hinged on the interview from one of those awful tapes. After running the recording through expanders, a dynamic range started to emerge. The results weren't sonically stellar, but what was being said was completely clear. The case was successful, resulting in jail time for the guilty. It was just like a *CSI* episode, and we played Archie!

Noise Gates

Controlling dynamic range is certainly the main function of compressors, limiters and expanders, but there's one type of dynamic controller that controls the dynamic range more as a happy accident than anything else—the noise gate. A gate serves to basically "turn off" the sound, based on the volume of the audio being fed through it. Much like a fence gate, if you push hard enough, you'll get through. If not, you're out of luck. Gates are similar to expanders in that they lower unwanted noise, but unlike expanders, sounds above the threshold are left unaffected and don't increase in volume.

Some gates have similar parameters to compressors, limiters and expanders like threshold, attack and release. However, others have a few different controls—range, hold, gate open, and gate closed. Gates that have a single threshold parameter can be difficult to use—sometimes, when audio plays in a range of volumes, the sound gets cut off inappropriately if the audio dips below the threshold. If you lower the threshold too far, you'll let some unwanted noises through while cutting off the audio. Unfortunately, there's no magic threshold where all of the desired audio is above that level and all of the unwanted audio is below it. This happens often with vocals, for example.

To avoid this issue, many gates replace the single threshold with gate-open/gate-closed parameters. The gate-open value works something like the threshold, to determine at what point the gate allows sounds to get through. The gate-closed is just the opposite, setting the point where the sound turns off. The two work together to set a range of volumes that are "allowed" and keep things quiet when unwanted sounds are played. Once the gate opens, it stays open until the volume falls below the gate closed level. That way, sounds that cross the gate-open level continue to play until the performance stops and then fall below the gate-closed level.

The range parameter sets how quiet the sound is when "closed." Most gates default to completely closed—sounds falling below the gate-closing volume simply don't play. However, this can yield unnatural results. You can tweak the attack and release so the sound turns on and off more naturally, but there may be no setting where a completely closed gate (-infinity dB) sounds natural. The range can be set to some value above -inf dB, so when the gate closes, it doesn't turn sound off completely—it just turns the sound down. This can reduce the unwanted sounds in your audio without creating unnatural artifacts. **Figures 1.92 and 1.93** show gates working at different settings.

Figure 1.92: A gate where the open and closed levels define the range of audio performance and the range is set to nearly –inf dB (or in this case, just past -80 dB).

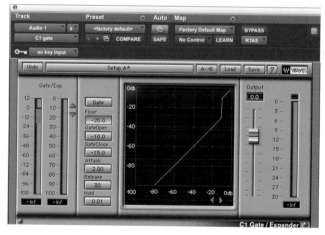

Figure 1.93: A gate where the open and closed levels define the range of audio performance and the range is set to -20 dB.

 DVD Track 58: Kick drum track without gating, with gating set to -inf dB and then with gating set to -20 dB. Notice how the noise is still there at -20 dB, but the kick envelope remains natural-sounding.

The "hold" parameter, measured in time, determines how long it takes for the gate to close, once the sound has fallen below the gate-closed level. The hold function works similarly to the sustain parameter in an ADSR, but while sustain refers to the level at which the sound is sustaining, the hold refers to the time. As the audio crosses the gate-open threshold, the attack sets how fast the gate opens. Fast attacks can result in sharp transients getting through, but can also create an audible Fourier click. Slow attacks remove the clicks but can soften the natural attack envelope of the sound. Once the audio crosses the gate-open level, the gate stays open until the sound crosses the gate-closed level. Then, the gate remains open for the length, after which the gate shuts at the pace set by the release.

Time-Based Effects: Depth

Depth is a term that is short for depth of field, or depth of image. It is a psychoacoustic term that refers to our perception of the position of a sound, which can be perceived as being nearer or farther than the actual distance of the listener to the monitors. DSP affecting depth manipulates time as its main parameter. Two common time-based effects are *delay* and *reverb*.

Delay

Delay is a relatively easy concept to understand—sound leaves the source and bounces off of a surface, returning to your ear at some point later in time. Underwater SONAR works in a similar fashion: A pulse is emitted and if it bounces off something, you can read the bounce and "see" what's out there underwater. The amount of time is significant—in outdoor spaces such as canyons and empty streets, the time of the delay can be seconds. The human ear cannot perceive two sounds as being separate unless they occur roughly 25 or 30 ms apart; to this end, delay must happen at values greater than 25 ms in order to achieve the effect.

Most studio delay systems (outboard or plug-in) have parameters for delay time, feedback and mix while others also have the ability to add a filter to the delayed sound and a certain amount of pitch manipulation, or warble. The delay time sets the time at which the incoming audio is delayed. In many cases, this can be linked to the tempo of the song and the delay can be set in time division, not just milliseconds. That means you can choose the delay to repeat in ¼ notes, ⅛ notes, etc. This is very handy in musical contexts.

Introduction to DSP Tools
Chapter 4:
Introduction to Time-Based
Effects—Delay

Figure 1.94: Some of the common parameters found in a delay plug-in.

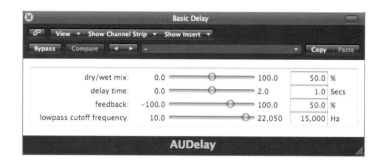

Some delays have a pair of parameters called rate and amount, which let users warble the pitch of the delay—how fast and how much. This is reminiscent of older, analog delay processing devices, which often had the ability to warble the sound this way. The feedback parameter controls how much of the delayed sound is routed back into the delay, which can create multiple delay effects. **Figure 1.94** shows a delay plug-in with common delay parameters, while **Figure 1.95** shows a vocal part before and after delay is applied. Notice that the delay is set to quarter notes and the individual repeats fall on the tempo-based grid. Check this example on **DVD Track 59**.

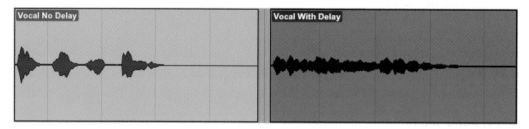

Figure 1.95: The waveform representation of a delay effect on a vocal part. Vertical lines represent quarter notes.

DVD Track 59: A vocal part without delay, then with delay effect repeated at quarter-note intervals.

These delay repeats are often referred to as "taps." While these two parameters are the most commonly used in delay settings, a third control—the mix level—also comes into play, but only if the plug-in is used in a certain way.

Time-based effects like delay and reverb don't function the same as EQ or compression—they don't necessarily sound very good if they affect the entire sound. For example, it might be odd to hear a high-pass filter employed on a sound and also hear the same sound playing in the mix without the filter. What would be the point? With time-based effects, however, hearing only the delay or reverb is a weird experience. There are cases where this might be a desired effect, but mostly, the original sound can get somewhat lost in the time manipulation. This calls for the ability to hear some of the sound processed with the time effect, while some of the sound plays normally. This is known as a *wet/dry mix*.

The wet part refers to the completely processed sound; the dry part refers to the unprocessed sound. When a time-based effect is used directly on a track, the mix parameter lets users set the balance between the wet and the dry mix, controlling the amount of the original sound used versus the processed sound used. One of the disadvantages of using time-based effects is that no matter how you set the wet/dry mix, some of the urgency or presence of the original sound is sacrificed for the increased depth of image. If you want a blend of both, without the sacrifice, you'll need to use the plug-in in a different way, known as the classic *send-and-return* configuration.

COACH'S CORNER

The value of the mix function on time-based effects (like delay or reverb) is often counterintuitive. For example, common sense dictates that an even split between the wet and dry sounds on a track would hover around 50% wet to dry. This is almost never the case. Try this at home—solo a vocal track and insert a delay or reverb. (This experiment is particularly effective with reverb.) Listen to the track starting at 100% wet, click and hold on the mix slider, then close your eyes. As you listen, slowly drag the mix slider down until your ears tell you that the wet/dry blend is good. Open your eyes and see the percentage—I'll bet it's less than half! Time-based effects are very strong to our ears and we usually like to hear a significant amount of the dry sound, as it is natural to us. Hearing the time-based effect in balance usually refers to its balance against the dry sound—which, again, we're used to hearing very well. Therefore, the mix tends to sound "even" when the mix is much lower than 50% wet.

 **DVD Track 60:** Vocal track with delay set to all-dry, 25% wet, 50% wet, and then 100% wet.

The send-and-return configuration involves having two tracks in your DAW—one for the dry sound and one for the 100% wet sound. DAWs often have sends, which take a copy of the audio and route it to the wet track. The details vary from DAW to DAW, but they're usually called auxes, sends or buses— or some combination of the three. (See an example in **Figure 1.96**.) The concept is to send the dry sound over to the track with the time-based effect, process that copy to 100%, then blend the two by raising or lowering their faders. The advantage here is that you'll have full control of the punch of the dry sound, with the depth of the wet sound.

Figure 1.96: A send-and-return configuration. Every DAW does it differently, so consult your manual for terms like aux, bus, returns, aux inputs, etc.

DVD Track 61: Vocal track with send/return to the same delay, with both faders at 0 dB and a send value of -20, -10, then 0 dB. Notice how the dry, punchy vocal retains those qualities as the delay level increases to match.

Reverberation (Reverb)

Reverb is short for reverberation and refers to the way sound behaves in an enclosed space. Remember, sound is a 360-degree energy wave and it tends to go everywhere it can, as often as it can, for as long as it can. In a small room, the sound will bounce off of every surface it hits, over and over, until it runs out of steam. Reverb DSP emulates the behavior of sound in an artificial room, or, occasionally, a model of an actual acoustical space. Reverbs have many parameters, but before we go into them, let's take a close look at how sound "bounces" around a room.

As sound leaves the source and emanates into the room, it travels everywhere it can before settling into your ears. In a studio control room, some of the sound hits you directly, coming right out of the monitors and into your ears. At the same time, the sound is also traveling at an angle out of the monitor and strikes off of a wall—say, the wall to your left. After it bounces once, it then finds its way into your left ear, just a bit later than the direct sound. It may have also bounced like a pinball off of the floor, the ceiling, the back wall, the painting at the back of the room, back onto the left wall, the dog, the lava lamp and then into your ear. All of these sounds arrive at your ear at different times—the direct sound, the first bounce, then the pinball bounce, as shown in **Figure 1.97**. The result is a combination of phase shift smearing and time shifting.

Figure 1.97: The many pathways that sound travels from the monitor to your ears.

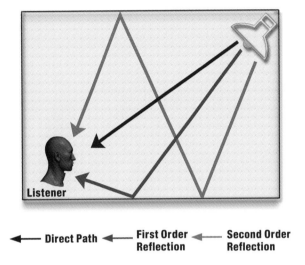

Think of reverb as delay, only multiplied by a few hundred million times. Delay occurs more often in the outdoors where there is a lot of space and a big surface for sound to bounce off of, like a mountain, wall or a building. Sound creates delay as it leaves the source in one big wave, travels to hit the big surface, then bounces back in almost the same condition it left—it doesn't sound all that different, it just happens later. Reverb differs from delay in that sound in an enclosed space usually doesn't have to travel very far to hit a surface and when it does, it tends to hit several of them at once, with a lot of energy still left to go. It then bounces as often as it can, off of every surface it can find—which, in a small room, is plentiful.

Not only is the sound bouncing all over the place, it's also bouncing into itself! Sound will leave the source, bounce off of the front wall then head back to the middle of the room. At the same time, it's bouncing off of the back wall and heading back to the middle, too. The two bounces meet and interact, causing a ton of phasing and summing at all kinds of frequencies— basically, it's a sonic mess. A lovely sonic mess, but a mess all the same! Now, multiply that by six main surfaces (four walls, the floor and ceiling) and any oddball shapes in the room, like a closet wall, window, the furniture and the mixing board itself, and you've got the glory of reverb.

The result is a huge cloud of delays that are smeared together into one big time shift of the sound. The original timbre is still in the sound but the details of the envelope have been blasted away through time and phase shift. This is not unlike an airbrushed painting, where the lines are gone and every edge has been smoothed away, leaving only shades that blend into each other. Reverb also has plenty of parameters to play with—some reverb DSPs have upwards of 40 of them. The basics are usually the same, though, and all relate to time, which is the first—and most important!

Time is measured as a function of the formula RT60. In short, this asks how long it takes for the reverb to drop by 60 dB. The RT60 is usually marked in the DSP as just time, ranging from as short as 150 ms to 10 seconds and beyond. One reverb I know has an infinity RT60 setting, meaning that as soon as sound enters it, it reverberates forever (or until you quit the DAW or turn the time down). Mix controls are also available on reverbs as they operate similarly to delays when it comes to blending the dry and the wet signal. In most cases, it's advisable to use the send-and-return configuration here, as well.

Figure 1.98: A simple reverb and its parameters. Notice how the time has been set to infinity.

Figure 1.99: A different reverb plug-in, with many more parameters.

COACH'S CORNER

Reverb is the emulation of the behavior of sound in a room. Many reverbs emulate fantasy rooms (with names like "Small Hall," "Large Hall," "Chamber," "Cathedral," "Hangar," etc.) in that the parameters are set to behave similar to an actual room—or how sound would behave if there were a room out there built that way. A recent advancement in reverb design is called convolution reverb, which attempts to simulate the behavior of an existing space: A real room is sampled and turned into an algorithm, which can be used on any sound source that feeds it. This lets users route their sound into that room—even if when they've never been there. Some convolution reverbs allow you to sample your own rooms—no matter how bad they might sound!

COACH'S CORNER

Imagine being at the far end of a very large church, where a choir is singing at the other end. (See an example of a reverb on a vocal in **Figure 1.100**.) You might imagine that you're hearing almost entirely reverb since you're so far away from the source and the sound has bounced so much that the singing and the words are unrecognizable. As you move closer to the source, the amount of the choir sound versus the reverb gets much more present and at some point, you start to hear the choir more than the reverb. There's a balancing point in there, more than likely closer to the source than the half-way point (similar to the "find the blend percentage" experiment listed above). There is, however, no place in the room where you can hear the choir as if you're right in front of them AND hear the reverb as you did in the back of the room. How could you be in two places at once? When you use reverb in a send-and-return configuration, you can create the experience of being both in the front of the room and the back of the room at once. Nice!

Figure 1.100: A reverb plug-in used on a vocal track. The settings seen are heard on DVD Track 62.

DVD Track 62: A vocal part heard dry, then with reverb inserted, set to 100% wet. Notice how the words and envelope of the original part are "airbrushed" out, leaving just the "cloud" of reverb.

DVD Track 63: The same vocal part as track 62, heard dry, then with reverb set to 100%, but in a send-and-return configuration. Notice that the dry vocal is still retained while the reverb is blended in.

Two other commonly used reverb parameters are pre-delay and diffusion. Pre-delay is the amount of time between the impulse of the sound and the responding reverb. A small amount of pre-delay can evoke the experience of being in a very big room, as the sound can take a few hundred milliseconds to cross the room, start hitting surfaces, and then bounce back to you. If used properly, pre-delay can almost give you a sense of playing backwards, as the reverb of the first impulse can play just before the second impulse. This gives the impression that the second impulse sounds backwards, as the envelope of the reverb of the first impulse ramps upwards, much like the envelope of a sound that's been reversed!

DVD Track 64: Vocal part heard with reverb send/return set at 100% wet, then, the same part with the same reverb, with pre-delay set to 300 ms. Notice how the reverb starts late compared to the original sound.

Diffusion refers to the amount of smearing in the reverb. Some rooms actually sound more like smeared delays than cloudy washes of sound. A low diffusion percentage has more of a slapped-back delay sound, while higher diffusion settings give the impression of more smearing. For example, in highly diffuse rooms, each time the sound bounces off a surface, it gets broken up into little sounds more and more. The end result is a very smooth reverb, made up of smaller "grains" in the cloud.

One of the least understood aspects of reverb is known as the early reflection. This defines the first reflections after only two or three bounces that occur, before the sound blooms into a cloud of reverb. Early reflections are highly useful for smearing a sound in time a little bit without smearing the punchiness or the envelope of the dry sound. Early reflections (ER) usually happen within the first 200 to 300 ms of the impulse and dissipate just as quickly. ER can be used very effectively on vocals to give the impression of space existing around the singer without smearing the crispness of the words. Again, there can be over 40 parameters to adjust in reverb but these few—time, mix, diffusion, pre-delay and early reflections—are plenty to work with for now.

DVD Track 65: Vocal part dry, then with reverb set to 100% wet, using only early reflections. Notice how the envelope is completely retained with a sense of ambience around it, but not a huge cloud of reverb.

Specialty Effects

The four horsemen of real-time DSP are EQ, dynamics, delay and reverb. These barely represent a fraction of the variety, categories and sheer numbers of plug-ins available today. We can't cover them all here—that's a whole different book that would need updating every month! There are two categories, however, that deserve mentioning here—correctors and emulators.

Pitch Correction

Pitch correction software seeks to analyze the pitches in the performance and correct them to the pitches that were intended. The biggest two advantages to this are a performance with solid pitch and the ability to keep a passionate performance without having to try it again. (See examples of pitch correctors in **Figure 1.101**.) Many of these tools come with significant artifacts—too much for some producers, just right for others. Many of these tools allow you to pick a scale that matches the song and conform all of the notes being performed to the notes in the scale only! If you don't know your scale, choose *chromatic*—the software will simply pick the closest note available and conform the performance to that note.

COACH'S CORNER

With the quality of pitch detection and correction, who needs music theory? Answer: Everyone. Don't trust the tools to do the artist's job—the tool might think a note is off and it might correct it, but it won't make a bad singer good. As always, try to use these tools tastefully. After all, the tool can fix the pitch, not the performance—well-tuned garbage is still, well . . . garbage.

When using the pitch corrector in this chromatic-automatic mode, the results can be unpredictable. Consider a singer who sings a note so sharp that the note is actually closer to the note above the intended one. In this case, the software would conform the note to the higher note, making the performance sound worse—it's on pitch, just the wrong pitch! In this case, you can sometimes get into a graphical mode and redraw the pitch by hand, note-for-note guaranteeing a perfect performance while minimizing the artifacts of pitch correction. This can give you the cleanest results, but it can take a long time!

Figure 1.101: Two popular pitch correction tools.

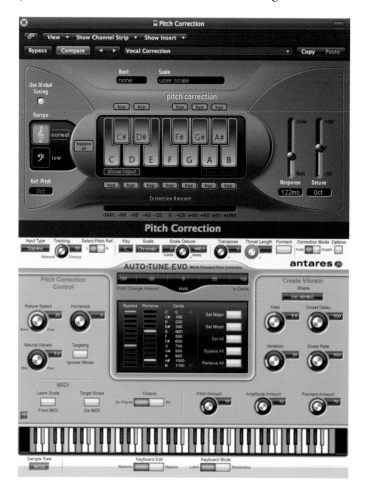

COACH'S CORNER

Some argue that pitch correction is highly audible and therefore fixes one problem but creates another. Many others claim that it's better to hear a note in tune than out of tune, regardless of the tonal changes. Others say that no amount of pitch correction can fix a weak performance, and the rest don't care. Like a very potent spice in the kitchen, pitch correction is often best when less is used. It's nice to hear the pitch being solid, but nasty to hear a voice sound robotic through over-correction. Of course, yet another group would say that the over-correction sound is the sound and the track just isn't complete without it! Early users of pitch correction created the sound of over-corrected pitch through misuse of the tool. However, once the "mistake" got out on records like Cher's "Do You Believe" and on various hits by Daft Punk, it has become ingrained in the expectation of pop and dance audiences. In fact, the hit isn't a hit without it!

DVD Track 66: Vocal part before and after tuning, in automatic/chromatic mode. Notice how the vocal is on pitch but has a "metallic" quality.

Emulation Plug-Ins

An emulator attempts to recreate the behavior of some real-world hardware in software form. This can be anything—a guitar amplifier (or 30 of them), an EQ, a compressor, a recording medium (such as tape) or another processor. There are lots to choose from and several of each kind. Guitar amplification emulators, for example, are plentiful—as of this writing, there are roughly ten different real amplifier emulation software manufacturers, all of whom make really good products. Some, of course, do a better job than others, but that's all up to your particular tastes. I'll leave out the conversation about whether or not software could ever truly emulate hardware well. You all can argue that one over beer—endlessly.

The process of making a piece of emulation software is rooted in technology called physical modeling. In modeling software, the original hardware is tested rigorously, down to the component level. Every configuration of the hardware is tested and measured—every knob, along with every type of knob—and the results are fed into an analysis program. The harmonic and dynamic results are then coded into a piece of software that behaves just like the hardware did. That way, the pieces that make up the timbre of the original are modeled and the software simply recreates that behavior. In the case of vintage guitar amps, one piece of software for $600 might come with models of 15 amps, each costing over $2,000, making the argument for software emulators very compelling.

Figure 1.102: A few varieties of guitar amp/effect simulators.

DVD Track 67: A guitar part recorded dry, then with a variety of amp simulators.

Another type of popular emulation software attempts to recreate the sound of analog audio processes like vinyl, cassette, 2-inch and ½-inch tape decks, vacuum tubes, antique EQs, etc. The idea is to "warm up" the sound of digital recordings. Since the early DAWs and I/Os were more affordable than building an analog studio with a 2-inch tape deck, would-be studio owners could open recording studios without the bigger budgets of the large studios.

However, they often lacked the microphone selection, the preamp selection, the great-sounding room and everything else that went into a high-quality analog studio recording. Therefore, many of these early digital studio productions came out sounding harsh, cold and brittle, creating a market for this emulation software. Additionally, early digital recorders were only 16-bit and only 44.1 kHz, and they were known for making harsher, edgier recordings. (Remember this from the digital audio basics section?) This necessitated both advancements in digital audio (16-bit became 24, 44.1 kHz evolved into 192 kHz, etc.) and the need for software emulation of the expensive hardware originals. However, just because a plug-in's user interface or screen appearance happens to *look* like a great guitar amp or classic studio device doesn't necessarily mean the software provides a similar effect or sound quality. Here again, it's important to rely on your ears to determine whether any particular tool—emulated or otherwise—fits the job at hand.

Figure 1.103: A variety of software-based emulations of analog processing gear.

RECAP

DSP, digital signal processing, refers to two things at once: software that processes the audio in some fashion and the computer hardware that runs the software. Software DSP can be used in real-time and non-real-time fashion. The non-real-time version renders a new file to the hard disk or overwrites the file completely with the new, processed one. DSP can process the audio in many ways—from gain adjustments (including the very handy normalize function), to phase inversion and file reversal, among dozens of others.

The four main DSP processors are EQ, dynamic control, reverb, and delay. EQ is the control of the frequencies found within a recorded or produced sound and allows you to either filter (remove), shelf (raise or lower beyond a chosen frequency), or notch a sound with a parametric (focus on a particular tone or range of tones and either boost or cut the tones). A great method of using EQ is "boost, hunt and kill".

Dynamic control is found in compressors and limiters (which reduce dynamic range) or gates and expanders (which increase dynamic range). Compressors and limiters reduce peak levels and let users increase the overall level of a track after reducing the peaks, thus making the average level of the track louder. Noise, however, also gets louder during the compression process. Expanders and gates seek to separate the noise from the sound, lower the noise and better expose (or increase) the level of the desired sound.

Time-based effects include delay and reverb, which are usually used in a blended fashion where all of the dry sound is blended with all of the wet sound. These effects seek to elongate the duration of a sound, or emulate the experience of a sound's behavior in a space—real, inside or outside.

Other DSP processes include correction processors (these fix specific audio anomalies) and emulation processors that are designed to re-create hardware processors. Keep in mind that there are hundreds of plug-ins available for all types of DAWs, and there's just no way to cover them all here.

"your monitors are among the most important parts of your studio; they are what you will be listening through for every project you work on . . ."

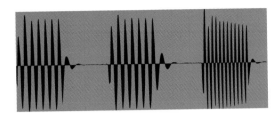

Studio Monitors

Monitors: The End of the Life Cycle

Music and audio production are rooted in the understanding that sound, in the end, wants to be free. That means that it wants to exist in a room, moving air molecules around and exciting someone at the other end of those moving molecules. Some of the sounds we produce come from moving molecules in the first place (players and instruments making music), and we try our best to capture these with microphones. Other sounds come from either pre-fabricated bits of captured sound (like loops, samples, etc.) or from devices that create sounds from electrical components (like synths). At the end of the day, however, that sound still needs to play out of a pair of audio monitors so that all of the work that we do in manipulating our productions will result in moving molecules that elicit an emotional response from the listener.

Studio monitors themselves becomes a part of the production process, as they greatly affect what we hear (or think we hear) in the studio and provide a means of predicting what will happen during playback on other speakers, from car radios to boom boxes to high-end audiophile systems. The quality of these predictions—i.e., how we think our work sounds in the studio versus how it will sound everywhere else—is known as its *translatability*, or its translation.

Tech-Speak: *Translatability*

Translatability is the measurement of sonic compatibility between the quality of sound reproduction in the studio versus the reproduction elsewhere.

Your monitors are among the most important parts of your studio. These are, after all, what you will be listening through for every project you work on. The goal of the monitor (and the studio as a whole) is to present the audio to you in an unbiased fashion, thus allowing you to make smart sound decisions in the studio and achieve a high level of translation in your productions. Many unbiased monitors do a great job of presenting the sonic information to you, but often, they just don't sound very good. In a way, these can be thought of as medicine—really good for you, but not necessarily fun.

Selecting Monitors

Choosing a monitor is a very personal process and requires a solid investment of time and testing. The testing process is usually good fun—you get to listen to music over and over through lots of different monitors until you find a pair that works for you! The idea is that they should sound good—to you. That means they help you enjoy listening to the music while revealing all of the subtle nuances that you expect in the music. A good idea is to show up at dealer or store with a handful of CDs—ones that represent the range of music you listen to and create and ones that you know extremely well. You'll need time to review each of your test CDs with little distraction—something not always available at the music store. In that case, consider renting pairs of monitors for a day of listening "shootouts."

You should also pay attention to what you're hearing. It's easy to get lost in the music, but you must stay focused on the sound and not the music. There are a few things to listen for, which should be no surprise: the frequency content, the dynamics and the imaging, as well as realism of left/right stereo sounds and the depth of reverb, etc.

When it comes to frequency response, try not to choose the pair that delivers the most exciting sound—this might be an indication that the monitors are hyped in some tones (by design) to get you to enjoy them more. This is one of the main differences between studio monitors (designed for accuracy) and home stereo speakers (designed to sound "good"). Clearly, the monitors you choose should sound good, but what you're really looking for is a blend of pleasing sound and accurate sound. Good monitors should reveal tones that you haven't heard before in the music you bring to the listening test.

For dynamics, the concept is the same—listen for the dynamic range to "come alive." This is where a high-quality recording of classical or jazz music might come in handy, as these records tend to achieve wider dynamic range than rock, pop or hip hop, etc. Good monitors present the dynamics boldly, while bad monitors don't. If you know a record that sounds very dynamic but the monitor sounds like it's 'putting the brakes" on the sound, don't buy them. As for imaging, a sonic image is the perception that the sound is coming from some space on the other side of the wall. It's a psychoacoustic phenomenon where the brain interprets the sound it hears as being three-dimensional. Good monitors improve the imaging; where bad ones hide the imaging.

Monitor Types

Monitors have evolved greatly over the last 20 years, in component quality and construction as well as overall performance. Some of the major advances come in the form of the materials of the physical monitor enclosure, the adjustability of the performance and the advent of the powered monitor. Monitors today are almost all self-powered, and some are intelligent enough to measure and compensate for the acoustical performance of your room! Powered monitors like this are generally comprised of a few bits of important components that make up the monitor system—the box, the drivers, the amp(s), the crossover and the control section (if any).

Remember the conversation about resonance and resonant frequencies? Well, monitors are subject to these issues, as well. That means that the monitor box itself runs a risk of resonating with the sound it reproduces, making the enclosure characteristics a part of the performance of the monitor. Resonance is generally something that designers seek to avoid. Monitor construction is often wood—a great resonator—for cost purposes, but a single sheet of plywood just doesn't cut it. In fact, some monitor companies use several layers of wood (one I know uses 21 layers of heavily flattened wood!) to create an extremely dense box that can withstand vibrations of very low frequencies at very high volumes. This makes for a very strong enclosure that will not interact with the sound being reproduced, thus making it better for translation.

The most popular type of powered monitor is the two-way monitor, where two different drivers work together to reproduce the sound. The driver is the actual speaker part, often called the woofer and the tweeter, for the bass and treble driver (shown in **Figure 1.104**). Generally, the larger the driver, the greater the degree of low-frequency reproduction. The driver works exactly like a dynamic microphone, but in reverse. In this case, we start with electricity (a line-level signal) coming from the DAW and going into the amplifier. The amp boosts the signal and sends the high-voltage electricity to the driver, which converts the electricity through magnetism (reverse inductance) and then pushes the driver out and in synchronously with the voltage. If the signal gets louder, the driver moves farther out, then back in. This motion creates an acoustical energy wave—free sound.

Figure 1.104: An example of a two-way monitor.

Traditionally, DAW outputs would connect to a volume control, then to a power amplifier, then to the speaker box. This works fine but adds a measure of noise potential, as there are more cables to run. Additionally, amps and speakers aren't always matched to each other in power or performance.

With powered monitors, the amplifier(s) lives in the box itself—just plug in an audio cable and go! Besides the convenience factor, having the amp built in to the monitor serves at least two very important functions—it shortens the distance between the amp and the driver, keeping unwanted noise to a minimum and it allows the manufacturer to match the right amp specs to the drivers, increasing the quality of the sound and the overall performance of the driver. The disadvantage to this versus having a separate amplifier/monitor combination is that if the amp goes down, the whole monitor goes down. With a separate amp, you can change out the amp and keep working while the original amp goes off for repair. (**Figure 1.105** shows signal flow to powered and unpowered monitors.)

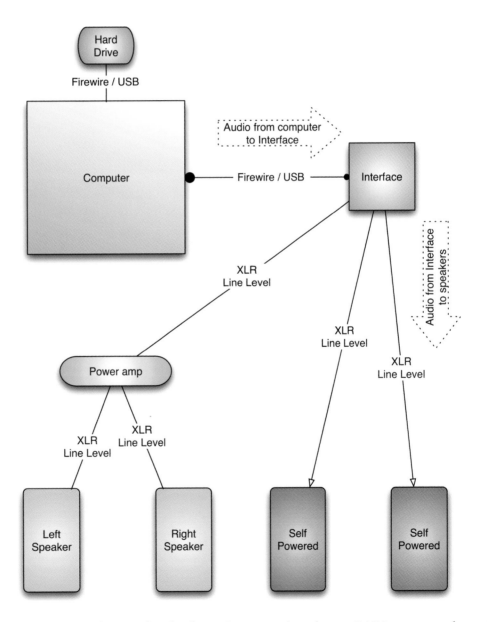

Figure 1.105: The signal path of a DAW-to-amp/speaker vs. DAW-to-powered-monitor.

The Crossover

No matter where the amp lives, there is always a challenge in monitor design once you go beyond one driver per box—how do you separate which sound goes to which driver? How does the speaker know to put the low tones into the woofer and the high tones into the tweeter? The answer is called a *crossover*. Think of it as a frequency splitter, where tones going into the crossover get separated at some predetermined frequency. A crossover is basically a network of resistors, inductors and capacitors—filters, really. The idea is that the signal is "copied" where one "copy" has the treble removed, then gets sent to the woofer. The other "copy" gets the bass removed and is sent to the tweeter.

Crossovers have a frequency at which the signal gets split, known as (surprisingly enough) the *crossover frequency*. Unfortunately, no filter is dead-accurate with its cut-off, and there is always a bit of "spillover" at the crossover frequency—the lows don't get cut off exactly at the crossover frequency; some of them still play just above the filter point as the filter drops the sound. The same holds true for the highs—there's always just a bit of sound above and below the crossover frequency. You might remember this as the slope—the rate at which filters remove gain in -dB/octave increments. **Figure 1.106** shows high-pass and low-pass filters, each with slopes of -24dB/octave slopes.

Figure 1.106: High-pass and low-pass filters, each demonstrating -24dB/octave slopes.

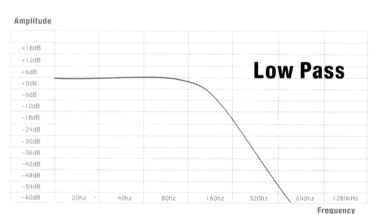

These two bits of spillover add together and can make a bump at the crossover frequency, unnaturally boosting that tone. For example, consider a crossover that functions at 3.2 kHz. In an ideal (theoretical) world, the woofer would get all sounds 3.199 kHz and below while the tweeter should get all sounds 3.2 kHz and above. In reality, the woofer gets all sound below something more like 3.4 kHz and the tweeter gets all sound above 3.15 kHz, etc. Between 3.15 and 3.4 kHz, there are "duplicate" tones from each side of the two filters, which can make the monitor sound like there's more 3.2 kHz in the mix than there really is! **Figure 1.107** shows the resulting bump of a crossover at 3.2 kHz.

Figure 1.107: The resulting bump from a loudspeaker system crossed over at 3.2 kHz.

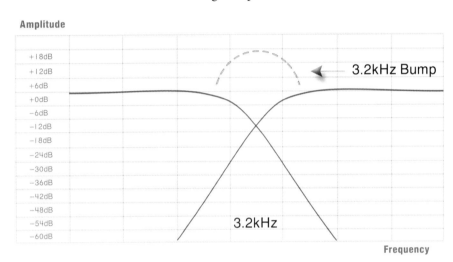

COACH'S CORNER

A 3.2 kHz crossover is just no fun. It's where the sound of fingernails on the chalkboard lives, along with wailing babies and that unbelievably bright pick sound that some beginner rock guitarists love so much. It's also where the human ear is highly sensitive and it's where a big bulk of the human voice lives. We hear it just fine, thank you very much, and if a monitor were to use 3.2 kHz as a crossover frequency, we might hear it in the box too. Look to see where your monitor crosses over—2 kHz might make the monitor "honky" and 4k might make it sound "sweet."

Usually, the crossover lives after the amplifier. That means that the sound is amplified, crossed over then fed into the drivers directly. This is a more cost-effective monitor design, as each monitor only needs one amplifier. In more expensive monitors, the crossover happens before the amplification stage. In this situation, the crossover splits the signal, and sends each part (the low and the high) to a unique amplifer for each driver. This is called bi-amping, where each driver has its own amplifier, making each amp more efficient and more capable of re-creating wide dynamic range.

Some monitor systems even let users change the crossover frequency manually! The idea is that the crossover frequency might happen at a point where the natural bump in tones around it accentuates tones that are very harsh or even resonating even more with your room. A *slight* adjustment in the crossover could make that go away. This adjustable crossover frequency is more rare than the norm—many manufacturers just don't want you messing with their hard-earned decisions and test results.

However, many powered monitors come with a series of user-definable parameters for monitors. These allow users to set how loud the monitor plays (independent volume adjustments) and provide options for turning boosting/cutting the bass or treble tones as well. This is a shorthand way of saying "we know you're shopping for a decent but affordable monitor but we also know that your room is likely an acoustical mess, so here are some adjustments that might help your situation."

In recent years, some companies have begun bundling microphones, test CDs and software combinations that effectively "read" the frequency response of the monitors in your room. The software takes the test CD sound, and routes it the to monitors, which play back the test tones. A microphone is placed in the listening spot and the results are sent back to the software for analysis. The software compares the input sound versus the sound coming out, and a chart or graph indicates what's going on in the room.

COACH'S CORNER

If you've ever done any serious work in your studio, and taken your new music creation to your friends to play for them, you've probably been disappointed at times when they just don't react how you'd like them to. This is not necessarily because the music is "bad." Things always sound different in different environments, and it's possible that the sound that excited you in your studio is simply not being reproduced properly at your friend's house. This is a function of poor translatability as much as it could be a testament to how bad your friend's stereo is!

The Translatability Issue

There are numerous scientific methods of measuring how translatable your studio listening environment is, but most of them are way beyond the scope of this book. Without getting too heavily into acoustics, let's say that the fact that something sounds great in your studio doesn't really count for much if it never sounds that good elsewhere. One of the key goals in production is to ensure that all of the care and critical decisions you've made during the process will come out in the final playback. So while we've been spending all of this time discussing how sound exists and how it gets into the studio, we now need to explore how sound gets out of the studio—or at least, how it gets out of the recording and back into moving air.

In the studio, accuracy is more important than sheer volume—we need to know what is really happening in the captured sound so that we can make good decisions. Like your computer monitor, studio monitors should simply "display" what is happening in the recording, and we generally like them to be "color-correct." Imagine having a two-monitor computer system where the left monitor was tinted blue and the left was tinted red! You'd be seeing things in 3-D (more headaches)!

Studio monitors usually come in three levels: near-field, mid-field and far-field. This should be familiar to you as these three types directly correspond to their microphone-technique equivalents. Far-fields are designed for playback a distance away from the listener, while near-fields are meant to be up-close and personal. In fact, these days, most near-field reference monitors are often termed as "personal monitors." Choosing which is right for you is something of a personal choice, but should take into account the distance between you and the monitor position. Louder is better—as long as the monitors are far enough away from you to avoid causing damage.

In the studio, volume of SPL can be a killer. Remember the Fletcher-Munson curves? Remember how our ears perform differently at different volumes? This may sound counterintuitive, but let's try going through the scenario of a production and talk about what can go wrong. As we listen to music louder—approaching 100 dB SPL, our ears perform very well, meaning that we hear bass tones and treble tones almost equally as we do midrange tones. It's a logical conclusion that we should always listen loud, so that our ears can do the best job possible of telling us what we're hearing out of the sound, right? Yeah, well … sort of.

The biggest problem with this approach is sustainability—never mind that your neighbors would never tolerate it! You just can't listen to audio for too long a time frame at that volume without either damaging your hearing or losing perspective on any sense of dynamics. After a few dozen minutes, your hearing acuity drops significantly and any sensitive parts just blend into the volume in the room. This phenomenon is known as ear fatigue, which is usually caused by listening too loud, for too long. Another problem is that Fletcher-Munson works whether you choose to listen loud or not. And you just don't know how loud your audience will listen. This is a big problem in translation.

COACH'S CORNER

Consider a piece of music that's very bass-driven, like much of today's dance music. The natural instinct is to listen loud enough to the music to really hear the kick drum and bass parts—key ingredients in the music. You turn up the volume until you're listening at roughly 95 to 105 dB SPL. It's loud; there's no question. Everything sounds great—especially the bass at this volume, just as you'd suspect from the Fletcher-Munson curves. In fact, you're hearing the bass so clearly, you now think it might actually be too loud! You tuck the bass in nicely with the kick and under the rest of the tracks, and now, your piece is done and ready for the audience.

As long as your audience listens as loudly as you did, they should get roughly the same balanced mix that you tried to give them. In the case of dance music, this is often the case, but plenty of folks listen to music from laptops or PC speakers during work, which are incapable of reproducing bass very well. Add to that the fact that they're at work, which means they can't play it loud anyway. This is the classic double-whammy, where two factors work against you.

Okay, perhaps they have a small personal monitoring system too, along with a subwoofer to reproduce the bass. Still, the challenge stems from their listening volume—it's significantly lower, more like 65 to 75 dB SPL. At this range, bass perception is much lower than it is at 95 to 105 dB SPL and as such, the listener no longer thinks that the bass is "tucked in nicely"—it's just too quiet. This leaves the guts of the tune lacking in volume, as presented to this listener. This is the crux of translation—making your productions sound "right" at as many volumes as possible.

Guidelines for Achieving Translatability

There are a few general rules of thumb here—again, without going into the science of acoustics. Here are some general principles that provide some quick and dirty methods of honing in on the translatability of your production environments.

☞ Pay attention to how loud you work. If you listen loud all the time, keep in mind how your ears function in that environment. Do they compress? Sometimes, ears that are exposed to high volumes actually compress the sound to attempt to protect your hearing. Here, the eardrums can go stiff and give you less-than-optimal hearing response when they're overly stimulated by loud sound. In this case, you won't hear dynamics well at all and you run the risk of over-stimulating your ears to the point of damage. If you listen too loud, you can experience tinnitus, which is a ringing in your ears at very high pitches. If tinnitus doesn't go away, your hearing is already seriously compromised.

☞ Listen to your work in as many places as possible to "hone in" on the real sound. Consider trying a car mix—an old and time-tested trick. When you finish a piece (or make some rough mixes along the way), go to the car for referencing. Hopefully, your creation will eventually play on the radio, so check it out on the sound system in a car. Many people listen to music in their cars more than anywhere else and therefore, you may know the sound of your car's system better than any other environment. Compare your work to the work of your favorite band or artist there, which should give you a sense of whether your piece has too much or not enough of anything. By going back and forth, you can get a feel for what it needs to sound like in the studio in order for it to sound good in the car. That's your sound!

☞ Do the bulk of your listening at modest volumes. Modest in this case means slightly higher than conversation, but less than club (i.e., threshold of pain) volume. The number varies from about 75 to 90 dB SPL, but most often in small rooms hovers at about 80 dB SPL. This lets you hear the dynamics of a performance and block out low-level noise, while keeping a high enough volume to get good performance out of your ears.

☞ Keep an SPL meter handy while you work. This will help you hone in on a range of volume at which you can balance the need to hear things well with the need to protect your hearing. SPL meters are cheap (about $40 at Radio Shack) and cheaper if you use an iPhone app. Some of those apps just don't seem to be very accurate but they're cheap—or free. Exactness doesn't matter at first—just a ballpark loudness level is good enough to start honing in on the right level.

☞ Repeat the mix/car/tweak process at different SPL levels in the room until you find a listening level in the studio that helps increase the translation between the two spots. Invariably, there will be a volume level at which the translation is the best. You might still have tonal issues (too much bass, hot enough highs, etc.) but settle on the one that comes closest. We'll explore other acoustic issues you might run into later, but first, let's get the volume right!

☞ Once you've determined a good listening level for the studio, keep listening at that level for a while. Play back several of your favorite tunes—or at least play tunes that relate to the music you're working on at that moment. Study how the tones play—are they bass-heavy or mid-heavy? Can you hear the dynamics? Is your piece much quieter than theirs? At what volume does their music sound best? All of this information will start to get you to find where the sweet spot is. I call this the Room's Volume Calibration Level (RVCL).

☞ Having determined your RVCL, go back to your piece and adjust the listening volume to that level. Use the SPL meter to see how loud you're listening—the meter will go up and down with the dynamics of the piece. Use the average level. Then, go ahead and remake all of your decisions, go do the car test and see how good the music sounds there versus at the studio. Go ahead and tweak the production until it sounds like it should in the car. Then, study that sound in the studio and learn it well—that's your final sound. That's the sound that has the translatability you've been looking for.

Factors Affecting the Studio Listening Environment

We know how loud to listen in the studio to increase translatability, but do we know whether we're even listening correctly? And just how do you listen to something *incorrectly*? Ever since the advent of stereo, there has been a *de facto* standard for listening to your works in the studio. This is not a technique involving your ears—literally, "how to listen"—but rather, a set of monitor standards that effectively reproduces the stereo image that has been sought after since stereo first started on the scene. It involves the two most important items in the studio—the monitors and the room—and a funny shape called "the triangle."

When listening in the near-field, there should be an equilateral triangle between you and the two monitors. If you sit five feet away from the left monitor, then you should also be five feet from the right monitor. Similarly, they should be five feet from each other. When setting up your room, you should start with this shape between you and the monitors to ensure that you hear the left/right balance properly and that stereo imaging can be accurately represented. Of course, your room just might not let you do this. Consider *your* room and how it sounds before settling on the final listening position.

Yes, just with onstage, at the club or in the recording room, the control room space is a part of our studio life. Every room has a sound and it affects everything that plays within it. In the case of the musician in the room, the interaction is key to eliciting a great performance out of the performance. In the studio, something of the opposite is desired—we often try to remove the room from the listening environment. That is to say, we are mostly interested in what's coming out of the monitors, not whether our studio room "sounds" great. In fact, having the room itself become a part of the listening experience goes against the whole concept of translation—the idea is that the sound coming out of the monitors is what you hear and only what you hear.

COACH'S CORNER

Consider the situation mentioned earlier about having a piece that sounds great in your room, but sounds thin elsewhere. Clearly, it's not a "wow" experience to have your piece translate poorly. Now consider how you'd feel if you were the client and you had paid for this piece to be produced at your studio. Assuming that they loved it in your room but were disappointed with how it translates, do you think they'd come back to you the next time?

The best way to make sure that what you hear is coming only from the monitors is to try to make sure that the room doesn't affect your sound. Thankfully, when listening in the near-field, the ratio of direct to reflected sounds is so large that the effect of room acoustics is greatly reduced—although not entirely diminished. But generally, beyond that there's only so much a person can do to acoustically treat a room, and even less so without good tools and a decent budget. The tools are designed to give you accurate readings of the performance of the room so you can decide what type of action to take when dealing with the room. Room acoustics is a complex science, but we can certainly dig into some of the basics—simple steps to help your room sound better.

When beginning the process of treating a room acoustically, the first thing you should buy is . . . nothing. There's really no purpose in buying anything until you know what's happening in the room. If you know how the room is affecting your sound, you can tackle the right problem with the right solution. All too often, people go out and buy a pre-fabricated packaged of acoustic material to solve their problem. The assumption that a one-size-fits-all solution somehow knows what kind of job to do about the sound issues in your room is flawed, because a one-size-fits-all solution rarely works properly for specific applications.

In order to do so, we need to revisit the conversation from earlier in this writing on the subject of noise—pink noise, to be specific. Remember that pink noise is a collection of all frequencies played at once, with a heavier "weighting" of the lower tones to the higher tones to approximate the human hearing process.

In an attempt to identify specific acoustical issues (or at least, identify the acoustical behavior of the room), one approach is to measure the playback of pink noise through the monitors and into a RTA (real-time analyzer)—affectionately known as "shooting the room." We know what pink noise sounds (and looks like) in an RTA, so it's easy to visually compare the noise entering the microphone versus the normal pink noise frequency "map." Once you see which frequencies are being accentuated and reduced, you can begin to uncover the room's effect on the sound. Be sure to use a measurement mic so you don't end up measuring the effect of the mic instead of the room! A rental RTA usually comes with testing microphones.

The RTA display will provide some good clues as to what might be happening in your room. For the record, the toughest part of the RTA process is trying to understand the bass response. The waveforms are so large and high in energy that they interact with each other in much broader ways than the high frequencies, and getting the bass wrong has drastic affects on the translatability of your productions. A good idea is to run an RTA test at the beginning of the process, just to get a starting perspective on your room. You can shoot the room before you move the monitors in the first place and use these results to gauge whether or not your adjustments have affected the response!

Monitor Placement

More often than not, a simple set of adjustments in the position of your monitors can make a huge difference in how you hear things in the room. Here are some simple guidelines for setting up your studio's monitors to help optimize the room/monitor interaction.

☞ Love the triangle. Monitors that are being set up for stereo work perform best when they're positioned at an equilateral triangle to your listening position. That means that they should be the same distance from each other as each one is to you. In the case of near-field monitors, this might be as close as four feet or as far as eight feet. The distance should be chosen based on your workspace, the size of the room and the RVCL of your studio. Lower RVCLs will likely precipitate having the monitors closer so they can perform well at lower SPL levels. This also applies to smaller monitors, as they tend to put out a lower SPL to begin with.

☞ Keep the triangle away from the center of a square room. This means that all of you bedroom producers (you know who you are) should realize that the center of your square 12×12-foot room is just about the worst place to be listening to sound. Square rooms with parallel walls, floors and ceilings are basically miniature echo chambers—sound bounces off of every surface and accumulates in the center of the room. Basically, it's a whirlwind of phase shift, and there's no way to get clean sound there. Try moving the listening position—where you sit—to either the front third of the room, or the rear third of the room.

☞ Farther is lower. This applies to volume as well as frequency. The farther you move from the monitors, the lower the SPL reaching you and the more low frequency you will hear. Remember that low frequency information has a long wavelength. This means that it needs a longer distance from the source to complete one of its cycles and begin the second. This also means that if you're closer to the monitor than the length of one cycle, you just won't hear that frequency. Find a sweet spot that's somewhere between too close and too far from the monitors in an effort to hear more low-end in your system.

☞ The long and the short of it: Not all rooms are squares—some are rectangles and others are just plain weird. Consider the direction your monitors will point if your room is not square—the long or the short pathways within the room. The advantage to the short way is that the wide part of the room is at your sides. Sound will spray into those areas and will have a harder time bouncing off walls and back into the listening position, dramatically minimizing phase shift. The advantage to having your monitors pointing the long way is that you can position yourself toward the back third of the room and potentially increase the low-frequency performance of your monitor system.

Acoustical Considerations

Once you've figured out the best listening position for your monitors in the room, you might still need to treat the room with acoustic material. This should be approached in small doses—in other words, less is more. Remember that sound goes everywhere, and if you want to remove what you hear in the room, you have to remove the interaction of the room from the sound. This can be done by adding absorptive material to the walls, floor and ceiling in strategic ways to minimize the phase shift at your listening position.

Many people rush out and cover the walls with thick blankets, egg foam from packaging material and other random items. (Carpets are popular in studios/rehearsal spaces.) Just because it's a heavy fabric material, doesn't mean that it's going to solve your issues. The secret is to properly identify the issue and then treat it with the right material. Sound treatment material comes in two main forms—absorption and diffusion. Absorption is basically designed to absorb sound at the surface so it doesn't bounce back into the listening position, while diffusion breaks up large energy waves into small energy waves, with little effect on the sound.

Rooms are almost never "flat"—they usually exhibit RTA results with big peaks and valleys, which are indications of reflections. This means that the sound leaving the monitors bounces off the walls, floor and ceilings before returning to the listening position. Unfortunately, these reflections usually arrive back at the listening position late, causing phase shift (which creates dips at phased frequencies) or summing (in the form of peaks). The solution is to strategically identify the points of likely bouncing and install absorption material, reducing the peaks and valleys at the listening position.

COACH'S CORNER

At one time or another, we've all been in rehearsal rooms where—in a well-meaning, but misguided attempt—someone covered the walls and floors with carpeting as a means of soundproofing. Seems like a good idea, but unfortunately this doesn't work at all. Anyone who's lived next door to someone with a loud stereo can tell you that most of the noise problems come from low frequencies. The wavelengths of high frequencies are pretty short and are easily absorbed by fairly thin materials like acoustical foam or carpeting, while larger waves generated by bass frequencies are largely unaffected by such materials. So the old "carpet the entire space" approach yields a room that's boomy and very-dull sounding. Ironically, since musicians' ability to perceive musical detail is compromised by the highly absorptive surfaces, they tend to turn up and play louder in such spaces, leading to more bass leakage than in an untreated room.

The RTA's display of large peaks or valleys in the sound, will tell you a lot about what's happening in the room. In the low frequencies, for example, seeing big dips in the bass should indicate there's some acoustic phasing going on between the floor, and likely, the ceiling. In this case, a good idea would be to purchase some kind of bass trap and mount it on the ceiling above the listening position. This is very common in studios and there are lots commercially available products for this task. Another source of bass problems comes from the corners of the room, where low frequency can accumulate, sum and return to the listening position. In this case, corner treatment is likely to be a good idea—if the bass gets stuck in the corners, it can't come back into the room and give you the wrong low-end information.

COACH'S CORNER

Many people end up building their own bass traps, which is fine—as long as it actually is a bass trap. Bass traps work best when they behave a bit like shock absorbers, using thick materials and/or resonating chambers to absorb the low-frequency energy. Good bass traps are usually at least four to eight inches thick and are comprised of a few layers of varying density material. Often, these have a layer of fabric (for design), a layer of fiber board, another layer of thick foam, then fiber, then foam with thick rubber in the middle. One good bass trap tip is mounting it close to—but not directly on—the wall/ceiling surface. A few inches off the surface should work. The idea is that low frequencies will not only hit the trap and be absorbed, but these could run behind the trap and get caught in the back. This extends the effective width of the trap by simply adding a few inches all around the trap.

Concerning high-frequency issues, there are many more solutions that work fairly well. Again, the key is to find the positions where sound energy coming from the monitors will likely bounce back into the listening position. A really handy approach to finding these spots involves a mirror and a friend. Sound reflections are simple in that they can only bounce in the direction opposite the monitor. Think of sound in this case like billiard balls—they always bounce off the rails at an opposite angle to how they hit the rails. In our case, the same holds true.

To perform the mirror trick, someone needs to sit with a mirror at the listening position while another person holds a mirror along one of the walls. When you can see the monitor in the mirror, you have an area of likely reflection. Mark that spot with a bit of tape or a thumbtack and continue this process until you've inspected every part of each wall. Once you've identified all of the areas of reflection, you can strategize which products best suit your needs.

Absorption material is available at just about any pro audio store and online. Many products serve the same purpose—absorbing frequencies in the mid and high ranges—although some products work better than others. While inspecting your RTA results, look at the bands with the worst peaks and valleys. If the trouble is in the low-mids or mid bands, you should consider getting thicker material. The thicker the material, the lower the frequency absorbed.

The Final Word

So, there it is—the life cycle of sound in your project studio! Keep in mind that this is a first pass at this massive world and there will be a few more passes through this life cycle as you grow your studio and the size and complexity of your productions.

Much like the harmonic series, any studio goes through octaves too—from one digital audio workstation to two; one mic to two and beyond; one synth to two and beyond; and so on. The good news is that every octave looks just like the first one, albeit with more gear and more complexity.

However, microphones will still need preamps, DAWs will still need I/Os (and more as you increase the number of mics), while vocalists will still need to hear more of themselves in the mix! Things do get more and more complicated as you increase the amount of gear in your studio, but the connections and the theories and principles listed here remain. So, go nuts—buy another mic and preamp! Upgrade your computer and pick up a few more EQ plug-ins and synths! Because once you've been bitten by "the studio bug," you're not likely to go back.

After all, I've never gotten a call to help someone make their studio smaller…

All the best until then,
—Your Friendly Neighborhood Pyramind!

About the Authors

Matt Donner
Author, Pyramind Instructor and Chief Academic Officer

Matt Donner has been playing music his whole life. He played throughout college while earning a bachelor's degree in quantitative business analysis but left that world behind to cut his producing and engineering chops in NYC.

He found himself working for high-profile studios like Sound on Sound (Diddy, Anita Baker) and Greene Street (Run DMC and Public Enemy) right after earning his master's degree in music and music technology at NYU. He went on to perform for various TV studios and John Cale (Velvet Underground), including three feature film scores using Pro Tools version 1.0 and a two-day live event to open the Andy Warhol Museum. After signing his band to an indie record deal, his cross-country tour brought him to San Francisco, where the drummer exploded—how typical!

Matt soon found himself in high demand in the studio scene as an experienced Pro Tools user, and became an award-winning Regional Technical Director for Guitar Center and the Pro Tools Support Lead for the Cutting Edge Audio Group, where he served as studio designer, installer and trainer for the likes of Joe Satriani, Metallica, and Benny Reitveld (Santana and the SF Jazz Fest), as well as hundreds of private studios including Wally World (N'Sync, Whitney Houston, Celine Dion and Walter A.) His crowning achievement during this period was installing, troubleshooting, delivering and supporting 50 Pro Tools work-stations for the legendary Skywalker Sound during production of *Star Wars Episode 1*. He claims no responsibility for Jar Jar Binks.

In January 2000, he and Greg Gordon began working together exclusively at Pyramind, where they began running the hybrid Production/Training businesses successfully. Matt has served as Chief Engineer, Senior Producer/Composer, Chief Technical Officer, Vice-President, Director of Education and now Chief Academic Officer. Along with Greg, he grew the Pyramind Training program from a single 24-hour class to the highly-touted 900-hour, 12-month Digital Sound Producer-Complete (DSP-C). He has trained hundreds of students and mixed/mastered another hundred or so records—including his own album, released in

2002—as well as having published several magazine articles. Matt has also written two texts on Pro Tools (*Pro Tools Overdrive V 6.9* and *V7* for Thomson Press).

Matt currently lives in San Francisco with his wife Kimberly and his two children, Marcus and Madison. He's been training in Mixed Martial Arts and Bak Mei Kung Fu for six years, and on good days, surfs the Pacific at Ocean Beach on his Al Merrick 6' 2" fish. The Pacific usually wins. Occasionally, he even takes the family dog Colonel for a walk in Golden Gate Park.

Steve Heithecker
Art Director, Pyramind Senior Instructor

Steve Heithecker is an accomplished composer, producer and keyboardist who's worked on more records than he can count and loves adding to that number. He has also written and produced music for live theater as well

as film and video productions. Before moving his studio to Pyramind, Steve was the co-founder of Digital Art & Music, a recording studio specializing in hip hop/rap and alternative rock music. Steve is a Pro Tools and Reason expert, who—as a senior instructor at Pyramind—constantly challenges his students to think and perform above and beyond the "bar."

As a writer, Steve co-authored the highly respected *Pro Tools 7 Session Secrets: Professional Recipes for High-Octane Results* for Wiley publishing—a book that brought numerous insider techniques to light for anyone using Pro Tools.

Steve is also an accomplished artist and graphic designer. He has designed dozens of albums and CDs over the years, and in his current position as Art Director for Pyramind, he is responsible for the look of Pyramind and Epiphyte Records, Pyramind's in-house record label.

George Petersen
Book Editor, Executive Editor of Mix magazine

Raised in San Francisco, George became interested in drums, guitar and electronics after his family moved to Italy, where he performed in rock bands opening for acts such as Ben E. King and The Searchers. Returning to America for college, he attained degrees in chemistry, technical theater and medical entomology, while at night working as an IATSE Journeyman doing sound reinforcement, 35/70mm motion picture projection, Dolby Stereo theater installs and film/video production. While working on a master's degree in film, he began writing for various magazines and joined the editorial staff of *Mix* in 1981.

During his three-decade tenure at *Mix*, Petersen has written five books and more than 1,000 articles on every aspect of audio production and has lectured extensively worldwide. He also operates a record label, ASCAP publishing company, 24-track recording studio and performs live with the Bay Area rock ensemble ARIEL in venues ranging from 100,000-person outdoor shows to small coffeehouse gigs, sharing the stage with acts such as Metallica, Santana, Jefferson Starship and endless local bands. George's production credits over the years include dozens of records (classical, rock, funk, folk, surf, rap, jazz, etc.) and broadcast documentaries.

One recent project is *Crazy Campsongs*, a book of slightly-whacked childrens' songs using the Tuneswapping® technology he developed, where the new lyrics can be sung to thousands of existing tunes. George lives with his wife and two semi-musical dogs in a 125-year-old Victorian house on an island in San Francisco Bay.

Index